PCH

WITHDRAWN

D1493509

Get **more** out of libraries

WITHDRAWN

Please return or renew this item by the last date shown.

You can renew online at www.hants.gov.uk/library

Or by phoning 0300 555 1387

 Hampshire
County Council

MARK DIACONO

THE NEW KITCHEN GARDEN

SALT · YARD
BOOK Cº

MARK DIACONO

THE NEW KITCHEN GARDEN

HOW TO GROW SOME OF WHAT YOU EAT
NO MATTER WHERE YOU LIVE

SALT · YARD
BOOK Co.

THE NEW KITCHEN GARDEN

OVER THE GARDEN WALL

DESPITE A REVOLUTION in our appreciation of flavours and recipes from other cultures, and a huge leap in our collective interest in where our food comes from, our idea of a kitchen garden has changed little.

For decades we've lived with the idea that a kitchen garden should be your best impersonation of the classic Victorian walled garden: a hardworking place of production, somewhere to coax the staples of life from the soil with sweat, a spade and a hoe. There is a dour undertone: growing food is about survival; self-sufficiency is your notional goal, however impossible; pleasure is incidental.

Let us write this down on a large sheet of paper and burn it before as many people as possible.

There should be more to it than this. Even if your main aspiration is to provide yourself with the core of your meals, your kitchen garden – whatever form it takes – can be a place of pleasure, of eye-opening flavours, where life's balance can (miraculously) be restored. Whether it's solitude, a place to share with loved ones, exercise or relax, your kitchen garden offers it in abundance.

Providing you bite off what you can chew and tailor your garden to your life – both of which I will talk about later – your kitchen garden should light up rather than weigh down your life. There's no need for your time to be overtaken with digging, weeding and watering: I'll be introducing you to ways of sidestepping almost all of that – which is not to say you should want to avoid them. I know many people who get real pleasure from the steady seasonal graft of digging over their allotment. Work isn't necessarily to be avoided, but then neither should we accept the hard-work version of the kitchen garden as the only kitchen garden there is.

There are choices, and I will place as many of them as I think will help in front of your eyes: take any as yours, or chip bits off each and make of the mixture what you will. Whether that produces something utterly outlandish or completely familiar, no matter: it should suit you, is all.

We need a new kitchen garden that relates to everyone; that marries how and what we eat with our ideas of how we grow. One that reflects that most of us live in cities and towns, that space and time are not necessarily unlimited and that (heaven forbid) we might fancy doing other things with our leisure time too. This new idea of what a kitchen garden can be has to reflect that, for many, growing some of what we eat is as much about pleasure as it is produce, that yield may not be the primary measure of success, and that there are other options for creating a kitchen garden beyond the traditional.

I hope to show you that the kitchen garden is a state of mind. A collection of pots by the kitchen door, a balcony, a walled garden, an urban farm or a community food scheme are equally worthy of the name. The kitchen garden is simply the place where you grow some of what you, and perhaps others, eat. If you allow your imagination to influence how you design and fill your garden, you are liable to have a far more rewarding time than if you feel compelled to fill the available space with commonplace plants because that is the norm.

How you do it is up to you. This book provides a series of invitations to grow on different scales, in company or alone, to commit varying degrees of time and labour, and, equally importantly, to grow the flavours and textures you like the idea of experiencing.

The trick, as in most things in life, is to find a happy starting point that suits you. This is essential. Many people overstretch and give up gardening quickly, often blaming the world for not telling them that growing food was so much work. This doesn't need to be the case.

If I gave you a pot of mint to look after, I suspect even the busiest among you would find it hard not to dedicate time to the once-in-a-while watering it requires. The key is to start small and build up, rather than overstretch and work back from the notion of the traditional kitchen garden. That's where I hope to help.

The traditional kitchen garden with its four-bed rotation is a popular way of growing and I am by no means suggesting we do away with it altogether. It recognises what farmers have taught us about the convenience of growing related crops together and the sense in moving them to a different patch the next year to avoid depleting the soil of the same nutrients and prevent the build-up of disease. It has many positives in its favour. That said, we mustn't let the ubiquitous map of the kitchen garden split into four — a quarter each for brassicas, roots and onions, legumes, and potatoes — turn into a prescription for a preponderance of the staples. There is, of course, absolutely nothing wrong with gardening using rotation, using four beds or growing only familiar staples, yet neither is it the only, or necessarily the best, way for you.

To some, none of the ideas in this book will be new. People have long grown even the most uncommon foods I've included here, edible gardens based on perennials proliferate in many cultures, and we have many fine books on growing in containers and in urban environments. What I hope this book will do is to draw the wealth of ideas and opportunities together for you to accept, decline or (hopefully) adapt as you like.

Another thing I hope to do is convince you that the familiar flavours are not necessarily the ones you'll enjoy most. The majority of the food found in supermarkets is there because its qualities suit the transport and storage necessary for it to reach the shelves in good visual condition. Resistance to disease is likely to have played more of a role in the selection of varieties than flavour. Essentially, the French beans you buy may not be that close to the finest they can be; and a mulberry or a wineberry is no less spectacular than a strawberry, despite their absence from the shelves.

Like everyone, I have favourites — flavours and approaches that I love or particularly connect with: I will be unable to keep some preferences from becoming apparent. Feel free to ignore me or disagree when that occurs. Or take it as a challenge to try that hated brassica one more time, a different way to how you've had it before — it may just turn out to be special.

In giving equal prominence to less-familiar foods and approaches, I shall remain equally enthusiastic of the well known: it is, after all, quite hard to improve upon the first new potatoes of the year or find many more gladdening sights than a beautifully tended walled garden.

And lastly, I'm expecting — hoping even — that I challenge and

15

infuriate from time to time: all of that is crucial to getting to where you should be, with the kitchen garden that suits you, that works for you and that provides you with fine food and enjoyment in equal measure.

LOVE WHAT YOU HAVE

MANY PERCEIVE THEMSELVES as in transition: on the way to that job, that house, more land, that perfect future. It rarely arrives, largely because we take ourselves with us. More often than not, any improvements we ask of life are more about ourselves as much as our lot — and so too with our garden.

To be alive where you are is the key to happy gardening. Imagine you will be where you are for years: often, that's exactly how it works out. Don't hesitate over planting an asparagus bed — the worst that happens is you move and leave something that will brighten the springtimes of those that follow for the next couple of decades. Scratch that: the worst that can happen is you don't plant it for fear of moving on, and three years later when you should be living off the tender green spears, you're still there, umming and ahhing about whether to plant or not. That was me at our last house. Within a few weeks of moving to our current place, out came the spade – I planted asparagus crown after asparagus crown. Don't waste the time I did in-between. Live like this is the only place you'll garden. If it's smaller than your ideal, use the free time as an opportunity to enjoy something else; if it's too large, share it.

Limitations are often to do with attitude and perceived ideals. Be positive. If your soil isn't perfect, you can improve it; if it's non-existent or truly awful, a raised bed or containers will overcome. While a sunny spot may allow you to grow the majority of plants that need plenty of warmth and light to produce well, there are leaves, sour cherries and currants among the many that find happiness in

the shade. Detach yourself from the myth that summer harvests are necessarily more desirable or delicious than those from cooler months — celeriac is no less fabulous than a tomato, a fistful of sprouting broccoli every bit as good as a pepper. There is always something delicious to grow whatever your patch. Find it and enjoy it.

Remember: almost always, there is a way of growing anything, whatever your space. Very dwarfing rootstocks can keep almonds and most other fruit and nuts to 1.5m in height and spread, blueberries will thrive in pots with ericaceous compost if your ground soil doesn't suit them, and a combination of rootstock and training can keep most fruit trees to a size that will flourish in a pot on a balcony. If there is a way, this book will show you it.

Lastly, love what you have because you might end up being exactly where you want to be. The next place isn't always better; the larger piece of land not necessarily an incremental pleasure. If you ask for something else, you might find it's not what you thought it would be — you might realise you already had it.

BEFORE YOU START

GIVEN THAT I have messed up in the most varied and complete ways that there are to, I feel qualified to offer a few thoughts on getting the most out of growing some of what you eat. They are not necessarily meant to be taken seriously or adhered to; laughing and pointing or ignoring is a perfectly sane response.

Bite off what you can chew

Growing too much food and using too much time and space to keep the rest of life in balance is the best way to find out what you'd rather be doing. It is also the best way of having your partner or other loved one reminding you of what they would rather you were doing. Start small, make it a success, then build up if you want to. Remember the rest of life: a bag of rude-looking carrots or a lemon coaxed from an unwilling plant is no substitute for a lack of summer spent with your family or friends. There's a seaside out there, a walk in the mountains and cultural pursuits aplenty to enjoy. I must write this out a thousand times and remember it myself.

Anticipate some unexpected pleasures

I hadn't expected to become fascinated with new discoveries or ways of growing, or for the hours spent outside, gardening, to become one of life's primary pleasures regardless of the harvest. It's also made me more of a food activist and interested in the provenance of the food I buy. Of course, not everyone will develop the same pleasures and interests but if you expect something unexpected you'll not be disappointed.

Choose your suppliers well

A plant or seed catalogue, whether online or in the hand, is a menu – the service takes a little longer than a restaurant, but nevertheless, whatever you choose will be served to you in due course, so take some time. Pick people who do it for a living rather than as an add-on to DIY supplies. Talk to other gardeners, either in the flesh or online, and get some recommendations for varieties — they are not all the same. Remember, it takes no more effort, money or time to grow the most flavoursome pea than it does the starchiest marbles.

Make your garden welcoming

Whatever 'beautiful' means to you, add some of it to your garden. Make it somewhere you want to be to just relax. Most of the best gardening, the learning and enjoyment comes as a result of just being in your garden with nothing better to do than be in it. Make places to sit, ideally something simple to cook on (a fire hole in the ground over which to hang a pot or grill for a barbecue is plenty enough) and, if you can, give yourself a little shelter from the strongest winds. A radio, an absence of radio, a deckchair, whatever makes it more welcoming, add it.

Consider becoming part of a community

I'm an unsociable sod and love few things better than being outside growing or inside writing or cooking on my own. That said, there is a thin line between the pleasure of alone-ness and loneliness, which often gets crossed when things aren't going to plan. Having a community of others doing similar to share with, whether virtually or physically, can make a huge difference to your state of mind. It's why allotments work so well — all that quiet companionship to call on, while always having the option of silence and solitude.

BE PREPARED FOR CHANGE

HARDLY ANYTHING APPEARS significant at the time. You might meet The One on that ordinary night when, for no reason, you decided to go out when you felt like staying in; you might unwillingly be dragged to a film, gig or play that turns out to make a left turn in your mind. Once in a while there's the hint of importance: choosing to live in this town or that may not change the direction of your career but many of the loves and friendships that'll colour your life may well come from that pool of people in Place A rather than Place B. Sliding doors are everywhere, however unobvious they may seem.

I walked through one when I semi-interestedly grew my first potatoes. And I'm not the only one.

Grow just a few pots of herbs and, however seemingly small its contribution to what you eat, these few mouthfuls grown rather than bought are likely to ignite a series of positive sparks. It's impossible to un-taste home-grown peas or asparagus, to dilute the pleasure of early salad potatoes lifted in late May or to un-experience the flavour of that first Sungold tomato of the summer. Even if you stop growing immediately, your sensitivities may well have been recalibrated. You'll appreciate what a real tomato picked at its peak tastes like, and you'll be forever in its search. My first peach, almost caught from our first tree, made me plant even more in the rather marginal dampness of Devon. Weirdly though, however much you think these glorious new flavours are branded into your being, by the time next year's harvest arrives it will have faded just enough for the reality to surpass even your expectations. It is what keeps many of us coming back for more.

But be warned: it might introduce an element of inconvenience to your life. You may well find you can't bear strawberries in November any more, or be less inclined to be taken in by the promise that those cricket ball peaches will ripen to aromatic loveliness at home. It might compel you to investigate local producers in search of flavour, and to seek out foods that appear in one season and leave us the next, and are all the better for it.

Growing some of what you eat is very likely to be life changing for many. You may well make the connection between small, local producers and an increase in freshness, quality and flavour. You may well become more inquisitive about where your food comes from and the story behind it as much as the taste.

In short, I believe that few people can grow a little food and remain

unchanged. You may not find that most hours of most days are consumed with it, but you will at least find the quality of some of your meals is gently improved, even if it is as seemingly insignificant as just buying asparagus from the local farm shop every spring, rather than from South America throughout the year. Your money will be keeping that producer in business, reducing the impacts of transporting food halfway around the world and you will be one of that secret society who knows those succulent spears as so entirely different to the tough Peruvian pencils.

You may, who knows, even become one of those producers. When I first stepped into my garden, I had no idea or ambition for spending all afternoon there, never mind all my time.

Once sensitised to that and with inquisitiveness amplified, it is perfectly common to become interested in the wider issues of how we feed ourselves. Our food system is alarmingly dysfunctional, dependent on peaking and insecure resources (especially fossil fuels), and it is characterised by appalling inequalities of access. Increasingly, the bases of our food supply — from land to seeds — are owned by fewer and more powerful interests, depriving us of diversity, security and (as usual) impacting on the less wealthy and the vulnerable disproportionately. There is much to get excited and active about. And in most instances the most powerful thing you can do is to grow a little, support local producers, eat seasonably, and speak up.

If you feel the urge to become more involved in the food system, collective efforts are generally more powerful: one person becoming self-sufficient almost always has less impact than a community taking small steps together. With few exceptions, there are only small steps. Our busy brains look for transformation, for leaps, but life is largely chain links rather than zipwire. As unexciting as it sounds, a small step taken by many creates more impact than a single maverick racing to the extreme.

For all that, I don't think I'd be doing what I do if the food didn't taste so fine. I'd like to think I care enough about the other spin-offs — being part of rebuilding our food system, supporting small producers above the supermarket giants, and so on — but flavour and pleasure, as is often the case, drive what we do.

Eating the best food there is, especially when I've grown it, makes me happy. It gives me satisfaction that we get to eat the best of whatever the season gives. And if that's the only thing that inspires you to sow the seeds, and to water the plants, so be it. It's the best reason there is.

The point is, how much you grow matters little in the scheme of things. How expertly you coax a harvest from a patch or pot is, beyond your pleasure, relatively unimportant. It doesn't matter how you come to grow some of what you eat, what that something might be, nor the scale at which you do it; all that matters is that you do.

CHAPTER 2

BEGINNING

IMAGINE THAT NO ONE had ever grown any of their own food. That we'd always only shopped at the supermarket. And that we lived with a sea of concrete under our feet.

Then imagine that whatever your version of the Almighty is appeared in the sky and announced that s/he is to bestow on each of us a little space. And that space will be called 'garden'. And in that garden we may grow anything we'd like to eat, with only the climate and our imagination to limit us.

Faced with all this beautiful possibility, the prospect of our favourite flavours and textures, of tastes and experiences we may never have tried but that take our fancy, what would you choose to grow?

I'm optimistic enough to think it unlikely that, fuelled by the excitement and freshness of new possibilities, most of us would dedicate the vast majority of our garden to the cheapest, most disease-prone, most widely available food there is. Or that most of our gardens would largely follow a broadly similar blueprint.

With a clean mental slate and no history of gardening to dominate our thinking, we would almost certainly come up with different choices to our neighbour: I love sprouts, number 46 loathes them; the family over the road wants a fruit forest, her neighbour favours a classic patch of veg planted in rows.

I like to think that, uninfluenced, we would display a touch of individualism, that our choices – and hence our garden – would reflect our personality, perhaps even be one of the ways in which we allow that self to develop. A garden will do that for you, if you let it.

If this book does one thing, I hope it will uncurl your fingers from accepted approaches and familiar choices. They may be perfectly fantastic, ideal for you even, but let them alone for now. They're not going anywhere: you can always grasp them again later if they're still the ones you want. Your choice will be stronger for considering all of the options.

Gardening is not just the 'what' you grow, but the 'how' you grow it. Allotments are largely laid out as they are because someone at some time looked up the hill and then replicated the farmer's lines in miniature. The brown spaces in-between remain, despite the lack of allotment tractors. Of course, done well, it looks fabulous, but not all of that bare space is necessary.

If you like that look, by all means plant your garden like that, but – as I will urge you to be about all the approaches in this book – be realistic. Most of your time will be spent not caring for the plants, but

hoeing off the weed seedlings that have germinated in the bare soil and standing with a hose replacing the water that has evaporated from that exposed ground.

There are other approaches, some older than the classic veg patch, some relatively new: each has their own pros and cons. Allow yourself to be tempted to look at them.

In the search for the kitchen garden that suits you, I will invite you to ask yourself a lot of questions. Do you want to grow expensive food rather than cheap; is flavour or yield more important to you; what is your favourite food; how much time do you want to commit?

There are no right answers, no approaches necessarily better than the next. If you want to grow potatoes, then do; if loquats are your fancy, give them space. If it seems like I might occasionally be taking against the traditional approaches, please have faith. Growing the historic staples of our diet in straight lines has dominated allotments and edible gardens for as long as we have had them — they have become the unchallenged norm and they can take a little examination. Like I say, if they appeal to you the most, they'll win through.

My only aims are that you grow something and that you grow it in the way that gives you most reward in whatever way offers you most pleasure.

CHOOSING WHAT TO GROW

CHOOSING WHAT YOU want to grow is really choosing what you want to eat. Almost. Let your taste buds decide for you; allow your sense of anticipation to lead your decision-making and you are unlikely to be disappointed when it comes to picking.

Start with a clean mental slate. The reason most allotments and other edible gardens tend to be alike isn't the result of people growing to suit very similar diets or because most of us happen to love the same foods, it's largely because there is an established culture of growing from a relatively narrow range of plants and doing so in a very set style. There is a silent expectation that you should grow the staples, leaving other foods for any space that remains around the edges. Ignore it.

I'm not wishing to discourage anyone from growing potatoes, onions, carrots and cabbages, but I do want you to consider all the contenders for your precious space. Allow unfamiliar possibilities the chance to make their case, and if at the end of all of that you choose to grow the usual suspects, then you will at least be sure that there is no

better alternative for you. Remember, you cannot have an incredible garden unless you open yourself to the possibility of one.

Take your time deciding what to grow (the 'how you'll grow it' comes later), and in doing so, ask yourself some questions: do I want gluts of crops, a steady supply or a mix of both; is saving money a priority; am I looking for some new flavours and experiences from my garden; would I like my garden to be beautiful? And plenty of others besides.

In my experience, it helps to consider what your potential choices can offer you, and any extra pleasures they may provide. There are no absolutes here: I won't be coming up with an order or ranking foods for you as it's a very personal consideration, but instead I want to suggest some useful ways to help you come to a decision about what to grow.

Favourites

Before you do anything else, get the flavours and textures that give you most pleasure on your list of things to grow. If you don't make the walk from garden to kitchen with salivating anticipation then something is amiss.

If I had to start again tomorrow, then asparagus, 'International Kidney' potatoes, Szechuan pepper, mulberries, lemon verbena, Babington's leeks and perilla would be among the first on my list. Each has flavour in abundance and, coincidentally, either can't be found in the supermarkets or is a whole world different when grown in your own garden.

Remember: in anywhere from a few short days to a year or two, you will be eating whatever foods you're busy choosing now, so be sure to prioritise your favourites.

Transformers

If you grow only one thing, let it be the transformers. Small in volume, large in flavour, transformers add zip and zest to meals, encouraging even the plainest ingredients into life. Some of the easiest plants to grow, they provide maximum impact from the least amount of effort.

Herbs, garlic, chillies, Szechuan pepper, Carolina allspice, and many others, all transform pretty much any foods they're combined with. In terms of flavour impact on what you eat, nothing beats them.

Tomatoes with basil, potatoes and rosemary, lamb with garlic; the perfect pairings are endless, and it's the small ingredient with the big flavour that makes the impact, which brings out the best of the larger

Carolina allspice

Szechuan pepper

33

one. For an experienced cook, transformers will already be high on the list of priorities; if you're a novice, let me encourage you to grow some, as they'll enhance the other ingredients you grow or buy and lift your meals to a higher level of pleasure and flavour.

Transformers have two other pluses: most are expensive to buy in the shops but cheap to grow yourself; and many (especially herbs) are repeat croppers — whatever you harvest is quickly replenished by the plant. They make a pretty compelling case for your garden, especially if you have limited space.

Multis

When you're putting together your wish list, think about the payoffs. Consider whether what you intend to grow gives once, or repeatedly: it can make a huge difference to the value you get from your garden.

Much as I love cauliflower, growing them involves a long wait for a single (albeit delicious) end, whereas sprouting broccoli may make you wait as long but it will give you repeated harvests over a longer period. I'm not suggesting you grow sprouting broccoli ahead of cauliflower,

Garlic

Rosemary

Lettuce

Mibuna

or indeed prioritise plants that allow you to harvest repeatedly, just that you consider these factors when finalising your choice.

It may be that there are ways of growing that can turn a traditionally single-crop food into one that gives repeatedly: most varieties of lettuce can either be lifted whole and hearted, or a cut-and-come-again approach utilised for repeated harvesting. It ain't (always) what you do; it's the way that you do it.

Secondary pleasures

As much as I emphasise the kitchen-end of the plot-to-plate journey, do take time to think about the lifespan of your relationship with the plant. Consider what it gives you throughout the year.

Ask yourself, what are the rewards and when do they come? What are the visual, aromatic, tactile and edible pleasures? Does the plant have blossom and, if so, is it edible or beautifully scented? 'More' doesn't necessarily mean better — the flavour of asparagus is enough to claim its space in my garden — and asking yourself these questions engenders conscious decision-making, and can help in prioritising one food over another.

The Szechuan pepper hanging out from the edge of the perennial garden is the place I stop most mornings for eight months of the year. Even the dog knows that's his cue to do his business. From the start of spring until the first real cold, its aromatic leaves punctuate the early walk — and any other walk — past it. From the moment the early soft golden edges start to uncurl, they carry the peppery citrus that sets the Szechuan pepper apart. As the leaves grow and become waxy, the intensity deepens. By early summer, its flowers — wide, almost umbelliferous heads — are helipads for the bees, a perfectly timed feast of pollen where there might otherwise be a lull. The peppercorns follow shortly after, first as small, pale green bobbles, then swelling and taking on a tinge of scarlet over the summer, before maturing to a deep, angry red into autumn. As the temperature drops, the leaves lighten from dark green, through oranges, browns and reds before falling, usually around the time the shell of the peppercorn splits and releases the black seed within. Even without the pepper itself, that's enough of a reason to grow it for me.

There are many others. Jerusalem artichokes provide midsummer sunflowers, plenty of compostable material and a seasonal windbreak, as well as their tubers for eating and repeat sowing. Courgettes give a succession of fruit, plus delicious young shoots and leaves, and

35

their flowers are a highlight of the early summer harvest.

For me, the breadth and depth of the pleasure a plant can give is part of the equation. Nasturtiums make me as happy for what they mean — less weeding and watering — as the flash of gaudiness and the flavour intensity of those amazing flowers.

And, of course, make your garden beautiful — whatever that means to you. If flowering plants are your thing, intermingle them; if sculptures, reclaimed oddments or a stuffed camel make you happy then include these too.

Save some money

Food is undervalued. We have a habit too of comparing potatoes with potatoes with potatoes, as if they are all equal. A bag of maincrop mashers might be as cheap as chips, but what price for a home-grown kilo of early season 'International Kidney', briefly boiled or steamed, within a few minutes of being lifted from the soil? And what is the true cost of most shop-bought potatoes, reliably high-yielding, often-bland varieties, grown using a cocktail of chemicals?

Even leaving aside the real cost of our food, your garden can save you considerable sums if you choose appropriately. Price in the shops tends to have little to do with flavour, size or nutritional value. Scarcity is a powerful driver. Asparagus and forced rhubarb are in season in Britain for a few short weeks in spring and command a price that reflects the work, risk and incredible flavour of both. Similarly, the shoulders of a harvest — those weeks at the very start and the very tail of a food's season — are usually when its price is highest. Generally speaking, expensive food is no more tricky to grow than cheap. Asparagus requires patience and weeding, forced rhubarb needs a forcing pot and (ideally) some manure, but they are both easy to grow. Similarly, with other short-season harvests, a little preparation and you are very likely to be saving yourself plenty.

Choice of varieties can really help in extending the season of foods that are usually in the shops for a short time. Planting a series of varieties — early, mid and late season — can give you a long steady harvest and plenty on those fringes of the season when they can be hard to find or expensive to buy in the shops. Even something as 'ordinary' as those festive staples, sprouts, can, with the right varieties, be yours for six months of the year — from October until March.

Relative ease of harvest also affects price in the shops. A tractor dragging machinery that lifts a fieldful of carrots in minutes is likely

Jerusalem artichoke flowers

Nasturtiums

to result in cheaper produce than, say, that which results from the manual snipping of globe artichokes from the plant. These aren't the same concerns that trouble you in the garden, where snipping artichokes is no more tricky than lifting a line of carrots.

Cost can have much to do with expectation too. We perceive herbs as something that makes us better cooks, more cosmopolitan even, so we'll pay well for a thin plastic sleeve of leaves that have been cut from a thriving plant, without much thought to the fact that the thriving plant could have been purchased for a similar price. Instead, we use half of the leaves at the weekend, allowing the rest to turn to slime in the foot of the fridge and then buy another packet a week later.

Packaging and preparation time can also contribute to cost — bagged salads are a perfect example. A few grams of leaves, cut, chemically washed and sorted to a supermarket's blend has a hefty premium; growing your own salad allows you to grow the amount you want, when you want it, do away with the chemicals and packaging, and you'll not have to live with the horrible little purple leaf that there's far too much of.

The shortcut to growing otherwise expensive food in your garden is to check your food shop receipts — ideally from different times of the year — and identify those foods you can grow for yourself. Look in the markets, shops and supermarkets for foods you might buy if they were cheaper and consider them too.

Make life easier

Many foods virtually grow themselves. This is not something to tell anyone who would otherwise marvel at your genius. Courgettes and squash, while very responsive to ongoing care and cosseting, are famously productive once set on their way as healthy young plants. Likewise, chard and spinach will stand most of the year with scant attention.

Of all the easy annual plants, legumes may be the most productive. Peas and beans are usually picked as pods containing their immature seeds — the more you pick, the more the plant produces in its race to reproduce itself. Pick them early, small and immature and the plant is under no illusions about its mortality; it will up its productivity until you either stop picking and its seeds mature or the season ends.

More often than not, easy productive plants are front loaders — you need to invest a little time and precision early on, after which they'll thrive with minimal intervention.

This is especially the case with perennials. Even most of our familiar fruit trees – apples, plums and pears – will happily give fruit each year once established, even if pruning is overlooked. Started off well and allowed to develop in favourable conditions, fruit trees will provide a harvest; offer them the pruning that guides their shape and allows light and air into their centre and they may do so more heavily, more consistently and with less likelihood of disease.

One of the main reasons perennials tend to be easy is that once established they are more resilient to fluctuating conditions at the surface than annuals. A young seedling has a hard job getting a physical and nutritional foothold in the soil, never mind then racing to grow to productivity; perennials have to do this only in year one, thereafter feeding in a lower level of the soil profile. This leaves

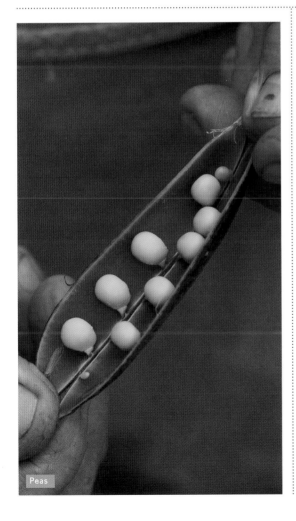

Peas

Runner beans

them not only anchored in subsequent springs — when the British weather may be anywhere between deepest winter and high summer — but drawing on water and nutrients from lower down, and therefore less susceptible to drought or deluge. This comparative resilience of perennials over annuals makes them low-energy crops, the basis of many permaculture systems, even though some take time to establish and become productive.

Staples

We dedicate most of our allotment space to the staples — maincrop varieties of carrots, potatoes and onions, with a few cabbages thrown in. Very fine they can be too. With their long storage life, they see us through the lean months when the allotment is less productive and form the basis for the traditional British diet.

On the face of it, it seems to make sense to dedicate the most space to growing food we eat the most of — grow the majority of what you eat and you can always buy the bits and bobs around the edges. True enough. This works well if your diet is predominantly made up of these core ingredients and you are striving for a high level of relative self-sufficiency. Grow enough of the staples and you are unlikely to be short of a meal, with something always to turn to in storage.

The staples are popular and have been so for many decades. This means there is a wealth of varieties to try that have been developed over many years — many are tried and tested, reliable and some with good levels of disease resistance. There should be little difficulty in sourcing or growing the staples.

Faders

At the other end of the spectrum from the staples are the faders. These are the harvests that, rather than store for weeks or even months, have only days if not hours before the decline in quality sets in.

Most often, this is the result of the conversion of sugars into starches — that tragic shift that makes asparagus a succulent treat on a Saturday but a woody chopstick on the Sunday. Any of the foods where this occurs — peas, asparagus, sweetcorn and baby carrots among them — are clearly almost impossible to buy at their best. In the odd case, notably with peas, the supermarket system manages to capture their finest qualities by freezing them within the window of perfection. Frozen peas are often sweeter than peas in the pod simply

Mulberries

Asian pears

Polytunnel companion planting

because freezing, which usually occurs within two hours of picking, arrests that shift from sweet to starch. Grow peas yourself and you can beat even these frozen ones — firstly, you can turn those hours into minutes and secondly, you get to choose the finest varieties to grow for flavour. This is the case with most of the faders: as fine as the best can be, grow them yourself and you'll find flavour that only comes with being home-grown. Simply, they cannot be any better than those you grow in your own kitchen garden.

Some harvests fade in vitality and texture rather than sweetness. Salad leaves can be conditioned by submerging in cold water, drying thoroughly then being stored in the bottom of the fridge, but their life is still relatively short. Peas, most edible flowers, mulberries (and to a lesser degree most other berries) and most of the annual herbs are quickly past their best once picked.

If you use a lot of these foods, or would like to, it makes sense to grow them yourself as there simply isn't an alternative in the shops to rival them for flavour or vitality.

Unbuyables

Your kitchen garden enables you to enjoy food and flavours beyond what you can find in the shops. But to get the most from that marvellous position, you have to let go of the widespread assumption that if a food was that good, it would have reached our shelves. That's really not how it works.

Supermarkets, especially, build their supply chain around reliability and shelf life — their ideal product has few pests, grows predictably and visually perfect, can be harvested mechanically, has a year-round season of supply and a long shelf life. This puts broad beans beyond most shelves, you'll rarely find the finest of all fruit — the mulberry — for sale, and in the supermarkets' search for us to fill our baskets each week with the same as last, even delicious (and easily grown) alternatives to the familiar, such as Jerusalem artichokes or boysenberries, will rarely be available. Hence, the selection in the supermarkets, greengrocers or even at the farmers' market is a slim section of the flavour and texture possibilities you can choose from.

I have mentioned the mulberry already: it has a day, perhaps two, after picking before it turns into a smoothie of its own making, yet its full flavour only develops when it reaches this state of perfect ripeness, so it can't be picked early. It is unbuyable, but not beyond the kitchen gardener.

43

Growing even familiar foods that are perfectly good in the shops opens another door to beauty, flavour and texture through the diversity of varieties. Crimson-flowered peas, yellow courgettes, golden raspberries (less prone to the birds' attentions) and the frankly incredible 'Sungold' tomato are all things I want in my garden every year that the shops do a different version of. With many foods, there's even the opportunity to grow them how suits you best — tall varieties for those with limited floor space or short kinds for those in a windy location.

Fruit

I'm waving a flag, shouting aloud and generally thumping the tub for you to consider fruit because many think only of vegetables and herbs when it comes to growing food.

Fruit is no more difficult or involved to grow than most veg — often much simpler — and with advances in developing new varieties and rootstocks, most of us can even find the space for a fruit tree.

Apricots, peaches, nectarines as well as the more familiar apples, cherries, plums and pears are among the many types of fruit that can now be sourced as dwarf plants, growing only to around 1.4m in height and breadth, which gives even the balcony gardener the option of home-grown fruit, and those with a standard urban plot the opportunity for an orchard.

Trained options of cordons, fans, espaliers and stepovers also allow you to grow many different types of fruit ornamentally, for structure, in tight spaces and/or against walls or fences. For more about rootstocks and tree shapes see page 345.

Challengers

Every year, I've grown at least a couple of foods I really don't like and much to my annoyance most of them I have at the very least enjoyed, and the odd few have become real favourites. It turns out that even my least favourite vegetable, celery, can indeed be really fine when paired with orange segments, mackerel and olive oil.

Approach every food like there is a delicious way of eating it, a combination in which it shines, and you take a big step towards eating ever-better meals. It's a simple way of keeping your mind open about food, which also stimulates your mind to stay inquisitive about the foods you already love. There are always discoveries to be made, even with the most familiar foods, and besides: who wants to

Tromboncino

eat just the same food repeatedly between now and the wooden box?

And of course, there are plenty of potentially delicious foods in the shops with little real flavour, which means we aren't necessarily familiar with how they should taste. When was the last time you actually really enjoyed a delicious, shop-bought sweet pepper? And if you've never eaten a peach picked when it's barely still hanging on to the tree, you'd have no way of knowing how bland and joyless most of the ones we buy are.

So grasp the nettle and grow a few crops that you really don't like. Choose annuals at first, perhaps, so that if they remain unloved there's little to be lost other than a few seeds. Look at the varieties available and choose the ones that sound most appetising (or least unappetising, if you really do need convincing). Even if you grow only a short row or small patch, resolve to eat the lot. Line up recipes before it's ready to pick and jump in: the worst that happens is you confirm you were right, the best is that you discover something delicious.

Newcomers

In the spirit of culinary adventure, please convince yourself, if convincing is needed, to grow a few things every year that are unfamiliar flavours, even better, that you've never heard of.

We eat a relatively narrow wedge of the foods that will grow perfectly happily in this country, and that wedge isn't necessarily the most delicious selection. As I've already mentioned, some foods — mulberries and medlars for instance — simply don't make it to the shops because they can't survive the journey when at their peak. However, there are others — such as kai lan (Chinese kale) — that are simply unfamiliar to commercial growers, or those, such as in the case of salsify, that are difficult to harvest without damaging. Your garden has no such limitations.

Read through the foods section and add a handful of those that are strange and unfamiliar to you. You may not get a 100 per cent success rate of new loves, but if you discover, as I did, desert island favourites like salsify, kai lan, Japanese wineberries, chervil root and Chilean guava by growing them yourself, your garden and kitchen will be the richer for it.

Pollinators

Most of us are aware of the appalling decline in bee numbers in recent years. It's a huge deal: we rely on bees to pollinate many of the crops

on which our lives depend. Many other pollinators are under threat too, with urban expansion and agricultural monocultures among the many pressures on their vital habitat.

The country's vast network of gardens and allotments can make the crucial difference to the health of pollinators: gardening with them in mind stitches another piece of fabric on to the national patchwork, which helps ensure they flourish. It also means more of your plants are pollinated (which means more produce to eat) and many pollinators are natural predators of pests that are likely to trouble your crops. Everybody wins.

Generally, almost any plant that is allowed to flower will draw in beneficial insects. Even unexpected sources can make a difference: rocket left to overwinter and flower provides an early, much needed refuge for early pollinators.

A combination of planting/sowing with pollinators in mind, and allowing some plants that you'd ordinarily pull up and compost (such as rocket and coriander) to stand and flower, is a slightly more relaxed approach that yields many positives.

There is more about companion planting, including non-edible plants that will attract bees and other pollinators, on pages 365–368.

Uncertainties

When I started growing at Otter Farm, I wasn't really sure what was possible and what simply wouldn't grow in our climate. That wasn't too hard to find out, but what I hadn't anticipated was a whole clutch of uncertainties that sat somewhere in the middle of the two.

Tantalisingly, many of these semi-possibilities are some of my favourite foods: peaches, almonds, nectarines, kiwis, pecans and apricots among them. I couldn't not give them a try.

Happily, with every year that passes, the grower's chance of a harvest increases; unhappily, that is at least partially due to climate change increasing the average temperatures and length of the growing season.

Many of the uncertainties grow into large plants, trees even, which a few years ago might have put them beyond the consideration of those with limited space, but new developments in varieties and rootstocks mean that many are available as true dwarf trees (see page 345).

A risk they may be, but with a sunny, sheltered spot – especially in the warmer, sheltered location of an urban garden – the prospect of your own peaches, eaten sun-warm from the tree, may prove enticing enough to give them a try.

Good companions

Most plants form a natural affinity with others: climbing beans will take advantage of sweetcorn as a scaffold to good light; onions help mask the scent of carrot foliage when interplanted, concealing their presence from the carrot root flies that would attack them. Conversely, there are negative relationships: walnuts, for example, release chemicals that inhibit growth beneath them.

Pairing your favourites up with plants that will help them in your quest for productivity is something to seriously consider. As well as upping the health and heft of your harvests, it makes for a lighter style of gardening, more concerned with encouraging a natural balance than chemical interventions.

The table on pages 366–367 will help with some of the most common companion pairings.

Winter harvests

Although this is really part of successional thinking (see page 347), I want to highlight the importance of deciding whether you want a productive garden through winter or not. Many reach the end of autumn and find a veg patch cleared of harvests and leafy remnants, with no thought of what was to come next. They walk away and return in five months. This is a perfectly sensible course of action, although I would recommend sowing green manures (see pages 356–360) to protect and enrich the soil in your absence.

That said, whether you have a traditional veg patch, a forest garden or anything in-between, there are many plants that will produce well through the cold months. Check the table on pages 212–231 for options.

Gluts or steady supply

Decide whether you want gluts of produce and sow accordingly: a fortnightly sowing of crops like peas and broad beans ensures seedlings are ready to take over as the older plants tire, or you can sow the whole lot at once.

This is most important for those crops with a brief window of picking or a short shelf life: dealing with 37 lettuces that might go to seed on a wet Wednesday is an activity that quickly adjourns to the compost heap – and is a waste of time, resources and perfectly good food. Essentially, if you are growing foods that go past their best

Elderflower

Hawthorn

Garlic mustard

Wild garlic

quickly, either have a plan for dealing with them while they are at their peak or make life more relaxed by sowing in batches so that they mature in a steady stream.

Another strategy is to sow all of the, say, broad beans at once, but allow them to develop in different conditions and therefore at different speeds. A line sown direct in the garden, another sown direct with a cloche covering and another started in root trainers under cover will all produce at slightly different times.

Fast returns

Many of the edible plants you can grow will give you long periods of abundance once they're established, and we love them for it. Plant them aplenty.

Save a little space for some that unwrap their present to you quickly too — those crops that can't wait for you to lift them from the soil or cut them from the plant to take to the kitchen.

Radishes, pea shoots and microleaves are among those fastest to move from seed to plate and each is full of flavour. There are others — the very first early potatoes, carrots grown under cover, courgette flowers to name just three — and their quick turnaround not only furnishes you with food, it is a tangible reward, something that tells you that it works, that you can grow. It builds confidence, ups anticipation and gives a welcome injection of energy.

Complement the wild harvest

Whether you live in the city or the wilds of the countryside, it's very likely that there will be plenty of food to forage. It might be leafy — sorrel, wild garlic or nettles perhaps; fruity — hawthorn, elderberries or crab apples maybe; or nutty, such as hazel. Whatever is available to you it's worth considering what might go well with it and possibly avoiding doubling up.

There may well be opportunities to grow a different variety of something locally forageable: I've a couple of American elder in the garden, which flower later than the native elder, giving me a long season of flowering that means I can make cordial, 'champagne' and endless elderflower puddings through the summer and into autumn.

Collaborate

As far as most of us are concerned, our space is limited: we want a little more. Equally, we find ourselves inundated with too much of

a good thing once in a while — courgettes being a prime example.

Consider pairing up with others, growing something they're not and vice versa and sharing the harvests. It effectively increases the flavours that you and they enjoy and helps to reduce that sinking feeling when it has gone almost too well and there's a surplus in danger of going to waste.

Collaborating can also save money. Deals are often available for large seed and plant orders, as well as saving money by sharing postage. Tools and other equipment can also be costly: having a group of people to exchange, barter, borrow and lend with can reduce costs and build a sense of community and common purpose.

CHAPTER 3

WHAT TO GROW

THERE ARE MANY thousands of options for what to grow in your kitchen garden. I urge you to treat every inch of space as precious and very carefully consider all your options before moving anything in.

In this section of the book are a couple hundred of the most delicious foods, all of which will thrive in most areas of the country.

Some will be new to many of you but don't let that make you suspicious of them: there's nothing in here I don't grow and love. Apart from celery, which I'm just about on speaking terms with.

VEGETABLES

AGRETTI

Salsola soda. Also known as: European barilla plant, opposite-leaved saltwort, monk's beard and barba di frate. Hardy annual. 🐛

Agretti has been a real fixture in my garden in recent years. Its slightly succulent texture and gentle mineral flavour work perfectly with eggs and fish and other seafood, and it adds delightful punctuation to almost any salad. Agretti has a wonderful texture and flavour raw, but is also happy to be cooked briefly – either steamed or sautéed. It's hard to find a finer lunch than an agretti tortilla.

VARIETIES: Generic.
STARTING OFF: Sow seed in late winter or early spring, as it needs cold to germinate. Sow in modules or direct into the ground 5–10mm deep. Germination can be erratic so sow twice as many seeds as you want plants.
POSITION: Full sun and light soil ideally – to suit its Mediterranean seaside origins.
SPACING: 20–30cm apart.

PRODUCTIVITY/EFFICIENCY: A great cut-and-come-again vegetable that's hard to find in the shops.
GROWING: Grows to full size (50cm height and 30cm spread) in less than two months. Each plant will grow into a small succulent bush that can be kept in shape with frequent harvesting. Easy to grow and pretty much pest free.
POTENTIAL PROBLEMS: Leaves can turn tough early in autumn. Seed is extremely short lived, with only a few months' viability.
HARVEST: Cut the green tops off the plants when they have reached 20cm – they will soon re-sprout and can be cut again.

ASPARAGUS

Asparagus officinalis. Hardy perennial. 🐛

In mid-spring, asparagus provides the vegetable equivalent of that first mouthful of cider on a summer's afternoon when you should be working – asparagus virtually defines springtime. It is the embodiment of the uniqueness of home-grown

60

Agretti

flavour – eat some cooked within a few minutes of cutting and you'll understand what makes otherwise grumpy old men and cranky old women leap from their beds brandishing asparagus knives during April and May. As good as food gets.

Asparagus needs little cooking – just a few minutes' steaming or simmering in water is plenty – it should be just tender. Hollandaise, mayonnaise, butter, pepper and Parmesan all go beautifully with asparagus. Do try it raw too – it has a flavour very like bright, fresh, unsalted peanuts.

VARIETIES: 'Darlise' is a very fine, vigorous French variety. 'Stuarts Purple' is one of the few purple varieties to retain its colour on cooking — tasty and tender. 'Connover's Colossal' is an old variety — flavourful and chunky, perfect for a late-season harvest.

STARTING OFF: Although asparagus can be started from seed, I'd suggest planting crowns — dormant clumps of roots — in early spring. Dig a ditch to a spade's depth and within it create a ridge, then lay the crowns over it. Cover with soil and water well.

POSITION: Sunny and well drained.

SPACING: 40cm apart.

PRODUCTIVITY/EFFICIENCY: A little work planting, some patience while they establish, but then low maintenance for a couple of decades of delicious productivity.

GROWING: Asparagus hates competition, so keep the bed weed free. Cut the stems back almost to the ground when they turn yellow in autumn/early winter.

POTENTIAL PROBLEMS: Watch out for asparagus beetle on mature plants (pick them off by hand), and protect young plants from slug damage.

HARVEST: Pick your first few spears 2 years after planting. In the following year, harvest for just 6 weeks then stop to allow the plants to build up reserves for the following year.

AUBERGINE
Solanum melongena. Frost-tender perennial.

I eat aubergines in more varied ways each year and, perhaps not by coincidence, I'm also getting better at growing them. Growing aubergines is a bit of a gamble:

you need to kick them off early with heat and light and then hope that the bit you can't control – the summer – is sunny and long. If all the stars align, late summer will present you with really superb aubergines – likely smaller than those in the shops, but with such fine flavour and texture. They are at their best, thinly sliced, lightly olive oiled and griddled. Their affinity for cumin (and, therefore, perilla) should be explored, especially in a curry.

VARIETIES: 'Moneymaker' and 'Slim Jim' are early and reliable varieties with taut, deep purple, shiny skins. They don't tend to grow too large, so are good for cool areas. You could also try the beautifully coloured 'Turkish Orange'. Perfect for a container, this Turkish heirloom variety produces small fruits that turn from green to orange, and have sweet flesh with little bitterness.

Aubergine

STARTING OFF: Aubergines need heat and light and a long growing season, so should be started off in February or March in modules or small pots in a heated propagator or airing cupboard. Once growing, pot on as the roots begin to show at the base until you reach a 30cm container. Either grow in the pot or plant into the ground in late May or June, ideally under cover.

POSITION: Full sun and shelter, in a well-draining soil or compost. Best in the warmth of a greenhouse or polytunnel.

SPACING: 60cm apart.

PRODUCTIVITY/EFFICIENCY: Rarely highly productive in Britain, but the flavour and texture of home-grown aubergines is very special. Plants need plenty of feeding and warmth.

GROWING: Feed with a comfrey or seaweed feed every fortnight as soon as your plants have flowered. When the plants reach 30cm tall, pinch out the growing tip to encourage side shoots, and be sure to stake your plants. For larger varieties of aubergine allow only 5 or 6 fruit to develop, removing all other flowers.

POTENTIAL PROBLEMS: Aubergines need really warm weather to perform well and may fail to produce fruits in cooler summers. Spraying with water to increase humidity should discourage red spider mites, but you can use a biological pest control Phytoseiulus persimilis if this doesn't work. Aphids can usually be rubbed off as they appear but also try companion planting with basil.

HARVEST: Cut fruits in late summer when they are firm and shiny.

BAMBOO

Various species - see below. Evergreen perennial. ✎

A few years ago, when my couple of bamboos were getting established, Martin Crawford (author of *Creating A Forest Garden*) cooked me lunch of bamboo shoots, Good King Henry and sweet cicely seeds - it was my first taste of freshly harvested bamboo and it was incredible. Happily, mine are now throwing up plenty of crisp, fresh shoots every year - they seem to go through a door, before which they are slow, after which they are highly productive. Shoots can

easily grow to 30cm in a couple of days, and should be picked no larger as they'll be tough. Their flavour isn't powerful, but rather like an interesting courgette. Non-bitter varieties can be eaten raw, or otherwise steamed for 10 minutes.

VARIETIES: There are many species of bamboo, all of which are edible. Generally speaking the Phyllostachys species are most productive in cooler climates like the UK. *Phyllostachys edulis* throws up shoots in spring whereas *P. aurea* produces them in autumn and both of which can be eaten raw. You could also try *P. viridiglaucescens* (early summer and also good raw) or *Pleioblastus simonii* (late summer, needs steaming to remove bitterness).

STARTING OFF: Source plants from a good supplier or divide established clumps.

POSITION: Tolerant of most moist soils and prefers light to moderate shade.

SPACING: This is dependent on species but running types such as Phyllostachys are keen to spread by throwing up new shoots, sometimes many feet away. Happily, once cut the shoots don't regrow and in this way the plant is easily kept within your chosen area.

PRODUCTIVITY/EFFICIENCY: Bamboos are very productive. With careful choice of varieties you can have young shoots from spring to autumn and with each variety producing new shoots over a period of 2–3 months. Some varieties like *Phyllostachys dulcis* begin putting up shoots in early spring when little else is around to eat.

GROWING: Little maintenance required. If harvested regularly then an annual mulch of compost will be needed or grow a nitrogen-fixing tree or shrub nearby.

POTENTIAL PROBLEMS: Control spread by cutting young shoots.

HARVEST: From spring to autumn, cut shoots at ground level, or just below, when it is around 30cm long. Remove the outer layers until you reach the tender pale green to white flesh.

BEETROOT

Beta vulgaris. Hardy biennial. ✎

I'm genuinely mystified as to the divide between beetroot lovers and haters - this is one of the must-

Bamboo

Beetroot

haves of my garden. Reliable, easy, provider of delicious sweet roots and really under-appreciated leaves – I can only put any dislike down to poorly pickled beets eaten in childhood. Sow a few rows of the varieties below in spring and see if you still dislike them by early summer when they're harvested. Roast washed, unpeeled beetroots with rosemary, garlic and a little oil to bring out the sweet end of their earthiness.

VARIETIES: 'Barbietola di Chioggia', with its glorious concentric candy stripes, and 'Burpees Golden', with its deep ginger flesh, are as beautiful as they are delicious. Essentials. For large, sweet, tender roots of classic deep rich purple, try 'Sanguina' or 'Bolivar'.

STARTING OFF: Sow 2 or 3 seeds on to each module in March, thinning to the strongest couple when they've germinated, planting them out in April, under fleece if you like. Subsequent sowings can be made direct every few weeks for a good supply throughout the summer and autumn months.

POSITION: Full sun is best, though will take a little shade. Well-composted ground is ideal.

SPACING: Thin to 7cm apart, or further apart if you prefer bigger beetroots.

PRODUCTIVITY/EFFICIENCY: Easy and cheap, needing little care as they grow.

GROWING: Water through extended dry periods.

POTENTIAL PROBLEMS: Generally trouble-free, though snails and slugs can make small holes later in the season and birds can occasionally bother the seedlings.

HARVEST: Harvest the largest bulbs in each row by gripping the stems and pulling gently. The bulbs should come up easily. Any neighbours left behind will swell to fill the space. For baby beetroot harvest from 7 weeks after sowing. Seedlings thinned out can be added to salads.

BORLOTTI BEAN

Phaseolus vulgaris. Frost-tender annual. ✑

I wouldn't grow many things just for looks – that'd be crossing over to the dark side where ornamental gardeners live – but for borlottis I'd make a rare exception. Lively climbing beans that skate up their support in search of light and heat, hanging glorious

B

63

Borlotti beans

red and cream speckled pods as soon as they can. The beans within are one of my favourites – nutty, creamy and flavourful in themselves yet happy to take on strong flavours like garlic, chilli and the woody herbs. Great used fresh and store well into and out of winter for hearty soups and stews. A must.

VARIETIES: 'Lingua di Fuoco' is the most common variety — available also as a dwarf, which is good for exposed sites. You can occasionally find 'Lamon' — large and tasty beans, and the traditional variety for pasta e fagioli.

STARTING OFF: Sow from March until midsummer for beans from summer to autumn. Sow into root trainers under cover, then plant out from mid-May on to a sturdy framework of canes. Sow direct from late April until mid-July if you prefer.

POSITION: Full sun and a light, well-composted soil.

SPACING: 20cm apart.

PRODUCTIVITY/EFFICIENCY: Borlottis take up little floor space but grow tall, so are good for those looking to get a good harvest from limited garden room.

GROWING: Tie young plants into canes to help them on their way. A liquid or manure feed will boost the size of your crops, especially if grown in a container. Save some of your crop for sowing the following year.

POTENTIAL PROBLEMS: Slugs can be troublesome when the plants are young.

HARVEST: Harvest beans in late summer into autumn to eat fresh while the pods are plump with beans, either when the beans are green or leave them on the plant and harvest when the plants are beginning to desiccate. You can use the beans demi-sec like this, or cut the plant at the base and hang it upside down to dry the beans for a few days more.

BROAD BEAN

Vicia faba. Hardy annual.

Worth growing just for the scent of the flowers – as happy-making as any ornamental – and the leafy tops which grow above the pods. Sliced off and stir fried they are one of the great unbuyable gardener's treats. The beans themselves are equally special, particularly if picked small – try to leave behind any attachment to size, as picked small they are sweet and less bitter than when allowed to plump up. Equally importantly, picking them encourages the plant to produce more, so you get no less in the way of yield.

VARIETIES: 'Bunyard's Exhibition' is my favourite with its reliably delicious, tender beans. For autumn sowing, 'Aquadulce Claudia' is a tough, hardy variety that grows slowly through winter to give early spring beans. 'The Sutton' is a dwarf that's ideal for windy spots or containers, but whatever your situation, make a little space for 'Crimson flowered' with its beautiful flowers.

STARTING OFF: Sow hardy types 5cm deep straight into the ground in autumn, or into root trainers under cover in late winter, planting out from March onwards. In spring you can sow direct too but I tend to start most of mine under cover to get them off to a good start out of the way of the slugs.

POSITION: Sunny, well drained and ideally sheltered.

SPACING: 20cm apart, with 60cm between rows.

PRODUCTIVITY/EFFICIENCY: A spring sowing will be ready to harvest in around 3 months. The secret with broad beans is to sow in repeated small batches every 3 weeks or so, to avoid gluts and give you a steady harvest. The legume family (of which beans are part) enrich the soil by capturing nitrogen from the air and making it available in the soil – cut the plant at the base when the beans are harvested, to improve fertility for the plants that follow.

GROWING: Sow every fortnight or so through spring and early summer for a steady harvest, with plants ready to replace those that tire. Broad beans are tall plants and may need support. Push canes into the ground at the ends of the rows and tie string between them. Pinching out the growing tips when the first tiny pods are beginning to appear will direct the plant's energy to the developing pods.

Broad beans

POTENTIAL PROBLEMS: Plants sown in autumn can weather badly, so cover with fleece or with a cloche if possible. Black aphids love broad beans — wipe them off with a cloth when you see them; pinching out the tips helps.

HARVEST: Beans will be ready three months after sowing. Small beans are sweeter than those allowed to grow on.

BRUSSELS SPROUTS

Brassica oleracea var. *gemmifera.* Hardy biennial.

One of my favourite winter vegetables, but I confess to growing only a small proportion of my consumption. Much as I love them – for the mini cabbages that sit on top of their trunk as much as the sprouts themselves – they are in the ground for an awfully long time (getting on for a year for later varieties). Much as they deliver in flavour, they take up a vast amount of space. A couple of lines, happily taken for tops and sprouts, are all I afford them – the rest I buy.

If you are a non-believer, try them thinly sliced and fried in olive oil with bacon, with thyme and cream, or in place of the cabbage in coleslaw. The tops are as fine tasting as any brassica – slice, steam and serve with lemon juice and olive oil.

VARIETIES: 'Noisette' is a particularly nutty early season variety for sprouts from October to Christmas. Traditional late varieties like 'Seven Hills' or 'Wellington' will give you sprouts when little else is around. You could also try 'Red Rubine' and 'Red Bull' for lovely purple and red sprouts.

STARTING OFF: Sprouts need a long growing season. Start them under cover in modules in early spring, potting on as needed and planting out from mid-May to June when around 10–15cm tall. Don't allow the plant's growth to be checked by delaying potting on. Firm them in well.

POSITION: Sunny position. Sprouts will do well in heavy soils. Preferably mildly alkaline soil, but not essential.

Brussels sprouts

SPACING: 60cm apart.

PRODUCTIVITY/EFFICIENCY: Sprouts need little maintenance and certain varieties can crop over a long period of time. Sow salad leaves, radishes or herbs around newly planted sprouts to make good use of space, or nasturtiums to cover the ground quickly, while retaining water and providing a harvest.

GROWING: Sprouts are tall but shallow rooting, so tread the soil down firmly when planting out and, if exposed, use a cane for support.

POTENTIAL PROBLEMS: Cabbage white butterflies and caterpillars can cause huge damage on unprotected crops. Plant nasturtiums as a sacrificial crop and/or use canes to create a cage of Enviromesh or fleece to exclude them completely – place it over the plants as soon as they are planted out.

HARVEST: If you want your sprouts to mature all at once, chop the top off the plant in October (or choose a cultivar that naturally matures its sprouts together), otherwise, snap the sprouts off using a downward action when they reach a suitable size.

BUCK'S HORN PLANTAIN

Plantago coronopus. Also known as: minutina, plantago and erba stella. Hardy perennial often grown as an annual.

This is a succulent salad leaf, sweeter and nuttier than spinach and with a faint hint of parsley. Harvest the leaves young and before the plant begins to flower, when they are at their most tender. Don't miss out on the flowers though as they are also great in salads. A native of coastal areas in Europe, it thrives in cool, rainy conditions, and also won't mind saline soil.

VARIETIES: Generic.

STARTING OFF: The seed is tiny so sow in trays under cover from February, prick out into modules and plant out when roots are showing. You can also sow direct in early spring.

POSITION: Most soils with good drainage. Sun or light shade.

SPACING: 20cm apart.

PRODUCTIVITY/EFFICIENCY: A small patch can provide you with leaves for salads or for steaming from April to June (longer if you cut back flower stems).

GROWING: Cut back flower stems to promote fresh leaf growth.

POTENTIAL PROBLEMS: Generally pest and disease free.

HARVEST: Pick young leaves while tender and before the plants flower. Leaves can be eaten fresh or lightly steamed.

Buck's Horn plantain

January King cabbage

CABBAGE

Brassica oleracea var. *capitata*. Hardy biennial.

I don't grow many cabbages, but I always, always have a line or two of 'January King'. It looks and tastes fabulous and the texture has the sort of stature you expect in a robust kale – making it perfectly happy to stand next to chilli, olive oil and garlic. Other than that, do consider a few spring cabbages – they may look tatty once they've hauled themselves out of winter, but beneath the outer leaves they're an early season smasher when there's little else around.

VARIETIES: With the right varieties you can be harvesting cabbage all year round. Try spring varieties 'Myatt's Offenham' or 'Pixie'. For summer cabbages I grow 'Hispi', 'Greyhound' or 'Marner Early Red'. Good autumn/winter varieties to try are 'Cuor di Bue', 'January King' and 'Best of All'.

STARTING OFF: Sow cabbages in modules under cover. Summer and autumn cabbages should be sown in March, winter cabbages in May, and spring cabbages in July/August. Plant out under fleece or Enviromesh 6 weeks later. Pot on and plant out when around 8-10cm tall. Cabbages, as with all brassicas, don't like their roots being checked, so plant out as soon as the roots are showing through the holes in the bottom of the pot.

POSITION: Full sun. Will do well in heavy ground.

SPACING: 25-50cm apart, depending on variety.

PRODUCTIVITY/EFFICIENCY: Cabbages will occupy space in your veg patch for around 16 weeks but without requiring much input from you. Make use of the space between your cabbages early on in summer and autumn by direct sowing leafy salad crops like summer purslane or herbs.

GROWING: Water in and firm the soil down well when planting. Water during dry spells to keep growth good and steady.

POTENTIAL PROBLEMS: Protect from cabbage white butterflies and caterpillars, and pigeons, with fleece or take your chances. Slugs can also do plenty of damage, so hunt out and pick off frequently. Clubroot can build up if brassicas are grown for too long in the same patch of ground, so don't grow them for consecutive years in one spot. Adding lime to the soil to increase its relative alkalinity can help rectify clubroot.

HARVEST: Use a sharp knife to cut the whole head once a firm heart has formed.

CALABRESE

Brassica oleracea var. Italica. Hardy biennial.

Another of my favourite vegetables (usually labelled as 'broccoli' in the shops) that I rarely grow. In theory, I should - they don't take too long before harvesting and I eat plenty of them - but I don't grow them well. Some things I'm prepared to persevere with but my patience has an elastic limit and with calabrese it snapped. Don't let that put you off - they aren't tricky; I just don't have the knack. It's frustrating, as I love calabrese steamed or broken into florets and roasted with lemon and olive oil.

VARIETIES: 'Chevalier' is reliable and has a good flavour. 'Green Comet' is good for early crops.

STARTING OFF: Calabrese is prone to bolting at any perceived slight, and won't take well to transplanting. Sow short rows direct into the ground from April to early summer, or sow in modules under cover from March until June and take care not to disturb the roots when planting out. You can also sow in October under cover for a spring polytunnel crop.

POSITION: Full sun in a well–drained and composted soil is ideal, though it can take some shade.

SPACING: 25–30cm apart.

PRODUCTIVITY/EFFICIENCY: You will have your first crops of calabrese 3–4 months after sowing, with little maintenance required.

GROWING: Steady growth is important, so prevent plants from drying out in hot weather.

POTENTIAL PROBLEMS: As with all brassicas, cabbage white butterfly, pigeons and clubroot are the main things to look out for. Try planting nasturtiums nearby to attract the butterflies or fleece against them (and the pigeons). Lime if clubroot is a problem and don't grow brassicas in the same place 2 years in a row. Soil must be kept moist or the threat of bolting rears its head again.

HARVEST: Heads can be ready to harvest 11 weeks after sowing. Take them when they are firm and before any of the buds have started to turn to flowers. You should find smaller side shoots appear providing you with a second crop.

CALLALOO

Amaranthus species. Half-hardy annual.

A delicious and beautifully ornamental plant, with leaves that taste somewhere between spinach and watercress. Hugely popular in West Indian cooking, this fast-growing, easy-to-grow plant produces leaves that can be coloured anywhere from green through to vibrant red. If allowed, it will grow tall and produce wonderful seed heads in late summer. Use the leaves as you would spinach.

VARIETIES: Callaloo seed is usually sold under the generic name common amaranth. You could try varieties 'Hopi Red Leaf' or 'Callaloo', which do well in cooler areas.

STARTING OFF: Sow seed in modules under cover in April. Pot on if necessary before planting out after the last frosts.

POSITION: Full sun and good drainage.

SPACING: Around 45cm apart.

PRODUCTIVITY/EFFICIENCY: Callaloo is a vigorous plant, taking up reasonable space but providing you with greens for several months from June. The seeds are also edible. Covers the ground well and is grown as a block, so needs little weeding or watering.

GROWING: Keep picking the shoots to prevent the plants from flowering and to encourage more shoots to form.

POTENTIAL PROBLEMS: Generally pest and disease free.

HARVEST: Pick leaves and shoots for steaming once plants are well established – usually from June until September.

Callaloo

Cardoon

69

CARDOON

Cynara cardunculus. Hardy perennial.

Life has to be pretty relaxed to find time to eat cardoons. Growing to 3m at times, and almost indistinguishable from globe artichokes, cardoons give structure and year-round presence to a garden. If you can be bothered, the leaf stalks (looking like bodybuilder celery) can be harvested and steamed to eat as a crudité with dips. They're actually rather good, but you know, life's not so long and I rarely get round to it.

VARIETIES: Cardoons are generally sold as unnamed varieties, but if you can find them try 'Argente de Geneve' or 'Gigante di Romagna'.

STARTING OFF: Buy as small plants or start seed in early spring in modules under cover.

POSITION: Tolerant of poor soils and grow well in shade, but happiest in full sun.

SPACING: 80cm apart.

PRODUCTIVITY/EFFICIENCY: Whilst cardoons do take up a large amount of space there is little work to do with them and the flowers are marvellous for the bees.

GROWING: Leave dead flowers and flower stems on the plant over winter and cut back hard in spring as the new leaves start to shoot. After a few years of growth, split clumps of cardoons in autumn and replant or pot up.

POTENTIAL PROBLEMS: Slugs can attack young plants, but beyond this vulnerable stage cardoons are trouble-free.

HARVEST: The edible part of cardoons is their celery-like stems. On a dry day in late summer, gather together the leaves, wrap a collar of card or thick newspaper around them, tie it in place and leave for around 4 weeks to blanch.

CARROTS

Daucus carota. Hardy biennial. 🐛

To my mind, there are two types of carrot: early, expensive to buy, occupy their space for a short time, sweet and small; and large, late, relatively cheap and perfectly fine carrots. I grow only the first, for reasons that I hope are obvious. Many of the earlies are eaten straight from the ground, soil brushed off and leafy tops cast semi-accurately at the compost bin. Lifted early, they free up space for another batch or a different crop.

VARIETIES: With a polytunnel, the right varieties and storage you can have carrots for a good part of the year. Try 'Nantes' and 'Chantenay' for a classic sweet and early carrot. 'Paris Market' is another early sweet variety – it comes golf-ball sized and shaped and is good for a heavier soil. Late winter storing varieties are 'Autumn King' and 'Flakee'. 'Rainbow Mix' is an early maincrop, which includes white, yellow and purple varieties.

STARTING OFF: Best sown direct. Early varieties can be sown successively from March to June outside for a good supply of small sweet roots throughout the summer, and from February to August if growing in a tunnel. Sow carrots for storage in May or June.

POSITION: Full sun in a well-drained and stone-free soil. Compost/manure isn't needed.

SPACING: Sow seed thinly in shallow drills 15cm apart or broadcast sparsely and rake in. Thin to around 7cm.

PRODUCTIVITY/EFFICIENCY: A small piece of

Carrots

ground can yield crops of carrots over a long period of time.

GROWING: Keep weeded and well watered.

POTENTIAL PROBLEMS: Carrot fly is the main culprit. Use fleece or companion plant with something oniony.

HARVEST: Pull early carrots as soon as they are ready from May onwards. You can leave maincrops to overwinter in the ground, but if rain or severe cold is threatening they can be dug up and stored (unwashed) in paper sacks or in crates or boxes with slightly damp sand.

CAULIFLOWER

Brassica oleracea var. *botrytis.* Hardy biennial. 🐛

I can't seem to not grow cauliflower, no matter how hard I try. I love them but they take an age to mature and, tediously, they will 'blow' with almost no provocation – turning from tight, pat-able heads into floating florets, losing much of their crisp texture in the process. But still, against my better nature, I continue to grow a few each year – more often than not a line split between coloured varieties and 'All The Year Round'.

VARIETIES: It is possible to have cauliflowers throughout the year with careful choice of variety. In grave infringement of the Trades Descriptions Act, 'All The Year Round' will give you cauliflowers from June to October. 'Purple Cape' is ready in March/April and 'Aalsmeer' in April/May when there's not much else around. Whatever time of year you are looking to harvest, there will be mini varieties, such as 'Igloo', to suit.

STARTING OFF: Sow when variety requires, starting in modules. Pot on into 9cm pots and plant out when 7–10cm tall.

Purple Cape cauliflower

POSITION: Full sun in a sheltered site on a moisture-retentive, well-manured/composted soil.
SPACING: 45–70cm apart for large cauliflowers, depending on variety, and 15cm for mini ones.
PRODUCTIVITY/EFFICIENCY: Winter cauliflowers in particular take up a lot of space (approx. 70cm) and for around 40 weeks of the year. Summer and autumn varieties will be in the ground for around 16 weeks.
GROWING: Cauliflowers do not like any check to their growth so ensure they are planted out in good time with the soil firmed thoroughly around them, and watered well in dry weather. To keep curds protected against the worst of the weather, bend a few of the outer leaves over them by snapping the central rib.
POTENTIAL PROBLEMS: Fleece against pigeons and any butterflies. Lime soil if clubroot is a problem.
HARVEST: Cut the stalk below the curd when the cauliflower has a nicely formed globe, and before it gets the chance to bolt (most likely in hot weather).

71

CELERIAC

Apium graveolens var. *rapaceum*. Hardy biennial.

A fine, rough and wrinkled ball of savoury earthiness that's one of winter's staple flavours for me. Its flavour is nominally of a potato crossed with celery, but far lovelier than that implies – there's an easy sweetness that sets off any gentle bitterness.

If you're not too worried about producing prize specimens, it's fairly easy to get a good crop, but for the plumpest, large celeriac they'll need sun and moisture and not to be held up in modules when they're ready to plant out.

Peel and either chop or slice celeriac depending on the recipe and submerge into acidulated water to prevent discolouring. It makes perhaps an even finer dauphinoise than the traditional potato version, and is superb in coleslaw – combine equal quantities of matchstick-sized celeriac, carrot and apple in a mustardy dressing.

VARIETIES: I can't tell varieties apart for flavour, but 'Prinz' and 'Tellus' are both reliable.
STARTING OFF: In February/early March sow seed in modules in a tunnel or greenhouse and plant into

Celeriac

CELERY
Apium graveolens var. *dulce*. Hardy biennial.

The single vegetable that I can't bear to eat as it is; even worse, paired with the wall insulation that is cottage cheese. As a flavouring I love it – in soup and stews especially, its savouriness is a must, though I am as likely to get it from the leaves of lovage or celeriac which are very similar in taste. If you like celery, grow the self-blanching varieties for ease.

VARIETIES: Older varieties such as 'Solid Pink' require blanching in a trench but many of the newer ones – such as 'Green Utah' and 'Golden Self-Blanching' – do it themselves, taking much of the grief away. The older varieties tend to be hardier with a more delicate flavour.

STARTING OFF: In March/early April, sow seed into modules under cover and plant into their final position as the soil warms up. The seeds are very small so sow as few as possible in each module and thin to one seedling.

POSITION: Tolerates some shade and needs a fertile moisture-retentive soil with good drainage.

SPACING: Self-blanching types are best planted in a block with 15–30cm between plants. Celery that requires blanching should be planted 30–45cm apart in the trench with 1.5m between trenches.

PRODUCTIVITY/EFFICIENCY: Self–blanching types will be in the ground for up to 16 weeks and trench celery for 9 months.

GROWING: Keep weed-free and water well in dry spells.

POTENTIAL PROBLEMS: Starting in modules minimises slug and snail damage. Planting out in May should reduce the risk of celery fly damage.

HARVEST: Self-blanching celery can be harvested when it reaches the desired size, from July until the first frosts.

final position as the soil warms up. The seeds are very small so sow as few as possible in each module and thin to one seedling.

POSITION: Full sun and tolerant of light shade. Keep soil moist in dry weather.

SPACING: 40cm apart.

PRODUCTIVITY/EFFICIENCY: Celeriac is pretty low maintenance but takes up space for a good part of the year.

GROWING: As the roots swell, remove the lower leaf stalks around the base to encourage larger roots.

POTENTIAL PROBLEMS: Largely disease free but slugs do appreciate them.

HARVEST: Except in the coldest of weather, celeriac can remain in the ground until March, digging as needed. If the celeriac is dug up for storage then remove leaves for longevity. Once established, feel free to take a few leaves to use in place of lovage, adding savoury stock flavours to stews and soups.

CHARD AND PERPETUAL SPINACH
Beta vulgaris var. *flavescens*. Hardy biennial.

Almost unnoticed, chard (and to a degree perpetual spinach) has edged its way on to my never-without list. As lazily productive as any vegetable I can think of, these glorious leaves can be harvested throughout the year. Once you get to know them, you'll appreciate their easy reliability, flavour and the generosity of crisp stalks and robust, yet not in any way tough, leaves. I'd not want to be without them.

VARIETIES: 'White Silver' for large and delicious leaves and a thick rib, 'Bright Lights' for smaller leaves with ribs ranging from yellows through oranges to red. 'Canary Yellow' and 'Lucullus' are some of the best for baby salad leaves.
STARTING OFF: Sow in modules in March/April and again in July, planting out when 3–4cm tall.
POSITION: Largely unfussy, and will tolerate some shade and a coastal spot.
SPACING: 10–15cm apart for baby leaves, 30cm between smaller varieties like 'Bright Lights' and 45cm for the largest.
PRODUCTIVITY/EFFICIENCY: From only 2 sowings you can have year-round cut-and-come-again leaves.
GROWING: Apart from watering in dry weather and keeping free of weeds, little else is required
POTENTIAL PROBLEMS: Slugs can make their mark on young plants and to a lesser degree in mature plants, but generally trouble-free otherwise.
HARVEST: Cut leaves 5cm above the ground and the leaves will regrow.

Chard

CHERVIL AND PARSLEY ROOT
Chaerophyllum bulbosum and *Petroselinum crispum tuberosum.* Hardy biennial.

These two really should have their own entry but I've put them together because I ate them for the first time on the same day, and because broadly you treat them the same. Limp, I know. Do, please, grow both. These relatively uncommon roots are delicious – chervil root has a sweet, chestnutty earthiness, whereas parsley root (aka Hamburg parsley) has just a hint of parsley about it. Try both roasted in olive oil or made into crisps.

VARIETIES: No named varieties.
STARTING OFF: Chervil root needs around 8 weeks of cold to germinate (stratification) so either sow direct in autumn or mix with damp sand and store in the fridge for 8 weeks before sowing in March. Parsley root can be sown direct in March.
POSITION: Sunny site, in composted soil.
SPACING: 10cm apart with 30cm between rows, or in blocks with plants 20cm apart in all directions.
PRODUCTIVITY/EFFICIENCY: As with most roots, chervil root and parsley root will spend at least 8 months in the soil before you can harvest, but being relatively small, they needn't take up a lot of room. Low maintenance.
GROWING: Water during dry weather and keep weed-free.
POTENTIAL PROBLEMS: Usually trouble-free.
HARVEST: From September through January. Their flavour will improve after a frost.

CHICORY
Cichorium intybus. Hardy perennial usually grown as an annual.

Embrace the bitter! So many of us are in search for the sweet that we often lose all appreciation of how wonderful a nip of bitterness can be. Try chicory leaves sparingly in mixed leaf salads or, even better, as heads cut in half lengthways and caramelised – you'll be turned. There are many great varieties for growing too.

C

73

VARIETIES: Many, and varied in their habits too. Some chicories are hearting like 'Sugar Loaf' and 'Palla Rosa'; some are loose-leaved such as 'Catalogna Frastagliata'. There are puntarelle types with finger-like growth, as well as cut-and-come-again varieties, such as 'Italian Dandelion'. Others like 'Witloof' can be 'forced' for use over the coldest winter months.

STARTING OFF: Sow from March through to August depending on variety.

POSITION: Chicory will do well in most soils except the lightest and heaviest. It will tolerate some shade.

SPACING: 20–30cm apart depending on variety.

PRODUCTIVITY/EFFICIENCY: Chicories can be in the ground for many months but much of it can be over the winter, when there is less demand on space. Takes well to pick and come again. They can supply you with greens in early spring when little else is around.

GROWING: Once established, chicory is very drought tolerant. May need protection over the coldest months.

POTENTIAL PROBLEMS: Usually trouble free.

HARVEST: Harvest leaves individually through the coldest months from loose-leaved varieties. Hearting varieties may re-sprout from the stump after cutting.

CHILLI PEPPERS

Capsicum annuum. Frost-tender perennial, usually grown as an annual.

Chillies are the quintessential transformers (see page 32), enlivening everything they come into contact with. With the right choice of varieties, chillies can give you everything from heart-stopping heat to gentle fruitiness, far beyond the narrow range of most shop-bought chillies. All take to pickling and freezing as well as being good stored under olive oil. I like to grow a few varieties at once, so I have different flavours and strengths to choose from.

VARIETIES: Many and varied ranging from mild to extraordinarily hot. Try 'Apricot', 'Padron' or 'Poblano' for something mild and fruity, a mid-heat 'Bulgarian Carrot' or 'Bird's Eye', or 'Scotch Bonnet' for something truly hot. Don't demonstrate your diminutive sexual organs by trying 'Dorset

Chilli peppers

Naga' – at over 1 million on the Scoville scale of chilli heat, they are hundreds of times hotter than most you buy.

STARTING OFF: In modules in a propagator or airing cupboard in February/March, potting on into 9cm pots and then again as soon as the roots show through the holes in the bottom. Generally speaking, it should be warm enough to plant in a tunnel or greenhouse by the end of April. Germination is usually slow.

POSITION: As hot, sunny and sheltered as you can give them, ideally a tunnel or greenhouse.

SPACING: 45–60cm apart.

PRODUCTIVITY/EFFICIENCY: Chillies are particular early on, needing care and to be started early with heat. Once growing and with the occasional feed, chillies can be hugely productive and carry much flavour in a small parcel.

GROWING: Whilst in pots, feed with liquid comfrey or seaweed every week or so.

C

POTENTIAL PROBLEMS: Fairly trouble free, though watch for aphids and deal with them in whichever way you prefer (see pages 366–368 and 370).
HARVEST: Depending on the summer, chillies are usually ready in September. Use them freshly picked or dry your excess on the lowest setting in your oven overnight.

CHINESE ARTICHOKE
Stachys affinis. Hardy perennial. ⌇

Popular in France where they are known as crosnes, Chinese artichokes resemble cream-coloured, segmented oca. Excellent raw in salads, lightly stir-fried or steamed, they have a nutty flavour and a pleasing water chestnut-like texture. An easy, delicious, un-buyable, underground treasure.

VARIETIES: No named varieties available.
STARTING OFF: Source tubers from a good supplier.
POSITION: Chinese artichokes are most productive in humus-rich, fertile soils. Tolerant of light shade.
SPACING: Chinese artichokes have a spreading habit, forming clumps, and are best planted 12cm or so apart and around 10cm deep.
PRODUCTIVITY/EFFICIENCY: Plentiful small tubers are produced with little effort on your part. Just re-plant some of the tubers to grow again next year.
GROWING: Little maintenance required except to keep them relatively weed free early in the year, and an annual mulch of compost.
POTENTIAL PROBLEMS: Generally pest and disease free.
HARVEST: Ready to harvest from late October, the tubers store happily in the soil over winter and can be dug as required.

CHINESE CEDAR
Toona sinensis. Deciduous tree/shrub. ⌇

Chinese cedar is one of the tastiest of the tree leaves, and hugely popular as a vegetable in China. The flavour is somewhere between garlic and onions - superb in stir-fries and salads. The leaves can be dried too (lay them in the sun in a greenhouse or polytunnel for a few days) and used as a spice.

VARIETIES: There are some named varieties but these have been bred for their ornamental qualities.
STARTING OFF: Can be started from seed but is unreliable. Best to source plants from a specialist supplier.
POSITION: A sunny spot and a moist but well-drained soil.
SPACING: A full-grown tree can reach 15m tall by 10m wide, but can easily be kept to 1–2m apart by coppicing and harvesting the shoots.
PRODUCTIVITY/EFFICIENCY: Once established, Chinese cedar will provide you with edible shoots with little work on your part, and can be underplanted with other edibles, as is common in Asia.
GROWING: Control its size by harvesting the young shoots and by coppicing occasionally.
POTENTIAL PROBLEMS: Generally pest and disease free.
HARVEST: Pick the young shoots before they exceed 20cm long, in spring and summer.

75

CHOP SUEY GREENS
Chrysanthemum coronarium. Also known as: shun-giku. Hardy annual. ⌇ (overleaf)

A peculiar thing, an edible chrysanthemum. The leaves and flowers have a distinctive, slightly aniseed flavour, best used in smallish amounts. Try young leaves and flowers in salads or more substantial leaves in stir-fries. Beautiful, too, bringing in beneficial insects as it flowers.

VARIETIES: No named varieties available.
STARTING OFF: Broadcast or sow in shallow drills from spring to September. Sow every few weeks for a good succession.
POSITION: Very happy in sun or part-shade.
SPACING: Thin to at least 5cm apart.
PRODUCTIVITY/EFFICIENCY: Harvesting is possible around 6 weeks after sowing and several cuttings can be had from each sowing.
GROWING: Water in dry weather.
POTENTIAL PROBLEMS: Fairly untroubled by pests and diseases but can become bitter in hot weather.
HARVEST: Cut when around 10cm high. The flowers are also edible.

Chop suey greens

CIME DI RAPA

Brassica rapa subsp. *rapa*. Also known as: broccolini, rapini, broccoli raab, broccoli rabe. Hardy annual. 〰

Cime di rapa is essentially turnip tops, where the plant has been bred to produce more leaves and no root. Deliciously green and brassica-y in flavour, and takes very happily to cut-and-come-again harvesting. Try chopped and sautéed in olive oil, with garlic and lemon juice.

VARIETIES: No named varieties available.
STARTING OFF: Sow in modules in March, planting out in April. Sow again after midsummer through to September.
POSITION: Full sun, in a well-composted soil.
SPACING: 30cm apart.
PRODUCTIVITY/EFFICIENCY: Cime di rapa is ready to harvest in around 60 days and can regrow several times.
GROWING: Water through dry periods.
POTENTIAL PROBLEMS: Fleece plants if flea beetle is a problem.
HARVEST: Leaves, stalks, flower buds and flowers are all edible. Cut 5cm from the ground as required and your plants should re-sprout.

COURGETTES

Cucurbita pepo. Half-hardy annual. 〰

Delicious, crisp cigars or hefty green water bags: the choice is yours. Harvest courgettes young and small to catch them at their best and the plant will quickly produce more for you. Thinly sliced, simply dressed and raw, they are a delight, as they are griddled. Make the most of the flowers too – peppery, with a crisp core, they are really good in salads, or stuffed, battered and deep-fried.

VARIETIES: 'Nero di Milano' and 'Tromboncino' are old varieties with the latter being vigorous and scrambling and producing swan-necked pale fruits. 'Romanesco' are ridged with huge flowers. 'Soleil' courgettes are yellow, 'Bianca di Trieste' are white and 'Rondo di Nizza' will give you round courgettes.
STARTING OFF: Sow seed individually in 9cm pots in April and plant out after the last frosts. Always sow

two seeds plus one for each person you are growing for. If there are two of you, that's four plants: one for the slugs, and three (ideally of different varieties) to keep you in delicious small courgettes.
POSITION: Full sun in fertile, moisture-retentive soil.
SPACING: 90cm apart.
PRODUCTIVITY/EFFICIENCY: Plants can crop from June until early October, each plant producing many courgettes.
GROWING: Courgettes need a lot of water to produce well so ensure a good supply especially in dry weather.
POTENTIAL PROBLEMS: Slugs like young plants so take whichever measures you favour (see pages 364, 370). Cucumber mosaic virus is largely untreatable. Powdery mildew is a potential threat late in the season, so ensure good ventilation.
HARVEST: Plants give you a harvest of both flowers and courgettes. Look for the male flowers (those without a courgette forming behind the flower) – picking them won't reduce your courgette harvest. Pick courgettes when small for best flavour and keep picking to ensure a good supply.

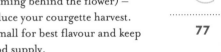

77

Courgettes

CUCAMELONS

Melothria scabra. Tender perennial often grown as an annual. ✑

A neighbour grew cucamelons seven or eight years ago and we were relatively unimpressed, but we both gave them another try the following year and picked them a little earlier – first time, I suspect they'd gone a little past their best. Picked ripe yet crisp, as grape-sized mini-melons, their lightly citrus-cucumber flavour and texture is really good in salsas, salads and cocktails.

VARIETIES: No named varieties available.
STARTING OFF: Sow direct in April or in modules, potting on before planting out after the last frosts.
POSITION: Full sun and in moist but well-drained soil.
SPACING: Around 40cm apart.
PRODUCTIVITY/EFFICIENCY: Many small fruits are produced on each plant and over a long period of time. Cropping starts 9-12 weeks after sowing. Easy, relatively drought resistant and largely ignored by pests.

GROWING: Pinch out the growing tip when it reaches 2m or so, and then pinch out any laterals when they reach 40cm. Provide support for the plants to climb up.
POTENTIAL PROBLEMS: Generally pest and disease free.
HARVEST: Pick cucamelons as they ripen from July to September.

CUCUMBERS AND GHERKINS

Cucumis sativus. Half-hardy annual. ✑

I'm very fond of the few cucumbers I grow, especially the very beautiful 'Crystal Lemon' – ovate, yellow and it seems to be cooler than the green varieties and without any hint of bitterness in the skin. Cucumbers are not easy to coax a decent harvest from, but along with gherkins they have a flavour very much more satisfying than those you buy. I use most raw in salads, but increasingly in cocktails and for ice cream – both are as refreshing as they sound.

Gherkins

Cucumbers

VARIETIES: 'Marketmore' for tasty cucumbers with good disease resistance; 'Crystal Lemon' has cool, crisp yellow fruit. 'La Diva' and 'Vert Petit de Paris' are small gherkins and good for pickling. 'Burpless Tendergreen' is a good ridge variety.

STARTING OFF: Start in 9cm pots under cover in April. Cucumbers can be planted outside after the last frosts.

POSITION: Full sun in a sheltered spot. Well-composted, moisture-retentive soil.

SPACING: 50cm apart for climbers and around 1.5m for ridge types to sprawl.

PRODUCTIVITY/EFFICIENCY: Cucumbers will produce from June until October if grown under cover.

GROWING: Cucumbers need a lot of water to produce well so ensure a good supply in dry weather.

POTENTIAL PROBLEMS: Red spider mite (treatable with the introduction of a natural predator, such as Phytoseiulus persimilis), cucumber mosaic virus (which is untreatable), and powdery mildew, which can be minimised with good ventilation.

HARVEST: Pick when a good size but preferably before they become too large.

DAUBENTON'S KALE
(AND OTHER PERENNIAL KALES)
(see page 90)

Brassica oleracea var. *ramosa.* Hardy biennial/perennial.

A delicious, perennial kale that was a Victorian favourite, and with all the classic green, bright flavour of a mid-green kale. Easy to grow, highly productive, and seems to be a little more robust in the face of the cabbage white butterflies than many.

VARIETIES: Other varieties to try include the very sweet 'Sutherland' kale, 'East Friesian Palm' kale and 'Walking Stick' kale, which can reach more than 3m tall.

STARTING OFF: Source plants from a good supplier. Daubenton's can be easily propagated from side shoots throughout the growing season.

POSITION: Perennial kales need a good fertile soil.

SPACING: This depends on variety but, as a general rule, space around 1m apart.

PRODUCTIVITY/EFFICIENCY: Once established,

Sutherland kale

Daubenton's kale is both easily productive for years and requires little effort.

GROWING: Give an annual mulch of compost.

POTENTIAL PROBLEMS: Net against pigeons and butterflies if they are a problem in your area.

HARVEST: Pick leaves as required throughout the year, but they are particularly valuable through the winter and early spring months.

DAYLILIES

Hemerocallis species. Hardy perennial.

A glorious, early flowering plant, of which all parts are edible. We use the leaves and flowers most – shredded leaves add fresh punch to salads, and the flowers are superb raw, as tempura, in salads or in soups where they are traditionally used as a thickener. Their flavour is green, fresh and peppery – more intense in the reds than the yellows/oranges. As their name suggests, the blooms only last for a day, so pick them in the afternoon, safe in the knowledge that they are about to fade in any case. Although all parts can be eaten, a piece of advanced horticultural advice: leave the roots where they belong – under the soil – as lifting them kills the plant.

VARIETIES: There are a multitude of species and varieties to grow. You could try *H. lilioasphodelus* for an early yellow flower or 'Sammy Russell' for a red flower. *Hemerocallis fulva* enthusiastically colonises any ground given to it.

Daylilies

STARTING OFF: Source plants from a good supplier or lift and divide established plants in spring or autumn.

POSITION: Tolerant of most soils and prefer full sun.

SPACING: 30–45cm apart, depending on variety.

PRODUCTIVITY/EFFICIENCY: With careful choice of cultivars you can harvest shoots, buds and flowers from spring to early autumn.

GROWING: Clumps may need dividing every 3 years or so.

POTENTIAL PROBLEMS: Pick off and burn any unusually swollen buds that refuse to open to deter the Hemerocallis gall midge. Protect from slugs and snails early in the year (see pages 364, 370).

HARVEST: Pick young leaves in spring, flower stems when no more than 12cm long, and the flowers that follow when they are fully open.

EARTH CHESTNUT

Bunium bulbocastanum. Also known as: great pignut and pignut, though not to be confused with the widely foraged *Conopodium majus*, which is also known as pignut. Hardy Perennial.

A relatively small (60cm each way) perennial vegetable with feathered leaves and white summer flowers. Leaves, flowers and roots are all edible - the green parts carrying a lovely parsley flavour and are best eaten fresh, while the sweet chestnut-flavoured roots need roasting or boiling before eating. Allow some of the flowers to remain unpicked and collect the seed in autumn - it has a similar flavour to cumin and can be used in the same way.

VARIETIES: No named varieties available.

STARTING OFF: You can sow seed in modules under cover in spring, potting on once before planting out, or source plants from a specialist supplier.

POSITION: Moist, well-drained soil in full sun.

SPACING: 50cm apart.

PRODUCTIVITY/EFFICIENCY: A versatile plant, using leaves as a salad ingredient, seeds as a spice or the roots during winter.

GROWING: Little maintenance required, but plants tend to live for only around 5 years, so it can be an idea to save a little seed to sow the following year.

POTENTIAL PROBLEMS: Generally pest and disease free.

HARVEST: Pick leaves throughout the growing season, cut flower stalks in autumn for drying the seed, and dig the tubers during winter.

EGYPTIAN WALKING ONION

Allium proliferum. A type of tree onion. Hardy perennial.

If you've a little patience to allow them to establish, walking onions will give you plenty in return. Early in spring they throw up tubular leaves to pick as chives. Any you allow to grow on can be pulled off as spring onions. Allow some to develop and small bulbils (mini-onions) will form on the end of the leaves. Pick some as they grow if you like, allowing others to grow on - as they do, they'll weigh down the leaves, bending

Earth chestnut

Egyptian walking onion

them until the bulbils touch the ground, where they will root and start the whole process off again – hence 'walking' around whatever space you allow them. Late in the season, the mother plant will have delicious shallot-like onions at its base – pick some, leaving the rest to provide the engine room for the following year. That's four delicious and different harvests from one perennial plant.

VARIETIES: No named varieties available.
STARTING OFF: Sow bulbils in small pots in spring or autumn.
POSITION: A reasonably drained soil in full sun, though they tolerate some shade.
SPACING: 30cm apart.
PRODUCTIVITY/EFFICIENCY: You can eat the onion bulbs that multiply at the base, leaves and bulbils. The onions will gently reproduce if given a weed-free bed.
GROWING: Needs very little maintenance and will travel around.
POTENTIAL PROBLEMS: Slugs – deal with them as you like (see pages 364, 370).
HARVEST: Pick bulbils from the top in spring when young and tender or later in the year when big enough to bother with peeling. These late ones can be dried for storage. Leaves can be picked at any time of year but don't over-harvest. Dig up to harvest the bulbs but don't forget to replant one.

ENDIVE

Cichorium endivia. Hardy biennial. ᏮᎦ

I don't grow endive every year but look forward to them very much when I do. A few of their bitter leaves in a mixed leaf salad adds a little zippiness that sets off the plainer leaves beautifully. But I like them best cooked face down in a hot pan with a few spoonfuls of olive oil and too much salt and pepper, until they wilt into a blond sweet-bitter wig.

VARIETIES: There are escarole types that are broad-leaved and hardy, and frisée types with frizzy leaves, which are happier in summer and autumn. 'Cornet de Bordeaux' will happily stand the winter; 'Blonde Full Heart' is excellent for hearts and 'Fine de Louvier' for leaves. 'Cuor d'Oro' blanches itself.

E

81

STARTING OFF: Depending on variety sow in modules from April and plant out after first frosts, or sow direct from May to midsummer.

POSITION: Happy in most soils but escarole types, in particular, need reasonable drainage.

SPACING: 30cm apart.

PRODUCTIVITY/EFFICIENCY: Endive can be sown as a cut-and-come-again crop, ready in under 7 weeks; otherwise it takes 3 months for a harvest.

GROWING: Little maintenance needed other than watering in a dry patch.

POTENTIAL PROBLEMS: Very few but check for slugs on any that you are blanching.

HARVEST: Blanch endive to make them less bitter by covering with an upturned pot for 3 weeks, with stones covering the holes. Cut entire heads by slicing through the stalk at ground level.

FLORENCE FENNEL

Foeniculum vulgare var. *azoricum*. A hardy perennial usually grown as an annual. ⌒

The glassy, firm bulbs of Florence fennel develop best in sunny, airy spots in a sandy, fertile soil. Of those conditions, I can rely only on 'fertility' in Devon, but don't let similar limitations put you off – the bulbs may look a little elongated compared with the ones in the shops but their flavour will be undiminished.

VARIETIES: 'Romanesco' and 'Finale' are reliable, delicious and bolt resistant.

STARTING OFF: Sow in modules under cover from April to July and plant outside from May. You can sow direct from May to July (or August for under-cover crops). Sowing every 2–3 weeks will give you a good succession.

POSITION: Sunny and warm in a good and well-drained soil.

SPACING: 30cm apart.

PRODUCTIVITY/EFFICIENCY: Fennel will occupy space for 10–15 weeks and while not hugely productive, it is packed with flavour.

GROWING: Keep weed free and don't allow the soil around to dry out. A good mulch will help with this.

POTENTIAL PROBLEMS: Few problems but slugs may have a nibble.

HARVEST: Cut the stem when the bulbs have swelled

Florence fennel

to a good size any time from late July through to November. Cover the stem with soil for a secondary crop of small shoots and don't forget that any thinnings are delicious too.

FRENCH BEANS

Phaseolus vulgaris. Half-hardy annual. ⌒

French beans are ever-present in most kitchen gardens – steadily and unspectacularly, they fill baskets every day or two from midsummer into early autumn. I say unspectacularly, but look at them with fresh eyes: their easy climbing habit, beautiful flowers (they were once grown as ornamentals) with the dangling pods to follow – they are as extraordinary as they are productive.

VARIETIES: French beans come in any combination of dwarf or climbing, flat or round and coloured purple, yellow or green. Try 'Rocquencourt' and 'Purple Teepee' for round pods, or 'The Prince' or

'Nassau' for flat pot dwarf varieties. 'Eva' (yellow) and 'Blue Lake Climbing' (purple) are fabulous climbers. Good varieties for drying include 'Cannellino' or 'Lazy Housewife'.

STARTING OFF: Sow in small batches (they are heavy croppers) in 9cm pots in April (March if harvesting under cover) and plant out after the first frosts. Do 2 more sowings, 6 weeks apart, for a steady supply. You can use dwarf beans for earliest and latest sowings, as these mature quickly and can be easily protected with a cloche or fleece.

POSITION: Sunny, sheltered spot on a reasonable soil.

SPACING: 20–30cm apart, depending on variety.

PRODUCTIVITY/EFFICIENCY: Many beans are produced over a long period of time from June into October.

GROWING: Keep weed free, water while the pods develop and give climbers something to twine themselves up.

POTENTIAL PROBLEMS: Aphids can be an issue as can slug damage on young plants.

HARVEST: Pick when young and tender for the best flavour and texture – it will encourage the plant to produce more pods. For drying, leave beans on the plant until they rattle, then pick, shell and leave to dry on a flat surface indoors for another couple of days.

French beans

Garlic

83

GARLIC
Allium sativum. Hardy perennial.

As much as I love regular bulbs of garlic, I grow more than half of my garlic to use early on in one form or another. Hardneck varieties produce stalks (scapes) that grow quickly in early summer – cut them while the flower is thin, closed and tear-shaped, for one of the harvests of the year. It is like garlic-flavoured asparagus. Hardneck varieties don't store well, so, as well as using the stalks, we tend to use the bulb as green garlic – picking them a few weeks before the individual cloves have formed. Roasted, they are mild, sweet and delicious. Softneck varieties tend to have a less complex, though stronger flavour and store well – we pick and dry these for using into winter.

VARIETIES: Before you choose a variety, consider how you want to eat it. Hardnecks should be used first – either for their leaves, as green garlic (see above) and as normal or dried bulbs. Softneck varieties store well and are best for using as you would shop-bought garlic.

Elephant garlic

SPACING: 20cm apart (25cm for Elephant garlic).
PRODUCTIVITY/EFFICIENCY: Garlic will be in the ground for 6–8 months but you have the possibility of scapes, green garlic and regular garlic bulbs. Many varieties store well for months, and it is one of the most transforming of flavours – just a little makes a great impact.
GROWING: Keep weed free. Tolerant of dry weather.
POTENTIAL PROBLEMS: Don't grow in the same place in successive years to reduce the risk of onion white rot and rust.
HARVEST: You can harvest garlic 'green' in May/early June for a mild flavour. The scapes can be harvested in early summer. Bulbs for drying will be ready in June or July once the leaves have turned yellow, with those planted before Christmas being a little larger and a little earlier than those planted later. Dry the bulbs in the sun for a few days and then store somewhere cool.

GARLIC CRESS
Peltaria alliacea. Hardy perennial.

One of the first and therefore most welcome leaves to emerge in spring, garlic cress grows reliably, with no attention, and adds punch and beauty to a spring salad when there's not much else to choose from. Pick the slim leaves early – as soon as the weather warms up they'll flower and bitterness follows. They make a fine pesto.

VARIETIES: No named varieties available.
STARTING OFF: Sow the seed in modules in spring or autumn and plant out in summer, or source as a young plant.
POSITION: Tolerant of most soils but likes some light shade. Plant in a permanent position.
SPACING: 20cm apart.
PRODUCTIVITY/EFFICIENCY: Can provide leaves most of the year.
GROWING: Will tolerate reasonable neglect.
POTENTIAL PROBLEMS: Generally untroubled.
HARVEST: Pick the leaves as desired. They are best between autumn and spring, becoming a little bitter over the summer when flowering. Happily, you can eat the flowers too.

'Picardy Wight' and 'Solent Wight' are two great-tasting softneck varieties that you can use well into winter, while 'Lautrec Wight' and 'Carcassonne Wight' are reliable and flavoursome hardnecks. Elephant garlic is more of a leek than a garlic, producing huge bulbs with a mild flavour – it is as tasty as it is impressive. Don't be tempted to grow from shop-bought garlic, as they are usually grown in warmer climates than Britain's and are more susceptible to viruses.
STARTING OFF: As garlic needs a certain amount of cold to induce it to bulb, plant by mid-February, ideally before Christmas. Separate the bulbs, discarding the tiny ones in the middle, and push individual cloves into the ground just below the surface with the pointy end up (10cm deep for Elephant garlic).
POSITION: Sun and free drainage.

Garlic cress

Garlic mustard

GARLIC MUSTARD

Alliaria petiolata. Also known as: hedge garlic and Jack-by-the-hedge, due to its liking for growing exactly there. Hardy biennial.

A delicious, tall nettle-like plant, with small white and yellow flowers, found in hedgerows, woodlands and riversides – anywhere where there's a good moist soil. Although it resembles a few wild plants, its bright green, heart-shaped leaves smell of garlic, distinguishing it from the others. A great leafy green for stir-fries and sides, and just the best in a cheese sandwich!

VARIETIES: No named varieties available.
STARTING OFF: Sow seed in modules from May to July and plant out when the roots are showing.
POSITION: Happy in most soils. Some shade preferred.
SPACING: 30cm apart.
PRODUCTIVITY/EFFICIENCY: This plant provides you with several crops over a reasonably long season. The young leaves are good raw. As they become older and hotter, they are better cooked. The seeds can be used as a peppery spice.
GROWING: Little maintenance needed.

POTENTIAL PROBLEMS: Generally pest and disease free.
HARVEST: You can start picking the young leaves in spring for salads and, later in the summer, use them in cooking. Harvest the seeds in summer.

GLOBE ARTICHOKES

Cynara scolymus. Hardy perennial.

It must have taken a hungry person to investigate the spiky armour of a globe artichoke in search of sustenance, yet somewhere underneath that threatening exterior lies culinary heaven. Harvested small, the immature flowers can be stripped of petals to reveal a pale, oval centre. Cut off the base to remove any petal remnants, then in half lengthways – remove any hint of fluffy choke from within. Immerse in acidulated water if not using immediately. Larger artichokes should be tackled in one of two ways. To demolish them in the classic 'French' style, boil them for 15–45 minutes (depending on size) and serve whole with a vinaigrette – peel off each of the petals, dip in the dressing and scrape the pad of succulent flesh from the petal with your teeth. To extract the heart for preserving or cooking, lay the artichoke on its side taken from established plants in April by digging up and gently separating the newer groups of leaves that have developed at the base. Plant these straightaway.

POSITION: Full sun and good drainage in a permanent position.

SPACING: Around 1.2m apart.

PRODUCTIVITY/EFFICIENCY: A relatively large space is taken up compared to the size of crop you get, but very low maintenance and any artichokes left to flower will be loved by the bees.

GROWING: Very little care needed. Replace plants every 3 or 4 years with some of the offsets they have produced.

POTENTIAL PROBLEMS: Slugs can bother small plants but otherwise trouble-free.

HARVEST: Small side-heads on 'Violet de Provence' can be harvested as early as May before any choke has developed. Cut the plant to the base for another crop around 2 months later. Otherwise, cut off the larger heads when plump and the scales tight between July and August.

GOOD KING HENRY
Chenopodium bonus-henricus. Hardy perennial.

Good King Henry has more noms-de-plume than Carlos the Jackal – poor man's asparagus and Lincolnshire spinach among them – which hints at its many uses. Its spears, leaves and flower buds are all equally, if differently, delicious. The spikes make for a wonderful pre-asparagus harvest in early spring – just cut them at 15-20cm and treat as you would asparagus. The leaves make a great spinach substitute, and the flower buds are amazing cooked in butter and garlic. A perennial that's as tough as old boots and with a long season of generosity.

VARIETIES: Generic.
STARTING OFF: Sow in modules under cover in March or sow direct.
POSITION: Prefers a reasonable amount of shade with only a couple of hours' full sun during the day. Avoid sandy or waterlogged soils.
SPACING: 30cm for good ground cover, which will help to suppress weeds.
PRODUCTIVITY/EFFICIENCY: A delicious and productive perennial, and easy to grow.

Globe artichoke

86

and use a bread knife to slice through the petals about 4cm from the base. Remove the petal stubs and any remnants. Ease out the fluffy immature flower (the choke) from the centre and discard. You are left with the heart. Either sauté or poach in a little wine and/or water until tender.

VARIETIES: 'Gros Vert de Laon', 'Violetta di Chioggia' and 'Violet de Provence' are classic and delicious varieties. 'Green Globe' is slightly hardier.
STARTING OFF: Growing from seed will give slightly variable results and takes time, so consider planting offsets/young plants. Sow seed in 9cm pots in spring and pot on once before planting out. Offsets can be

Good King Henry

GROWING: Allow plants to establish without harvesting any in their first year, building themselves up for years of delicious productivity.

POTENTIAL PROBLEMS: None.

HARVEST: Good King Henry will produce spikes early in the spring – cut them just below the soil level when young and tender – and leaves throughout the growing season, with the flower buds in summer.

GROUND NUT

Apios americana. Also known as: the potato bean. A tuberous, climbing hardy perennial.

A lively climber with beautiful, chocolate-coloured flowers and really tasty tubers – like nutty potatoes in flavour though more like yams in texture. I like them best roasted, though they can be fried or boiled, as you would potatoes. It can be slow to start growing in spring, but once underway there's no stopping it.

VARIETIES: Named varieties are increasingly available, all of which taste the same to my taste buds but they do yield a little more than the generic.

STARTING OFF: Source tubers from a specialist supplier or propagate by potting up or planting out tubers from established plants.

POSITION: Prefers moist but well-drained soil and is tolerant of reasonable amounts of shade.

SPACING: Around 30cm apart.

PRODUCTIVITY/EFFICIENCY: Takes up little space as it can be planted next to small trees or shrubs up which it likes to climb. As it is a nitrogen fixer (see page 357–360), it improves the fertility of the soil as it grows.

GROWING: Give them a structure – even just a few canes – to climb up. Allow to establish for a few years after planting before harvesting some of the tubers.

POTENTIAL PROBLEMS: Generally disease free, but mice may go for the tubers if left over winter, so protect.

HARVEST: The tubers are around 5cm in diameter and can be harvested at any time of year, though you will upset the growing plant less if you pick them in autumn or winter. Remember to leave some tubers in place for the plant to regrow.

Ground nut

HOPS

Humulus lupulus. Deciduous perennial climber.

Apart from enriching some of my favourite ales, hops make a really good vegetable – with the young nutty shoots taking to a quick steaming very well. I tend to eat them as a simple side veg with olive oil, or as part of a stir-fry. They look beautiful too, scrambling over an arch or other structure, offering shade to plants beneath.

VARIETIES: You could try 'East Kent Golding', which climbs to around 6m. Or, for an easier-to-reach hop, try 'First Gold' that won't reach half that.
STARTING OFF: Source young plants from a good supplier, or take root cuttings or divide plants in spring for best results.
POSITION: Prefers any humus-rich soil and sun or semi-shade.
SPACING: Plants will reach around 1.5m in width.
PRODUCTIVITY/EFFICIENCY: Growing up through existing trees or trellises means hops take up little space, providing you with greens in the spring and cones for beer-making in the autumn.
GROWING: Either prune back to 50cm or so after harvesting or leave old stems for the new ones to climb up.
POTENTIAL PROBLEMS: Aphids can be a nuisance in summer, but generally pest and disease free.
HARVEST: Pick young shoots in spring for cooking, allowing some to grow on and survive. Cones (mature flowers) can be harvested for beer as they ripen in autumn. They are ripe when they have a strong 'hoppy' aroma and leave yellow lupulin powder on your fingers when you touch them.

HOSTA

Hosta species (see below). Hardy perennial.

A favourite not only of the slugs, but also much of Asia and increasingly inquisitive eaters in the UK. Widely grown as an ornamental, with most unaware that many Hosta species are also edible. The emerging shoots are very good harvested in spring and steamed quickly, with butter and pepper.

VARIETIES: Many of the Hosta species are edible. *H. sieboldiana* are large-leaved and you could try 'Big Daddy', 'Bressingham Blue' or 'Elegans'. The flowers and flower buds of *H. fortunei* are reputedly the most delicious.
STARTING OFF: Source plants from a good supplier or divide established plants in autumn or winter.
POSITION: A shady spot with moist soil.
SPACING: Depending on variety space 30–90cm apart. Err on the close side if you want good groundcover.
PRODUCTIVITY/EFFICIENCY: Hostas can take a few years to establish but will be productive year after year. Little effort, other than encouraging a healthy population of frogs and other slug predators.
GROWING: Little maintenance needed.
POTENTIAL PROBLEMS: Protect from slugs when young (see pages 364, 370).
HARVEST: Harvest the hostons (rolled-up leaves) as they emerge in spring by snapping off at the base from the outside of the plant. Younger hostons need less cooking and can be lightly fried, whilst older, loosely furled hostons will need boiling briefly. The leaf-scales at the base of the hoston are slightly bitter and best removed. Allow the shoots that come up to replace those harvested to grow on and keep the plant alive.

Hosta

Jerusalem artichoke flowers

J

89

JERUSALEM ARTICHOKE

Helianthus tuberosus. Hardy perennial.

Along with celeriac, these egg-sized tubers shout their subterranean origins in their hearty earthiness more than any other underground harvest. They are perhaps the easiest vegetable to grow: plant them once and any you leave unharvested will regrow the following year. They are one of the most generous plants too – cut its sunflowers for the house in summer, lift the tubers through winter and cut the tall stalks and leafy growth to compost as you harvest. And the flowers will attract plenty of beneficial insects to your garden. Jerusalem artichokes contain inulin, which isn't readily broken down by the body – this can cause 'interesting' results, but the body often quickly builds a tolerance and effects are diminished. Wonderful roasted, when they collapse a little and take on the flavours around them, or as the basis of a soup or risotto.

VARIETIES: 'Fuseau' is the least knobbly (hence easiest to peel) and highest yielding but 'Gerard' is said to have a smokier flavour if that appeals.
STARTING OFF: Jerusalem artichokes are perennial so find a permanent spot and plant tubers 15cm deep.
POSITION: Sunny with reasonable drainage.
SPACING: Around 60cm apart.
PRODUCTIVITY/EFFICIENCY: High-yielding crop requiring very little attention, though appreciative of the odd mulch with compost in spring.
GROWING: They make very tall plants producing beautiful yellow sunflower-like flowers in late summer. Their height and mass of growth make a good summer windbreak.
POTENTIAL PROBLEMS: None.
HARVEST: Jerusalem artichokes don't store well so dig as needed from October to February. Leave a few tubers in the ground for next year's supply.

Kai lan

K

KAI LAN

Brassica oleracea var. *alboglabra*. Also known as: Chinese broccoli, Chinese kale, gai-lan or kailaan. Hardy perennial.

Depending on when you harvest and how you grow it, kai lan is either one of the tastiest little-known harvests or a tough waste of time. The secret is to cut the growth while young and lush rather than let it become too leggy and woody. Get it right and you'll have succulent asparagus-crossed-with-sprouting-broccoli; leave it too long, and you'll have something with all the flavour and tenderness of a pencil. Eat it as you would asparagus or sprouting broccoli.

VARIETIES: No named varieties available.
STARTING OFF: Sow in modules under cover in February/March, for planting out as soon as the roots are showing. Sow again from July to September, direct if you prefer.
POSITION: Full sun in a composted and reasonably drained soil.
SPACING: 30–40cm apart.

PRODUCTIVITY/EFFICIENCY: Early sowings are ready to pull whole in 20 days or so. Later ones can be cut several times from around 2 months after sowing. Kai lan is a perennial and if you want to treat it as such, cut it back to 5cm in late autumn and allow to regrow in spring.
GROWING: Keep weed-free and watered in dry weather.
POTENTIAL PROBLEMS: Fleece against flea beetle, butterflies and pigeons if they are a problem.
HARVEST: Leaves, stems and flowers are all edible. Pull up whole plants from early sowings and use all parts – these are likely to run to seed too quickly for you to use as cut-and-come-agains. For seed sown after midsummer cut the stems a few centimetres above the ground when 15–20cm tall and before they flower. You should be able to cut the stems twice more.

KALE

Brassica oleracea var. *acephala*. Hardy biennial, mostly grown as an annual.

Kale comes in as many distinctive and delicious varieties as tomatoes and chillies do, encouraging the gardener to try at least three or four. 'Red Russian' is my favourite, picked early, small and sweet for salads. This joins the dark, iron-y 'Cavolo Nero' for summer-into-autumn leaves with the substance to stand up to olive oil, chillies and garlic. 'Redbor' is a beautiful winter leaf, adding colour and variety to the other two. There are many perennial kales to be found – 'Sutherland' is the sweetest of the ones I've tried.

VARIETIES: 'Red Russian', 'Redbor' and 'Cavolo Nero' are each delicious and distinct from each other. 'Sutherland' kale is very sweet. 'Daubenton's' kale (see page 79) is one of a number of fine perennial forms, as are 'East Friesian Palm' kale and 'Walking Stick' kale, both growing to an impressive height.
STARTING OFF: Sow seed in modules under cover from February to early August, depending on variety, potting on into 9cm pots. Plant out when 10–15cm tall. You can sow direct from April. Sowings made before May will give you a summer crop and those after, an autumn/winter one.

POSITION: Tolerant of some shade and an exposed site but soil should have reasonable drainage.
SPACING: 30–80cm apart, depending on variety and whether you plan to pick leaves when small.
PRODUCTIVITY/EFFICIENCY: Kales are productive over a long period of time and provide greens when little else is around. The immature flowers also make good eating.
GROWING: Keep weed free and don't allow to dry out.
POTENTIAL PROBLEMS: Fleece against flea beetle, butterflies and pigeons if they are a problem. Crop rotation will help deter clubroot (see page 368).
HARVEST: Pick individual leaves of summer kale when small and sweet and as required from autumn/winter plants.

Kale

Kohlrabi

K

91

KOHLRABI

Brassica oleracea var. *gongylodes*. Hardy biennial, mostly grown as an annual.

Very possibly top of the 'What on earth do I do with that?' vegetable list. In the days before I found some culinary homes for it, I remember using a few for a particularly close game of boules in the River Cottage kitchen garden. These days, while I'm still happy to tennis-racket any slug-ruined kohlrabi into the pig pen, the best of the harvest goes into remoulade and coleslaw, and also gratins with whichever of the green leaves are flourishing.

VARIETIES: 'Azur Star' is great for quick-growing roots, 'Gigant' for a large size and winter storage, and 'Luna' for sweet baby roots.
STARTING OFF: Sow in modules under cover from February to August, planting out as soon as its roots are showing.
POSITION: A sunny site with reasonable drainage.
SPACING: 25–30cm apart.
PRODUCTIVITY/EFFICIENCY: Crops can be ready in as little as 5 weeks.

GROWING: Keep weed free and watered in dry weather.

POTENTIAL PROBLEMS: Fleece against flea beetle, butterflies and pigeons if they are a problem for you. Crop rotation will help deter clubroot (see page 368).

HARVEST: Pull kohlrabi as soon as it reaches the required size. Winter crops can withstand light frosts so dig up and store in paper sacks if you want to use over the winter. The leaves are also edible.

LEEKS

Allium ampeloprasum var. *porrum.* Hardy biennial, mostly grown as an annual.

With every year that passes, I grow more leeks. Their combination of fresh green flavour with sweet, mild onioniness wakes up everything from potatoes to red and white meat. They're relatively easy to grow well, and they add structure and height to the veg patch. Any left unharvested will sprout the most impressive flower heads late in the season – the mini-florets are very fine scattered through salads or in a mayonnaise.

Leeks

VARIETIES: Early varieties include 'Hannibal' and 'Monstruoso de Carentan', with 'Saint Victor', 'Bleu de Solaise' and 'Musselburgh' good for later in the season. 'King Richard' is a good, very early variety that also makes for superb baby leeks.

STARTING OFF: Sow seed in modules under cover from February and plant out when 20cm tall using a dibber or narrow pen. Trim down the roots to a few centimetres before putting in the hole and water in but don't backfill the hole with soil – leave the leeks loose in the hole. Leeks can be sown outside from March to early May. You could also try multi-sowing 4 seeds per module.

POSITION: Moisture-retentive soil in full sun.

SPACING: 15–25cm apart, depending on the size of leek required. For baby leeks, space at 1.5cm within the row and 15cm between rows. Space multi-sown leeks about 23cm apart.

PRODUCTIVITY/EFFICIENCY: Leeks take up little space and are very easy to grow, occupying the ground over autumn and winter.

GROWING: Keep weed free and watered in dry weather. Earth up for larger white parts.

POTENTIAL PROBLEMS: Use crop rotation (see page 368) to help prevent leek rust and fleece if leek moth is a problem in your area.

HARVEST: Dig as required, lifting baby leeks when around as thick as a pencil.

LETTUCE

Lactuca sativa. Hardy annual.

My teenage self probably ate less salad in a year than I do in most weeks now. While a lot of the reason for that must rest with me simply being a teenager, at least part is down to the terribly thin choice at the time. So many good lettuces are available in the shops now, but the very best leaves are those that you grow yourself. I tend to grow half for cut-and-come-again leaves, growing the rest into hearting lettuces – many of them butterheads for summer salads. Do try some winter lettuces too – as well as salads, they make fine soups; try them with peas and a little lovage.

VARIETIES: Innumerable, with huge variety in looks, flavour and texture. Careful choice, some protection and different methods of harvesting can

Flashy Butter Oak

Red Oak Leaf

L

93

give you year-round lettuce. Try 'Buttercrunch' for a butterhead type that will withstand heat fairly well, 'Reine de Glace' or 'Pinokkio' for a bit of crunch, or 'Marvel of Four Seasons' and 'Winter Density' for lettuces to take you through the colder months. Most varieties can be planted for cut-and-come-again crops, but 'Red Oak Leaf' or 'Flashy Butter Oak' are particularly good.

STARTING OFF: Sow successively in modules under cover from January, and direct from March to September. Plant out as soon as the roots fill the modules (they may need some fleece or cloche protection). Sow seed in the evening during the warmer summer months, as seed needs cooler temperatures to germinate. Lettuce can bolt in hot weather so cut-and-come-again is a good option for this time of year.

POSITION: Ideally, a moisture-retentive but well-drained soil. Needs some shade in hotter months.

SPACING: 4–35cm apart, depending on harvesting method and variety.

PRODUCTIVITY/EFFICIENCY: Lettuces are quick from seed to harvest and a very efficient use of space, especially if grown as cut-and-come-again or harvested 'in the round'.

GROWING: Keep moist during dry weather and provide some shade in the hotter months, perhaps by growing on the north side of your bean poles.

POTENTIAL PROBLEMS: Your chosen slug and snail deterrents may be necessary (see pages 364, 370).

HARVEST: For cut-and-come-again, harvest a couple of centimetres above the ground when a suitable size and leave to regrow, or pick individual leaves. By growing as a hearting lettuce but picking off individual leaves from the outside, you can harvest a single lettuce over a very long period.

Mashua

MASHUA

Tropaeolum tuberosum. A herbaceous climber that is borderline hardy.

Like the potato, mashua originates from South America, and also like the potato, it is mighty fine to eat. Treat them as you would most underground harvests - boil, roast or fry - to bring out their very gentle aniseed and pepperiness. Peel large tubers before cooking. The leaves are very similar in look and taste to nasturtiums, and the flowers are also edible: try both in salads. Above ground, it is a perennial climber that will scramble across the ground if given nothing to latch on to.

VARIETIES: Try *T. tuberosum pilifera* for white tubers and fiery orange flowers or *T. tuberosum* 'Ken Aslet' for early flowers and yellowy-red flowers.
STARTING OFF: Source tubers from a good supplier or pot up tubers from an existing plant.
POSITION: Full sun in a moist but well-drained soil.
SPACING: 40cm apart.
PRODUCTIVITY/EFFICIENCY: Leaves, flowers and tubers of this beautiful climber are edible. Very productive over a long period.
GROWING: Lift tubers before the cold weather and store in moist sand or sawdust over winter.
POTENTIAL PROBLEMS: Generally pest and disease free. Late frosts can knock back new growth, but they will usually recover. A long summer is needed for good-sized tubers.

HARVEST: Leave tubers in the ground for as long as possible to allow them to swell, but dig up before the ground freezes. Leaves and flowers can be harvested throughout the growing season and the seeds (like nasturtiums) can be picked in autumn and used like capers.

MEXICAN TREE SPINACH

Chenopodium giganteum. Hardy annual.

One of the prettiest leafy plants in the garden, Mexican tree spinach is one of those plants you need only grow once to have a friend for life. A close relative of fat hen (commonly thought of as a weed), it is one of the earliest leaves to emerge in spring –

Mexican tree spinach

M

94

and is likely to do so randomly, within wind-blowing distance of its parent, if you let it go to seed. Growing to more than 2m, and with leaves than carry splashes of vivid pink that intensify the hotter the sun, Mexican tree spinach can be used as you would spinach – in salads or wilted in any number of main courses.

VARIETIES: No named varieties.
STARTING OFF: Sow in modules in March under cover and plant out as soon as the roots have filled them. Sow direct outside when the soil is warming up.
POSITION: Full sun and tolerant of most soils.
SPACING: Plants will grow to around 1.5m if given enough space, but grow 5–10cm apart for a cut-and-come-again crop.
PRODUCTIVITY/EFFICIENCY: A small patch of cut-and-come-again will give you several harvests.
GROWING: Little maintenance required.
POTENTIAL PROBLEMS: Very trouble free.
HARVEST: Pick individual leaves from large plants or cut whole shoots when around 20cm tall if grown closely together, allowing them to regrow for a second or third harvest.

MIBUNA

Brassica rapa Japonica Group. Hardy annual. 🌱

Greener in colour and flavour than mizuna, mibuna sits ever so slightly more on the brassica side of things too. I was never that taken with it until I tried 'Green Spray' – an altogether fresher variety, that's pretty hardy and reliable. I prefer its more balanced flavour and that, for some reason, its leaves seem to avoid the flea beetle a little better than regular mibuna. A great salad leaf when small; when larger, use wilted in place of spinach.

VARIETIES: Few named varieties but try 'Green Spray'.
STARTING OFF: For an under-cover crop, sow from mid-February to mid-April in modules, planting as soon as the roots are showing. Sow outside after mid-June, as it will bolt if sown in the approach to midsummer.
POSITION: Moisture-retentive and well-drained soil. It will tolerate some shade.
SPACING: 25cm apart.

Mibuna

PRODUCTIVITY/EFFICIENCY: Each plant produces masses of long narrow leaves, which you can cut 3 or 4 times.
GROWING: Little maintenance required.
POTENTIAL PROBLEMS: Flea beetle shouldn't be a problem for sowings made after midsummer.
HARVEST: Cut leaves about 3cm above the ground as required. They will re-sprout and can be cut and harvested 3 or 4 more times in this way.

MICROLEAVES

Any midsummer birthday cards I get usually end up cluttering the dining table because the window sills (where my daughter likes to put cards) are taken up with lengths of guttering. A few inches of compost in each is all that's needed to nurse any of these punchy vegetables and herbs, which can be picked at just 5–6cm tall. Snipped just above the surface or pulled free and brushed clean of compost, many of the best have an intensity and cleanliness of flavour far superior to their full-grown version. And they're ready as quickly as a week after sowing in summer. Wonderful strewn in leafy salads, as a small salad of their own, or to add zip to all kinds of recipes, especially baked fish.

95

Microleaves

VARIETIES: Try fennel, rocket, radish, chervil, sorrel, coriander, nasturtium and any of the oriental leaves such as 'Red Giant' mustard or mizuna.
STARTING OFF: Sow in a seed tray or guttering throughout the year.
POSITION: Somewhere warm and light like a window sill or polytunnel.
SPACING: Sow thickly.
PRODUCTIVITY/EFFICIENCY: A very quick harvest from a small space, and (with the right choice of micros) offering huge flavour from a small harvest.
GROWING: Keep the compost lightly moist.
POTENTIAL PROBLEMS: None.
HARVEST: Microleaves will be ready from 7–20 days, depending on what you are growing and the time of year. Harvest by lifting and brushing free of compost, or cutting, when no taller than 7cm.

MIZUNA

Brassica rapa var. *Japonica*. Hardy annual.

One of the easiest oriental leaves to love, mizuna looks like a more deeply incised version of rocket, marrying a gentle pepperiness with fresh green flavour. You'll probably have eaten plenty of it, as it makes up one of the key components of many salad bags because it takes very well to cut-and-come-again harvesting and grows reliably for much of the year. As with most oriental leaves, pick them small for salads and use the larger, more peppery leaves in place of spinach.

VARIETIES: Few named varieties but try 'Mizuna Purple' for purple-tinged leaves or 'Broad Leaf' for a bolt-resistant mizuna.
STARTING OFF: Sow in modules under cover from mid-February to mid-April, planting out as soon as the roots are showing. Direct sow from mid-June to September. If sown from May to early June, plants will bolt.
POSITION: Full sun or light shade in a moisture-retentive but well-drained soil.
SPACING: 15cm apart for cut-and-come-again leaves and around 25cm for larger leaves for stir-frying.
PRODUCTIVITY/EFFICIENCY: Ready to harvest in 4–6 weeks with 3–4 harvests possible from one plant if growing as cut-and-come-again.
GROWING: Ensure soil around plants is kept moist.
POTENTIAL PROBLEMS: If growing after midsummer flea beetle shouldn't be a bother, otherwise fleece against them.
HARVEST: Cut entire plant at the base if harvesting large leaves for stir-frying. For cut-and-come-again leaves, cut 3cm above the ground when around 10cm tall.

MOOLI

Raphanus sativus var. *longipinnatus*. Also known as: daikon or Chinese white radish. Hardy biennial.

I tried growing mooli years ago, to no great effect, but recently met Japanese grower Shige Takezoe who had dedicated a fair stretch of his polytunnel to his beloved mooli. He convinced me to try again, giving them the sunniest spot I could find and plenty of water – I owe him. Their crisp, fresh texture is really special and their radish brightness is altogether more pure and satisfying than many of the regular radishes you can grow. They're very fine used as you would regular radishes, but I especially like them lightly, briefly pickled.

VARIETIES: No named varieties.
STARTING OFF: Sow seed direct from late July to early September into well-prepared soil. Seed can be sown successively for a continual supply of young roots.
POSITION: Likes a deep soil – moist but well-drained – and in full sun.
SPACING: Thin to 10cm apart within rows with 25cm between rows.
PRODUCTIVITY/EFFICIENCY: Great for a quick crop where summer veg have been lifted.
GROWING: Water during dry spells.
POTENTIAL PROBLEMS: Generally pest and disease free.
HARVEST: Harvest baby mooli 7–8 weeks after sowing. Later sowings of mooli are harvested in November before the frosts and will keep for a week or so in the fridge.

Mooli

Mushrooms

MUSHROOMS
Many edible species. Perennial.

As summer slips into autumn and the weather gets wetter, you'll find (largely) bearded or be-hatted men sneaking off to closely guarded secret sites in the hope of finding delicious (as opposed to poisonous) fungi. Much fun it is too, but it is perfectly possible to grow mushrooms in the comfort of your own garden or even your home. More than that, you can tweak the conditions to make them just right for mushroom production for much more of the year than the wild harvest. Oyster mushrooms are a good first stop – an old book indoors or a bin bag of straw are all it takes for your first home-grown fungi.

VARIETIES: Shiitake, oyster, lion's mane, shaggy inkcap and Stropharia to name but a few.
STARTING OFF: Spawn usually comes in the form of grain or pegs. Refer to suppliers' instructions on how to start your chosen variety.
POSITION: Often on straw, bark chippings or hard or softwood logs. Refer to suppliers' instructions for your particular mushroom.

Mushroom spawn

SPACING: Dependent on type of mushroom. Refer to suppliers' instructions.

PRODUCTIVITY/EFFICIENCY: Once started off, mushrooms can largely be left to their own devices. Depending on mushroom type they may crop over many months — or even years — if their food source is replenished.

GROWING: Refer to supplier for specifics of each variety.

POTENTIAL PROBLEMS: Employ your chosen slug deterrent.

HARVEST: This is often in autumn after a cool rain following a warm spell. Refer to information from your supplier for specifics.

NEW ZEALAND SPINACH

Tetragonia tetragonoides. Hardy evergreen perennial.

For some reason, perhaps best known to botanists, New Zealand spinach seems to dodge every ailment that besets regular spinach and other similar leafy greens. So its lightly glossy, gorgeous triangular leaves not only taste fabulous, they make you look like a champion gardener. It's a perennial that covers the ground quickly, retaining moisture and swamping out weeds but, alas, hard frosts see it off, so it'll only flourish all year round under cover in the warm.

VARIETIES: No named varieties.

STARTING OFF: Soak seed overnight to speed up germination. Sow in 9cm pots under cover around 3 weeks before the last frosts (6 weeks earlier if you are growing it under cover) and plant out after the last one.

POSITION: Full sun in moisture-retentive and well-drained soil.

SPACING: 30–45cm apart.

PRODUCTIVITY/EFFICIENCY: New Zealand spinach will be ready for harvesting around 2 months after sowing, forming a fairly spreading plant. From a single sowing you can harvest until the first frosts. A spinach that won't bolt.

GROWING: Water only in the driest weather.

POTENTIAL PROBLEMS: Generally pest and disease free.

HARVEST: Pick individual leaves and leaf tips throughout the growing season.

New Zealand spinach

OCA

Oxalis tuberosa. Borderline hardy perennial.

Oca looks like a knobbly new potato and shares many of the qualities of an early potato – a lovely nuttiness and a firm texture, especially. But they differ in a number of crucial ways. Oca isn't susceptible to blight and neither does it turn green when exposed to the light – instead, its gentle just-harvested, lemony edge sweetens in the sun, giving you a range of flavours at the end of the season when they're ready to lift. Keep a few back to sow next year and you have an un-buyable harvest year after year for only the expense of starting in year one. I use them grated raw in salads as well as in most of the ways I do new potatoes.

VARIETIES: Usually sold as generic rather than named varieties, though tubers can be pink, yellow or white.
STARTING OFF: Start oca under cover in April by sowing one tuber per 9cm pot and plant them outside in May once the last frosts are over.
POSITION: Full sun in moisture-retentive and well-drained soil.
SPACING: 30–40cm apart.
PRODUCTIVITY/EFFICIENCY: Oca will occupy the ground for 6 months and can produce around half a kilo of tubers per plant. Needs little attention.
GROWING: Mulch to retain moisture around plants.
POTENTIAL PROBLEMS: Generally untroubled by pests and diseases.
HARVEST: Tubers form very late, so don't dig until a couple of weeks after the leaves have been killed off by frosts. If a hard frost is forecast, it will be worth protecting the soil to prevent the tubers from freezing.

ONIONS

Allium cepa. Hardy bulb.

Every year I grow fewer traditional onions – something has to give when you've only so much space and time, so it's the harvests that are relatively inexpensive and taste reasonably similar whether bought or grown that tend to get left off the list. The exceptions are red onions, which are often inexplicably pricey, and a short row of one or two white varieties that I change

Drying onions

every year. The saved space is dedicated to shallots and a few trials of new flavours I've not grown before.

VARIETIES: 'Centurion' and 'White Ebenezer' are reliable and tasty white varieties; and 'Red Baron' and 'Red Electric' are fine red ones. Choose varieties well for flavour that's superior to most shop-bought onions.
STARTING OFF: Sow several seeds per module under cover in February/March and plant out when around 10cm tall, or sow direct in April. Plant sets from September to November or in March, pushing the set into the ground so that only the very tip is showing.
POSITION: Full sun in a well-drained, moisture-retentive soil.
SPACING: Spacing will determine onion size. 25cm apart for multi-sown modules. If sowing in rows, space 4–10cm apart within rows and 30cm between rows.

Drying onions

PRODUCTIVITY/EFFICIENCY: Onions can be occupying the ground from between 20 weeks for a spring set planting, and 40 weeks for autumn-sown seed.

GROWING: Onions dislike competition so keep weed free.

POTENTIAL PROBLEMS: Rotate to avoid onion downy mildew and white rot (see page 368). Don't store any soft onions, as they may rot.

HARVEST: In dry weather pull up onions once their foliage has died down and lay out to dry for a couple of days, turning occasionally. Onions grown from seed in autumn don't store well.

OSTRICH FERN

Matteuccia struthiopteris. Also known as: shuttlecock fern and fiddlehead fern. Hardy perennial.

Not one that's going to keep the wolf from the door, but certainly a delicious treat that's happiest growing in damp shade, where there is little else screaming for the space. The young emerging shoots - known as fiddleheads - are crisp, with a fine flavour somewhere between asparagus and calabrese, but they must be cooked for at least 15 minutes or they can cause stomach upsets.

Ostrich fern

VARIETIES: The hard-to-source 'Jumbo' lives up to its name – growing to 2m.

STARTING OFF: Source plants from a good supplier or propagate by division in spring.

POSITION: Moist but well-drained neutral to acid soils. Prefers light shade.

SPACING: 60cm apart for good ground cover. Plants can reach 1.5m in height.

PRODUCTIVITY/EFFICIENCY: Plants will easily colonise the area they are given by spreading via rhizomes. They give an asparagus-flavoured treat when other greens are scarce.

GROWING: Little maintenance needed.

POTENTIAL PROBLEMS: Generally untroubled by pests and diseases.

HARVEST: Harvest the young shoots or 'fiddleheads' in spring when the leafy section is still tightly furled – they can be 20–50cm tall at this stage, although the lower part of the stem is likely to be tough and will need removing. Plants can be forced in the winter for an earlier crop. Wash and remove the hairs before cooking.

101

PARSNIP

Pastinaca sativa. Hardy biennial, mostly grown as an annual.

I eat a fair amount of parsnips through the winter, and while I can't hope to grow all of those that I use, I usually sow a row or two because they seem to grow so happily here. I'm easily flattered. Occasionally, I let some grow on for a second year, when they'll flower tall and beautiful - their umbelliferous heads catching the eye and drawing in all manner of beneficial insects.

VARIETIES: 'Tender and True' and 'Gladiator' are delicious. 'Half Long Guernsey' is tasty, with good disease resistance.

STARTING OFF: Sow direct in March/April as the soil is warming up.

POSITION: Full sun on a sandy, well-worked soil.

SPACING: Sow in rows 30cm apart and thin to 15cm between plants. You can also grow parsnips closer together for smaller roots, which are good for summer harvesting.

PRODUCTIVITY/EFFICIENCY: Parsnips are in the ground for around 10 months of the year.

Flowering parsnips

GROWING: Germination is erratic and slow. It's a good idea to sow with radish at the same time — by the time you harvest the radish, your parsnips should be showing.

POTENTIAL PROBLEMS: Root rot and canker can be a problem on heavier soils, so grow a resistant variety and avoid very early sowings.

HARVEST: Dig as desired after the first frosts.

PEAS

Pisum sativum. Hardy annual.

Unless you eat very few peas or have plenty of space and time, you are unlikely to get anywhere near growing all the peas you'll want to eat. Don't let that stop you for a second from growing them though – picked fresh from the plant and eaten before you've had chance to walk more than a few feet from it,

they are the ultimate garden treat. I don't suppose I've ever cooked any that I've grown – they're too good straight from the plant! Growing your own also opens the door to pea shoots, and the finest sugar snap and mangetout varieties.

VARIETIES: Try 'Douce Provence' for a dwarf, hardy and productive pea for sowing year round or 'Alderman', 'Hurst Green Shaft' or 'Ne Plus Ultra' for a sweet, productive climbing pea. 'Markana' is good for an exposed site, or you could try 'Purple Podded Pea' for some colour. Sugar snap peas such as 'Sugar Ann' will give you some sweet crunch or try a mangetout variety such as 'Norli' or 'Weggisser'.

STARTING OFF: Timing depends on variety, so check the packet. Start under cover in root trainers or guttering for early crops, planting out when the plants are 10–15cm tall. Sow outside once the soil is warming up. Either sow little and often (every 2–3 weeks) or in larger quantities in spring, summer and autumn.

POSITION: A sunny spot with a moisture-retentive, free-draining soil.

SPACING: Direct sow peas 5cm deep, in trenches 20cm wide. Space peas at around 7cm apart, with 60–90cm between trenches. Plant out seedlings at similar spacing.

PRODUCTIVITY/EFFICIENCY: Peas produce over a long period of time if you keep picking. Climbing varieties will make more efficient use of space, particularly important if you're short of ground space. You can have crops from May to September.

GROWING: Little needed other than support. Twiggy hazel branches are best if you can get them. Leave roots in the ground when plants have gone over, as they are nitrogen rich and will break down to feed the soil.

POTENTIAL PROBLEMS: Mice like the seed and slugs the young plants. Start in root trainers to avoid the worst of this. Fleece against pigeons if they are a problem. Plants should outgrow pea and bean weevil attacks. Sow quick-growing peas early and late to avoid pea moth or grow mangetout varieties.

HARVEST: Pick pods whilst the peas inside are a good size but still young and succulent. Don't allow any pods to completely mature, as this will stop the plant from producing any more flowers/peas.

Peas

POTATOES
FIRST AND SECOND EARLIES

Solanum tuberosum. Half-hardy perennial, mostly grown as an annual.

The first handfuls of 'International Kidney', 'Belle de Fontenay' and the unromantically named 'BF15' make me ridiculously happy. Sweet, firm and cooked in just a few minutes, they are a spring-into-summer treat of which I never tire. They are rightly expensive in the shops too, so growing them saves a hatful of money.

VARIETIES: There is a huge variety of flavour, shape and colour available. Try first earlies 'Foremost', 'Epicure' and 'Lady Christl'. For second earlies

(more productive and taking slightly longer to mature), try 'British Queen' or 'Yukon Gold' for an excellent chipper and roaster.

STARTING OFF: Chit potatoes for a few weeks to induce sturdy young shoots, by placing your seed potatoes on a tray, eye-side up, in a light place. Plant out in trenches or holes from mid-March, covered by around 10cm of soil. Alternatively, cover your potato bed with 8–10cm compost and top with mulch matting, cutting holes to plant through (big enough for leaves to emerge from) – this removes the need to dig trenches/holes or earth up (see 'spacing').

POSITION: A sunny site with well-drained soil.

SPACING: Variable, depending on the size of your chosen cultivars and how large you want your potatoes to grow. Plant 35cm apart along rows with 50cm between rows. You could also try a closer spacing if using the mulching method (see 'starting off'). I've tried planting at 30cm between tubers, neither mulching nor earthing up – just allowing the foliage to shade the tubers, and although smaller tubers result, the hassle of earthing up is avoided.

PRODUCTIVITY/EFFICIENCY: Earlies will be in the ground for around 4 months. The yields will not be as large as for maincrops and are best eaten soon after they have been dug.

GROWING: To prevent your tubers turning green, earth up or mulch with compost, leaf mould or similar when shoots are around 15cm tall and again before the leaves touch.

POTENTIAL PROBLEMS: Much fewer than maincrop potatoes – they are usually dug up before blight and slugs become a serious problem.

HARVEST: Most varieties of early potatoes are ready to harvest when they flower. Dig up as you want to eat them. Some varieties are suitable for baking and roasting if left in the ground and grown on.

POTATOES
MAINCROP

Solanum tuberosum. Half-hardy perennial, mostly grown as an annual.

For years, I grew pretty much only early varieties of potato, but recently I've been risking a row or two of maincrops to the scourge of blight. 'Mayan Gold' make

P

103

P

Harvested potatoes

incredible crisps and roast potatoes with the perfect blend of crisp shell and buttery centre, which is a huge incentive. But I've always loved 'Pink Fir Apple' – perhaps too much, as I can't bear losing them to blight. On my head be it.

VARIETIES: Maincrop potatoes are the highest yielding and a huge choice is available to you. 'Cara' or purple-skinned 'Arran Victory' have creamy flesh for roasting and baking, or try 'Pink Fir Apple' for a maincrop waxy salad potato. 'Sarpo Mira' is the one for blight resistance — and growing it helps boost the commercial market for it, which means more potatoes grown without the huge chemical additives most come with.

STARTING OFF: Chit potatoes for a few weeks to induce sturdy young shoots, by placing your seed potatoes on a tray, eye-side up, in a light place. Plant out in trenches or holes from mid-March covered by around 10cm of soil. Alternatively, cover your potato bed with 8–10cm compost and top with mulch matting, cutting holes to plant through (big enough for leaves to emerge from) — this removes the need to dig trenches/holes or earth up (see below, 'spacing').

POSITION: A sunny site with well-drained soil.

SPACING: Variable, depending on the size of your chosen cultivars and how large you want your tubers to grow. Plant about 40cm apart if you are using a mulching method (see above, 'starting off'), or 35–45cm apart along rows and 65–75cm between rows if earthing up.

PRODUCTIVITY/EFFICIENCY: Maincrop potatoes will occupy the ground for around 5 months and will risk blight, but many varieties store over winter.

GROWING: To prevent your tubers turning green, earth up or mulch with compost, leaf mould or similar when shoots are around 15cm tall and again before the leaves touch.

POTENTIAL PROBLEMS: Maincrops are more susceptible to blight than early potatoes so grow a more resistant variety and cut leaves to the ground if blight hits, lifting them as soon as you can. Slugs living in the soil like tubers — a no-dig system can help here.

HARVEST: Dig up your potatoes when the foliage dies down, usually in August. If storing, keep only the perfect ones.

105

Chitting potatoes

PURSLANE
WINTER AND SUMMER

Portulaca oleracea. Half-hardy annual. Also *Claytonia perfoliata.* Hardy annual.

Winter purslane is as tough as it appears delicate, being not only frost resistant but tolerating poor soils and shade. Leaves may be small but they are abundant and easily harvested – and they make especially welcome crop through winter. Delicious, crisp of texture and high in omega-3.

Summer purslane has a peppery edge to its flavour, and it is best used raw in salads, or steamed. As with winter purslane, it is very high in omega-3. Way less tough than winter purslane, summer purslane is nevertheless perfect in the heat of summer.

VARIETIES: No named varieties of either but there are golden and green forms of summer purslane, with golden purslane tasting a little more of lemon. Winter purslane is also known as claytonia and miner's lettuce.

STARTING OFF: Sow summer purslane successively from April to August (earlier and later if cropping in a tunnel). Sow winter purslane successively from June to September. The seed is very small so it is easiest sown direct very sparingly.

POSITION: Tolerant of most soils.

SPACING: Thin to 15cm apart.

PRODUCTIVITY/EFFICIENCY: A small patch will keep you in leaves for a considerable period.

GROWING: Little needed.

POTENTIAL PROBLEMS: Generally problem free but summer purslane is a half-hardy annual and won't tolerate frosts.

HARVEST: Pick shoot tips and individual leaves as required. The plant will send out side shoots for harvesting at a later date.

Summer purslane

QUINOA

Chenopodium quinoa. Half-hardy annual.

Quinoa is a high-protein seed (although commonly thought of as a grain), cooked just like rice, with a couscous-like nutty flavour. It grows as a tall plant, like a spinach crossed with sweetcorn, its big flowers developing into seed-rich heads in the run up to harvesting. The seeds can be a number of colours – most commonly, yellow and red – and this bitter-coloured coating of saponins helps protect them from the birds' attentions. Soak them in water to remove the coating before cooking to avoid any soapiness.

VARIETIES: 'Temuco' and 'Rainbow' crop well in a damp climate due to their open seed heads.
STARTING OFF: Sow seed in modules under cover in early April, potting on once before planting out after the last frosts.
POSITION: Full sun in a moist but well-drained soil.
SPACING: 50cm apart. Plants can reach 2m tall in a good year.
PRODUCTIVITY/EFFICIENCY: Quinoa gives very high yields in relation to the space it takes up, occupying the ground from late May to late September.
GROWING: Provide support, as these are tall shallow-rooted plants.
POTENTIAL PROBLEMS: Generally pest and disease free.
HARVEST: Quinoa is ready in September when the seeds are changing colour and come away easily from the plant when rubbed between your fingers. Cut the stems and hang up to dry out for a few days, then rub the seed heads between your hands whilst holding over a bowl or sheet. You will be left with a pile of quinoa and chaff, which needs spreading out to dry for a few more days. When dry, pour the seeds from one bowl to another outside when there is a light breeze. This blows away the chaff, leaving you with just the seed.

RADISH

Raphanus sativus. Hardy annual.

If you're starting off, sow radishes. They'll be ready in no time and reassure you that this growing lark really isn't so tricky. Home-grown radishes really are

Radishes

a very different prospect from those in the shops – pick them early, before any woodiness or all-out heat takes them over. They can be anywhere from cool to hot, crisp to sweet, depending on variety. They're also good sown in short-lived gaps between crops, being quick to harvest. Don't be too hasty to pull up any plants that go to seed – the seed pods are full of flavour.

VARIETIES: Try the classic white-tipped 'French Breakfast' or 'Scarlet Globe'. 'Icicle' is a long white radish, or try the yellow 'Szlata'. Mooli (see page 96) can be sown in late summer for a larger autumn/winter radish. 'Rat's Tail' has been specifically bred for its tasty pods.
STARTING OFF: Sow summer radish little and often outside from March to September. Sow thinly in rows that are 15cm apart or broadcast. Autumn mooli varieties should be sown in July or August.
POSITION: Full sun or partial shade on a moisture-retentive soil. Don't over-manure before sowing.
SPACING: Thin to around 2–3cm apart.
PRODUCTIVITY/EFFICIENCY: Radishes are ready to crop in about 4 weeks and can be sown around crops that take longer to reach maturity.
GROWING: Keep soil around radish moist to keep a nice steady growth and prevent them splitting.

107

POTENTIAL PROBLEMS: Very few.
HARVEST: Pull when roots are young and tender. Mooli can be dug as required through late summer, autumn and into winter. Pull the seed pods whenever they reach a size, flavour and texture you like.

RED VALERIAN

Centranthus ruber. Not to be confused with *Valeriana officinalis*, which is used medicinally. Hardy perennial.

I've only just started growing this gorgeous pink/red-flowered plant in the last couple of years, but I'm already hooked. The young leaves and shoots have a similar flavour to broad beans and are really good either in salads or as a side dish of their own. Easy to

Red valerian

grow in well-drained conditions, it can even self-seed and remain evergreen in sheltered, sunny spots.

VARIETIES: Available only in its generic form although there is also white-flowered generic form.
STARTING OFF: Source plants from a good supplier or start from seed. Sow in spring in modules under cover, potting on once before planting out.
POSITION: Full sun in well-drained soil. Poor soils are tolerated. Valerian also grows well in walls and will do well in a container.
SPACING: 40cm apart.
PRODUCTIVITY/EFFICIENCY: Centranthus can provide leaves year-round in some milder areas where it is evergreen.
GROWING: Cut back flower heads if you prefer fresh new greens over attracting butterflies.
POTENTIAL PROBLEMS: Keep watered during dry weather to avoid the leaves becoming bitter whilst the plant is flowering.
HARVEST: Pick shoots in spring, and young leaves as desired throughout the year — though avoid any during extended dry spells as they can become bitter.

ROCKET

Rucola coltivata. Hardy annual.

Like pasta and duvets before it, rocket invaded our country at some point during the last series of Starsky & Hutch and now we can't imagine life without it. Fair enough: it is one of the most delicious and reliable salad leaves, it's easy to grow, and it's productive too – taking well to cut-and-come-again harvesting. It also makes a fine, punchy pesto.

VARIETIES: Wild rocket is very productive — growing steadily for months of repeat harvesting, and is the one to grow through the summer. Rucola runs to seed more quickly than wild rocket, so I tend to grow it for all but the hottest months.
STARTING OFF: Sow from February to October directly, avoiding May and June if you want to avoid any risk of bolting.
POSITION: Sun or partial shade in a moisture-retentive, well-drained soil.
SPACING: 5–15cm apart, depending on how large you want the leaves.

PRODUCTIVITY/EFFICIENCY: Rocket can be ready to eat in as little as 3 weeks and so can be sown at the base of other crops.

GROWING: Keep moist in dry weather. Grow in partial shade during hotter months.

POTENTIAL PROBLEMS: Fleece if flea beetle is a problem.

HARVEST: Cut leaves when young and tender at around 2cm above ground level, leaving them to regrow. Leave some to run to seed, as the flowers are edible too.

ROMANESCO

Brassica oleracea var. *Botrytis* 'Romanesco'. Hardy biennial, mostly grown as an annual.

Thought by some to be a kind of cauliflower, sometimes known as Italian broccoli, and many consider it a vegetable all of its own. I'm in the latter camp: its logarithmic pattern of self-replicating spirals is as uniquely beautiful as it is delicious. It's a reliable grower too – none of that 'pick it today or it's blown' nonsense you get with a cauliflower. Roast it with oil and garlic and/or shred finely and stir-fry with garlic, anchovy, chilli and olive oil for a fine pasta sauce.

VARIETIES: Usually sold as generic, but you may find 'Veronica' available.

STARTING OFF: Sow seed in modules under cover from February to May, potting on into 9cm pots and planting out when the roots are showing.

POSITION: Full sun in a well-drained, moisture-retentive soil that has been mulched with compost.

SPACING: Between 25–60cm apart, depending on the sized head you want.

PRODUCTIVITY/EFFICIENCY: Romanesco takes up a considerable space for around 4–5 months of the year, but they are reliable to grow and expensive to buy.

GROWING: Keep soil moist to avoid checking growth.

POTENTIAL PROBLEMS: Fleece against flea beetle, butterflies and pigeons if they are a problem for you. Use crop rotation and lime the soil if your brassicas have clubroot (see page 368).

HARVEST: Harvest between August and January, cutting when the required size.

Runner beans

RUNNER BEANS

Phaseolus coccineus. Half-hardy perennial, mostly grown as an annual.

The mistake many make with runner beans is to cook them. If you're in any doubt about their marvellousness, take one from the plant when it's no wider than your third finger and you'll find them sweet, crisp and full of life. I've genuinely never known anyone not be converted by their flavour and texture. Otherwise, pick them small, steam them briefly and be generous with the olive oil and garlic.

VARIETIES: 'Polestar', 'Kelvedon Marvel' and 'Scarlet Emperor' are delicious red-flowered varieties. 'Polestar' is one I've never known to go stringy. 'White Lady' has white flowers and 'Pickwick' is a short variety needing very little support, so it's good for an exposed site or container.

STARTING OFF: Sow under cover in April in root trainers, planting out after the last frosts. Sow direct from May to July.

POSITION: Sunny spot with well-composted, moisture-retentive soil.

SPACING: 15cm apart within the row and 60cm between rows for tall varieties. For block planting dwarf varieties allow 25–30cm apart in all directions.

PRODUCTIVITY/EFFICIENCY: Plants are very productive over a 3-month period. You can make a second sowing in early July for runners into autumn.

GROWING: Provide support for tall varieties and water well in dry weather to encourage more flowers and good fruit set.

POTENTIAL PROBLEMS: Plant marigolds and other insect-attracting flowers to draw in aphid predators. Buy seed from a good supplier to avoid halo blight. Birds can peck flowers off, but in my experience they rarely do.

HARVEST: Pick from 10–17cm, eating the smallest ones whole. By picking often you will keep the plant producing. Flowers are edible too, but you will not have so many beans. At the end of the season try letting the bean mature inside the pod for using like butter beans.

SALSIFY AND SCORZONERA

Tragopogon porrifolius. Hardy biennial, mostly grown as an annual.

If you grow carrots or parsnips (or are considering either), you have to grow one of these two. As easy to grow as any other root vegetable, salsify and scorzonera both taste of globe artichokes, a little of asparagus and have something of the sea about them – though I confess to picking up neither the oyster flavour they're supposed to have nor any difference between the two of them. They are undeniably fine though – boil for 15 minutes, slip off the skins in cold water and push them around a pan with cream, parsley, salt, pepper and Parmesan, and be convinced.

VARIETIES: 'Mammoth' and 'Giant' are reliable and delicious varieties of salsify, and 'Russian Giant' or 'Black Giant of Russia', of scorzonera.

STARTING OFF: Sow direct in April at 1cm deep.

POSITION: A sunny position in a well-prepared soil.

SPACING: The seeds are large so it is easy to space them at around 5cm apart, thinning to 15cm as they grow.

PRODUCTIVITY/EFFICIENCY: They will occupy the ground for almost a year, but require little input while they grow.

GROWING: Keep weed free but be careful not to damage roots by hoeing.

POTENTIAL PROBLEMS: Relatively untroubled.

HARVEST: Harvest the roots from October to February. Earth up, or cover with an upturned pot (holes covered), any that you don't eat over winter and the plants will provide you with two or three cuttings of tender green shoots to eat.

SEA KALE

Crambe maritima. Hardy perennial.

A seashore favourite that can be grown in the garden for an early spring harvest when there is little on the menu. The young leaves are pretty good – mild and succulent in salads – but the shoots are incredible, with a flavour like asparagus and the finest hazelnuts. Cover plants as you might rhubarb to force shoots early. The flowers, with their bright honey flavour, shouldn't be overlooked – try them raw in salads.

VARIETIES: You could try the variety 'Lily White' or the larger species *C. cordifolia*.

STARTING OFF: Source plants from a specialist supplier or divide established plants in spring. You can also sow seed in pots in spring, planting out when around 10cm tall, but germination can be very slow.

POSITION: As you might imagine given its origins, it will tolerate most well-drained soils and a certain amount of exposure, and grows well in coastal areas. Prefers neutral and alkaline conditions and full sun, but tolerates some shade.

SPACING: 60cm apart.

PRODUCTIVITY/EFFICIENCY: You can make two or three cuttings of young shoots every year and begin cropping the year after planting out. Shoots, young leaves, flower heads and roots are all edible.

GROWING: Little maintenance required.

POTENTIAL PROBLEMS: Protect from slugs (see pages 364, 370).

HARVEST: Blanch young shoots with a forcer in early spring and cut when a good size. Pick young leaves in spring, flower heads in summer, and dig the roots around the outside of the plant in winter.

SHALLOTS

Allium cepa ascalonicum. Hardy bulb.

I grow more shallots each year, and I suggest you do too. They are expensive to buy, but easy to grow and with such an array of sweet to full-on flavours to choose from. Peeled and used whole in stews, cooked to a soft glossiness in red wine or used as you would onions, shallots really are worth what little trouble they ask of you.

Shallots

Sea kale

S

111

VARIETIES: Try 'Echalotes Grise' for a highly prized, mild gourmet shallot, and 'Longor' and 'Jermor' for delicious and long shallots. 'Red Sun' is round with a reddish-brown skin, or you could try the 'Banana' shallot, which is a cross between an onion and a shallot and combines the best of both.

STARTING OFF: Push sets into the soil in February or March (November/December in milder areas) so the tips are level with or just below the surface. Growing from seed, shallots will make a single bulb in the first year so broadcast sparingly in March or April in wide drills covering with a thin layer of soil.

POSITION: A sunny spot in soil with good drainage.

SPACING: 20cm apart in all directions, if planting in blocks, or 15cm apart and 20cm between rows. For seed-grown shallots thin to 3–4cm.

PRODUCTIVITY/EFFICIENCY: Shallots will occupy the ground for around 4 months.

GROWING: Keep weed free and water in dry weather as bulbs are swelling.

POTENTIAL PROBLEMS: Generally trouble free.

HARVEST: From July, pull the shallots as the leaves begin to yellow. Dry them in the sun for a few days and they should store happily through the winter.

SIBERIAN PEA TREE

Caragana arborescens. Deciduous small tree.

The combination of nitrogen-fixing, soil-enriching qualities, lovely yellow flowers that are adored by the bees and tasty, pea-like pods make the Siberian pea tree a real favourite. The pods have a fine flavour when raw or lightly steamed, but don't let them get too big as they become progressively tougher and lose their charm. The peas can be dried and kept for some time, but they will need soaking overnight and boiling for 20 minutes like other dried pulses.

VARIETIES: You could try *C. arborescens* 'Pendula' for a weeping form or 'Nana' for a more compact version.

STARTING OFF: Source plants from a good supplier or sow seed in pots, potting on until a suitable size for planting out is reached.

POSITION: Full sun and well-drained soil. The Siberian pea tree is happy on poor soils and exposed sites.

SPACING: Reaches 3m high by 2m wide in a UK climate but can reach twice this in a warmer climate.

PRODUCTIVITY/EFFICIENCY: A very productive small tree which begins to fruit in its fourth year, and whose pods and seeds can be eaten fresh or dried for later use.

GROWING: Little maintenance required.

POTENTIAL PROBLEMS: Slugs and snails can be a nuisance to young plants, but once established they are pest and disease free.

HARVEST: Pick young pods in midsummer when around 3cm long. Pods larger than this can be shelled for the peas inside. For peas for storage, harvest pods that have turned brown and allow them to dry further under cover before shelling.

SMALL-LEAVED LIME

Tilia species. Deciduous tree.

After three years, the small-leaved limes I've been growing, not far from a watery ditch that runs through one of the fields here, suddenly became hugely productive. Their thin, delicate leaves, picked small and succulent, provide substance and nutty flavour to salads, especially in spring when the garden is less productive than summer and autumn.

VARIETIES: Small-leaved lime *Tilia cordata* but you could also try *T. platyphyllos*.

STARTING OFF: Source plants from a specialist nursery.

POSITION: Happy on most soils and in sun or shade.

SPACING: If allowed to grow to full size, *Tilia* species can reach 20m tall and 12m wide. Happily, they coppice well and can be kept to around 4m in width.

PRODUCTIVITY/EFFICIENCY: Young leaves are produced from spring until autumn. Leaves are mineral rich and will fertilise the area in which they grow.

GROWING: Coppice at around 6 years old and thereafter every 3 or 4 years.

POTENTIAL PROBLEMS: Generally pest and disease free.

HARVEST: Pick young leaves throughout the growing season.

SOCIETY GARLIC

Tulbaghia violacea. Half-hardy perennial. ✿

This fabulous perennial is my favourite of the society garlics. Its long thin leaves and stems are fine enough, but it's the pale pink flowers I'm after – they have a full-on flush of garlic flavour but without a hint of harshness. They lose texture and flavour when cooked, so I use them scattered raw in salads and floating in more cocktails than is good for me.

VARIETIES: The named varieties have been bred for their differing ornamental characteristics rather than flavour; however, 'Silver Lace' has larger flowers.

STARTING OFF: Source plants from a good supplier or sow in modules 5cm or so deep, under cover in spring or autumn. Pot on once when the roots are showing and then plant out. You can also divide established plants in autumn.

POSITION: A sunny, sheltered spot with moisture-retentive and well-drained soil. Does well in a pot.

SPACING: 50cm apart.

PRODUCTIVITY/EFFICIENCY: A single plant will give a supply of flowers and leaves from early summer into autumn.

GROWING: Protect with a deep mulch over winter in more northerly areas or grow in a tunnel or greenhouse.

POTENTIAL PROBLEMS: Generally pest and disease free.

HARVEST: Pick leaves and flowers throughout the summer and autumn.

Society garlic

Solomon's seal

SOLOMON'S SEAL

Polygonatum species. Hardy perennial. 🌣

A well-known plant, largely grown as an ornamental but with delicious early shoots that taste like the very sweetest asparagus. Not the most prolific plant in the garden, but one that loves a damp, shady spot – and there's not much that will give you such a delicious crop from those conditions.

VARIETIES: Most *Polygonatum* species are edible, although *P. commutatum* is the largest of them. Variegated varieties tend to produce less than others.
STARTING OFF: Source plants from a good supplier or divide established plants in spring.
POSITION: A moist but well-drained soil in light or deep shade.
SPACING: 30cm apart.
PRODUCTIVITY/EFFICIENCY: This plant is a slow coloniser and will take some years to establish enough for cropping.
GROWING: Little maintenance required.
POTENTIAL PROBLEMS: Use your chosen slug deterrent on young plants.
HARVEST: Cut shoots at ground level when they are around 25cm tall, leaving the growth that follows to grow on and sustain the plant.

SORREL

Rumex acetosa (Broadleaved), *Rumex scutatus* (Buckler leaved) and *Rumex sanguineus* (Red-veined). Hardy perennial. 🌣

With a glorious lemon sharpness, not dissimilar to rhubarb or gooseberries, sorrel is one of my favourite leaves. Picked young and small, the leaves add brightness and zip to mixed leaf salads but are perhaps at their very best thrown into a pan of hot new potatoes with butter and shaken to create the silkiest of sauces. Sorrel is really fine with fish and eggs too.

VARIETIES: Broadleaved with its large leaves is ideal for cooking or try Buckler leaved, which is small and perfect for a salad. You could also try Red-veined sorrel, or pick some from the wild.
STARTING OFF: Sow in spring or autumn in modules under cover or direct, planting out as soon as the roots are showing.

Sorrel

POSITION: Tolerant of most soils. It will run to seed less quickly if given some shade.
SPACING: 30cm apart.
PRODUCTIVITY/EFFICIENCY: You will get a good supply of leaves early and late in the growing season.
GROWING: Water during dry weather to slow running to seed.
POTENTIAL PROBLEMS: Generally untroubled.
HARVEST: Pick or cut leaves as required.

SPINACH

Spinacia oleracea. Hardy annual. 🌣

I used to grow vast swathes of spinach. I love its grassy freshness wilted in omelettes, tarts, gratins and uncooked in leafy salads. But I've discovered so many other fabulous spinach-alikes, such as Mexican tree spinach and New Zealand spinach (see pages 94 and 98), which deserve some room that something's had to give. I'd still not be without regular spinach, and if anything, I love it all the more for being one on the spectrum of fine spinachy leaves.

VARIETIES: 'Giant Winter' is good for an autumn sowing as it withstands cold well. Use bolt-resistant varieties such as 'Matador' and 'Medania' for June to August sowings.

S

Spinach

S

STARTING OFF: Sow successively from February to September in modules under cover and plant out once roots are showing. Direct sowings can be made from March.

POSITION: A moisture-retentive soil in part shade in the hottest months. Spinach will crop happily from an early or late sowing under cover.

SPACING: 5–7cm apart for baby leaves and 15–20cm for larger ones, with 30cm between rows (less for baby leaves).

PRODUCTIVITY/EFFICIENCY: This is a quick-growing crop especially if grown for baby leaves. Plants can regrow after harvesting.

GROWING: Keep soil moist by watering and mulching to prevent bolting.

POTENTIAL PROBLEMS: Very few, though slugs can be a nuisance to young plants and flea beetle similarly so, once in a while.

HARVEST: Cut leaves at 3cm or so above the ground.

SPRING ONIONS
Allium cepa. Hardy bulb.

As with radishes, spring onions are exactly the thing to grow if you're looking for a swift confidence boost. Quick, easy and reliable to get to harvest, their sweet-sharp flavour livens up salads, soups or (even better, if you ask me) griddled to go with pretty much anything.

VARIETIES: 'North Holland Blood Red' and 'White Lisbon' are classic and delicious. 'White Lisbon Winter Hardy' will give you an overwintering crop for early harvest. 'Purplette' forms a round bulb, which can be grown on for pickling if desired.

STARTING OFF: Sow successively outside from February to June and again in August/September for an early spring crop.

POSITION: A sunny well-drained spot but will tolerate some shade.

SPACING: Thin to around 10cm apart.

PRODUCTIVITY/EFFICIENCY: Spring onions take up little space and are ready around 2 months from sowing.

GROWING: Keep weed free and water in dry weather. Protect winter crops in harsh weather.

POTENTIAL PROBLEMS: Use crop rotation (see page 368) to avoid onion downy mildew and white rot.

HARVEST: Pull when around 15cm.

SPROUTING BROCCOLI
Brassica oleracea var. *italica.* Hardy biennial, mostly grown as an annual.

Easy to grow and with a long season of repeated picking, sprouting broccoli is a wonderful cold weather harvest. Much as I love calabrese in the summer (see page 68), the depth of flavour and nuttiness of sprouting broccoli has me looking forward to the dark months. Slice off the flowering heads, steam and serve with melted butter – better still, with an anchovy or two mashed into it.

VARIETIES: 'Rudolph' is a good early variety, producing from October to January, or try 'White Eye', 'Red Arrow' or 'Late Purple' for crops from February to April.

Sprouting broccoli

STARTING OFF: Sow seed in modules under cover from March to May, planting out in June when 10–15cm high.

POSITION: Full sun in a composted, well-drained but moisture-retentive soil.

SPACING: 60cm apart.

PRODUCTIVITY/EFFICIENCY: Each plant will produce spears over 2–3 months. The later varieties are particularly useful, being harvested during the hungry gap.

GROWING: Keep the soil weed free and moist.

POTENTIAL PROBLEMS: Fleece against pigeons and butterflies. Rotate crops (see page 368) to avoid clubroot and plant deeply (up to first true leaves) to avoid cabbage root fly.

HARVEST: Cut spears when the buds are showing but before they flower. Regular harvesting encourages more spears and plants can be cropped for around 2 months.

SQUASH

Cucurbita species. Half-hardy annual.

A word of advice: admire the gourds, hollow out the pumpkins, and eat only the squash. Better still, be very, very particular about which squash you grow. The best varieties really do sit head and shoulders above the rest of the crowd. As with tomatoes and chillies, grow a few varieties – it will offer you insurance if conditions don't suit one variety, while giving you a range of textures and flavours. Squash is very adaptable in the kitchen – I love it roasted with garlic, olive oil and rosemary, puréed for puddings, and diced and simmered in stock for pasta sauces.

VARIETIES: A huge variety of colour, shape and texture is available. 'Uchiki Kuri' produces good harvests of sweet, onion-shaped squash. Productive and sweet butternut squash are 'Ponca' and 'Early Butternut'. Try 'Crown Prince' for sweet flesh and a

Harvested squash

duck-egg blue exterior. 'Acorn Table' has a beautiful leaf-shape and produces many incised, dark-green fruits.

STARTING OFF: Sow in 9cm pots in April, with the seeds on their edge vertically rather than laid flat to prevent rotting, and plant out from early June to the end of July.

POSITION: Full sun in a rich, moisture-retentive soil.

SPACING: At least 1m apart. In general, trailing vine types need more space than bush varieties but trailing varieties can thread their way through other crops.

PRODUCTIVITY/EFFICIENCY: Squash will occupy the ground for around 3–4 months, and require little more than watering once in a while.

GROWING: They like moist soil so keep watered in dry weather.

POTENTIAL PROBLEMS: Protect young plants from slugs and snails for the first few weeks.

HARVEST: Cut squash and pumpkins once they sound hollow, leaving a 5cm stalk to prevent rotting. Keep them outside with their undersides upwards in order for them to fully ripen. Bring the squash inside before the first frosts and store somewhere light and cool.

STINGING NETTLES

Urtica dioica. Hardy perennial, mostly grown reluctantly.

If there's one thing most of us grow well, it's nettles. Weeds to most, nutritious greens and a source of nitrogen-rich leaves for making a plant feed to a few. As long as you can keep nettles and your other precious plants apart, there's no reason you can't learn to love them – try young leaves steamed or wilted in place of spinach in tarts especially.

VARIETIES: Needs little introduction and is readily available almost everywhere.

STARTING OFF: If you need to introduce it, start from seed or, easier still, pull up runners and plant where you wish them to grow.

POSITION: Prefers a rich soil but will tolerate most, as well we know.

SPACING: 70–80cm apart.

PRODUCTIVITY/EFFICIENCY: Provides nutritious greens when little else is around. It is also a mineral

Stinging nettles

accumulator, drawing up many nutrients from deep in the soil, making a great liquid feed or mulch.

GROWING: Cut back flowering stems to check spreading and also to promote fresh young growth.

POTENTIAL PROBLEMS: Generally pest and disease free.

HARVEST: Wearing gloves, pick the young tips in spring.

SWEDE

Brassica napus var. *napobrassica.* Hardy biennial, mostly grown as an annual.

One day, very shortly if I have anything to do with it, there will be a revival in swedes' fortunes. As with turnips, most of us see swedes as livestock feed, when, with good varieties and care in the kitchen, they are every bit the equal of squash. Steamed or boiled until just cooked, mashed and over-peppered they make a fine side, as well as a sweet-savoury root in all manner of stews and gratins. Try a short row and I promise you'll expand it next year.

S

119

VARIETIES: 'Ruby', 'Willemsburger' and 'Helenor' are all good.

STARTING OFF: Sow direct from May to early June. Earlier sowings can be made in February under protection.

POSITION: Full sun in moisture-retentive and well-drained soil.

SPACING: Space rows 35cm apart and thin to around 20cm. If block planting, space maincrops 30cm apart in all directions and early ones at half that.

PRODUCTIVITY/EFFICIENCY: Maincrop swedes are in the ground for around 6 months and can be eaten up to December, after which they risk becoming woody.

GROWING: Keep soil moist but don't water too heavily at once after a dry spell as the roots can split.

POTENTIAL PROBLEMS: Fleece against flea beetle. Control slugs (see pages 364, 370) to prevent them eating swede tops as this can encourage rotting.

HARVEST: Begin harvesting when roots are the size you want them. Harvest as needed.

SWEETCORN
Zea mays. Half-hardy annual.

Barbecued sweetcorn, fresh from the plant, smothered in butter, lime juice and too much pepper and salt is about as good as summer outdoor eating gets. They are easy to grow but a little hit and miss, needing a long hot summer to thrive. Take care with varieties – there are plenty of very sweet ones, but I prefer the ones with a balance of wider flavours.

VARIETIES: 'Sweet Nugget' and 'Sweetie' are among the sweetest varieties. 'Golden Bantam' and 'Stowell's Evergreen' have a good balance of flavour and sweetness, the latter being a very old variety that will stay ripe on the plant for a long time. You could also try 'Minipop' for baby sweetcorn or 'Strawberry' for your own popcorn.

STARTING OFF: Sow in 9cm pots in April under cover and plant out as soon as the last frosts have past. Sow direct from May to June. Sweetcorn can be grown under cover and baby sweetcorn works well in pots.

POSITION: Warm and sheltered in a composted, moisture-retentive and well-draining soil.

SPACING: 15–30cm apart, depending on variety, but do plant in blocks rather than rows as this makes wind pollination more effective. Make sure you leave at least 8m between super-sweet and non-super-sweet varieties, or you may find that cross-pollination makes the super-sweet less so.

PRODUCTIVITY/EFFICIENCY: Sweetcorn will occupy the ground for 8–20 weeks. You will get around 8 mini cobs per plant and 2–3 large ones, with harvests possible from August to October with the right varieties.

GROWING: Growing courgettes and squash around your sweetcorn will help keep it weed free. Grow in blocks rather than rows, as sweetcorn are wind pollinated and success rates are improved. Provide support if growing on an exposed site.

POTENTIAL PROBLEMS: Sow in pots and transplant if you have mice and bird problems.

HARVEST: Larger cobs are ready when the tassels turn brown and the juices are milky when you push the cob with your thumbnail. Pick baby sweetcorn when around 7cm long.

Harvested sweetcorn

Sweetcorn

SWEET PEPPERS

Capsicum annuum. Half-hardy annual.

I have to admit, I rarely grow sweet peppers – I'm loath to give up any of the under-cover space that chillies could take, and I prefer the sweet, mild chillies such as 'Apricot', 'Padron' and 'Poblano' to sweet peppers. That said, if you like them, they aren't tricky to grow, but they are particular. Choose good varieties, start them early, give them heat and light throughout their lives and feed them often and you'll be rewarded in all but the coolest summers.

VARIETIES: 'California Wonder' for a traditional bell shape, 'Marconi Rosso' and 'Jimmy Nardello' are long, red and sweet. 'Hamik' is possibly the sweetest of all and 'Tequila' is early ripening and purple.

STARTING OFF: Sow in modules in a propagator or airing cupboard in February/March (no later than April), potting on into 9cm pots and then again as soon as the roots show through the holes in the bottom. It should be warm enough to plant in a tunnel or greenhouse by the end of April. Germination is usually slow.

POSITION: For best results grow in a tunnel or greenhouse.

SPACING: 45–60cm apart, depending on variety, although they are also happy grown in pots.

PRODUCTIVITY/EFFICIENCY: Yields vary greatly between varieties but you should be able to pick peppers from midsummer to early autumn.

GROWING: A weekly comfrey feed is essential if growing in pots.

POTENTIAL PROBLEMS: Rarely affected by pests and diseases.

HARVEST: Harvest from green through to red when they will be at their sweetest.

SWEET POTATO

Ipomoea batatas. Half-hardy perennial climber.

Slowly, these tropical/sub-tropical favourites have been selected and bred to stand more than a racing chance in our cool climate, and you can now expect to get a good harvest in a sunny location. Unlike more familiar potatoes, sweet potatoes grow as a trailing, scrambling vine that can cover 1–2m but it won't climb even if you give them a structure to ascend. I like them best mashed, roasted and as chips.

VARIETIES: 'Georgia Jet' is very reliable in the UK climate or try 'Beauregard Improved' or 'Henry', which with its compact habit is very good for containers.

STARTING OFF: Source slips (unrooted cuttings) of named varieties from a good supplier. The slips may look wilted when they arrive but are easily revived by putting in water overnight. Pot them up so that the stem is in compost right up to the first leaves and then put them in an unheated propagator or cover the pot with a clear plastic bag until they have rooted. Plant sweet potatoes out after all danger of frost has passed. They grow best in temperatures of 21–25°C and are very happy in a polytunnel or greenhouse. If growing outside, warm the ground with black polythene some weeks before planting and plant through the polythene. Covering with a fleece or a cloche will help them grow.

POSITION: Fertile, humus-rich and well-drained soil in a sunny sheltered spot.

SPACING: 30cm apart along the rows with 70cm between each row.

PRODUCTIVITY/EFFICIENCY: Sweet potatoes will occupy the ground for 4–5 months.

GROWING: Plants growing under cover will be more vigorous and support may be needed. Feed plants in containers every couple of weeks with a liquid seaweed or comfrey feed.

POTENTIAL PROBLEMS: Generally pest and disease free but can be a risk in cooler parts of the UK.

HARVEST: Tubers are ready when the foliage starts to turn yellow in late summer/early autumn. For larger tubers, leave in the ground for as long as possible but dig them up before the frosts arrive. If the sweet potatoes are for storing then leave to dry in the sun for a couple of hours after digging and then cure further in a greenhouse or polytunnel for around 10 days. Store somewhere cool and dry after this.

TOMATILLOS

Physalis ixocarpa and *P. philadelphica.* Half-hardy annual.

Mexican in origin, tomatillos unsurprisingly take perfectly to the salsas and sauces that characterise that fine, fresh cuisine. Similar to tomatoes in habit and appearance, the flavour of tomatillos is on the fence between sweet and citrus, and once you get your mind past the expectation that it should be sweet like a tomato, they really are very good in the kitchen. And it's hard not to love something that comes in its own papery wrapper.

VARIETIES: Try 'Dr Wyche's Yellow', 'Tomatillo Verde' and 'Tomatillo Purple'.
STARTING OFF: Sow in modules on a window sill, or in an airing cupboard or heated propagator 6–8 weeks before the last frosts, potting on once when the roots are showing at the bottom of the module.
POSITION: Sunny and warm with a rich well-drained soil.
SPACING: Allow around 60cm apart in all directions if providing support, and double that if allowing them to sprawl on the soil (they may produce more fruit this way).
PRODUCTIVITY/EFFICIENCY: Tomatillos are prolific and can produce 10kg of fruit per plant.
GROWING: Tie in the tomatillos as they grow if you are using support.
POTENTIAL PROBLEMS: Very few.
HARVEST: Harvest when the papery cases split open. Fruits are produced from July to October.

Tomatoes

Tomatillos

T

123

TOMATOES
Lycopersicon esculentum. Half-hardy annual.

It is absolutely compulsory to grow 'Sungold' tomatoes at least once in your life. Although it may be something that brings you considerable unhappiness: every shop-bought tomato will disappoint from that day forward. Their blend of sweet and sharp with a juiciness and fine texture is hard to match. I'd suggest growing tomatoes in all three main sizes: 'Sungold' as cherry tomatoes, 'Black Krim' or 'Black Trifele' as medium-sized tomatoes, and 'Costoluto Fiorentino' as fine hand-filling fruit. I always grow a few different varieties each year, for different flavours, sizes and textures.

VARIETIES: An enormous variety is available to you ranging from white through yellow, orange and red to black, and from the size of a currant to as big as your hand. 'Sungold' (F1) and 'Honey Bubbles' are small and sweet yellow varieties for an early harvest. 'Black Cherry', 'Japanese Black Trifele' and 'Black Krim' have a beautiful flavour, and 'Costoluto Fiorentino' and 'Big Brandwine' are delicious larger red varieties.

STARTING OFF: Sow in modules in February or March and put on a window sill or in an airing cupboard or propagator. Pot on when the roots are showing. Plant out when the flowers are just opening on the first truss, making sure this is after the last frost if growing your tomatoes outside.

POSITION: As much sun and warmth as you can give them and in a composted soil with good drainage.

SPACING: 45–60cm apart, depending on variety.

PRODUCTIVITY/EFFICIENCY: Tomatoes will supply you with a steady stream from June/July to October.

GROWING: Indeterminate varieties (those that grow high) require support as the main stem grows. Growing tips should be pinched out when the plant reaches the height you want it. For outdoor-grown indeterminate varieties, pinch out the growing tip when there are 4 or 5 trusses of fruit to encourage

Black tomatoes

Pinching out

ripening. For those growing under cover, most people pinch out when there are 7 or 8 trusses. Pull off the lower leaves to the next fruiting truss to keep airflow good. Bush varieties won't need pinching out at all. Pinch out the shoots that grow between the stem and the side branches — this helps direct the plant's energies to the fruit, rather than unnecessary green growth. Water regularly, making sure it is the soil or compost that gets wet, not the plant — wet leaves and fruit encourages disease. Once the plant flowers, feed every fortnight with a high potassium feed (see page 362).

POTENTIAL PROBLEMS: Blight is your main worry. Water at the base to minimise blight problems and don't overwater as this can reduce the flavour. Grow basil around your tomatoes to deter whitefly.

HARVEST: Pick cherry tomatoes a little under-ripe as they can split when fully ripe. Other varieties should be picked as soon as they have reached the colour appropriate to the variety. As cold weather approaches, pick your last tomatoes green. They will ripen in the warmth inside.

TURNIPS

Brassica rapa. Hardy biennial, mostly grown as an annual. ✑

Before you consign turnips (along with swede, see page 119) to the pigeonhole labelled 'livestock feed', try the varieties below. When you get them to the kitchen, roast them with honey, or dice them small to take the place of the rice in a risotto where they'll soak up the flavours from the stock and herbs. The leaves are really tasty too – a nutty, yet sweet brassica flavour that makes a fine pasta sauce when wilted in olive oil.

VARIETIES: 'Snowball Early White' will give you sweet globe-shaped turnips through summer and into autumn. 'Noir d'Hiver' is a black-skinned performer in cold weather or try 'Purple top Milan' for purple-flushed baby turnips.

STARTING OFF: Sow quick-maturing varieties direct every 2–3 weeks, from March to July. Sow maincrops direct in July and August.

Turnips

POSITION: Moisture-retentive and well-drained soil in sun or part-shade.

SPACING: Space quick-maturing varieties 15cm apart in all directions in blocks and 22cm in all directions for maincrops.

PRODUCTIVITY/EFFICIENCY: Quick–maturing varieties can be ready in 5 weeks and are great for catch-cropping. Maincrops can occupy the ground from July until New Year, or longer if you harvest their leaves.

GROWING: Water in hot dry weather to prevent splitting or bolting.

POTENTIAL PROBLEMS: Fleece against flea beetle, cabbage root fly, pigeons and butterflies.

HARVEST: Pull quick-maturing varieties when around 5cm in diameter and maincrops when they are around 10cm.

VIOLA 'HEARTSEASE'

Viola tricolor. Also known as: wild pansy and heartsease. Hardy annual. ✑ (overleaf)

This one's a bit of a no-brainer. Unless absolutely every square centimetre of soil is covered, you've room for a few viola scattered around the garden or in pots. They'll bring in insects for pollination and to keep the balance of pests-to-beneficial-insects in your favour and, as well as being beautiful, they're delicious and productive. Their flavour, while not mouth-slappingly heavy, is gently sweet and mildly peppery – really good as a little garden nibble or in salads and floating in cocktails.

VARIETIES: None available.

STARTING OFF: Sow in modules in March and again in September, planting out when the roots are showing.

POSITION: Will tolerate some shade and most well-drained soils.

SPACING: 15cm apart.

PRODUCTIVITY/EFFICIENCY: Plants will keep producing flowers for around 5 months, so 2 sowings should give you nearly year-round flowers.

GROWING: Little attention needed.

POTENTIAL PROBLEMS: Few problems.

HARVEST: Pick flower heads as desired.

T
V

125

Viola 'Heartsease'

YACON
Polymnia edulis. Half-hardy perennial. ᝌ

A fabulous South American tuber that I grow every year: lush, tall, leafy growth is occasionally topped (in the hottest of summers) by small, gorgeous yellow flowers. Underneath this distracting loveliness, tubers are developing. Often swelling disconcertingly late in the season, the tubers come in two sorts: the large ones for eating and the smaller ones to be stored with a little of their growing tip (where next year's shoots emerge) for replanting next year. Buy it once and you have it for life. Their glassy texture is similar to water chestnuts and they are similarly good in stir-fries, but do try them fresh after a day or two of them sweetening in the sun – their flavour is pears crossed with the earliest sharp apples.

VARIETIES: No named varieties although tubers can be yellow, pink, purple, orange or white.

STARTING OFF: Source tubers from a good supplier and plant in damp compost under cover, planting out after the last frosts. You can also split the crown of established plants in spring, ensuring that each section has some root attached.

POSITION: Somewhere sunny and hot in fertile well-drained soil. They are hardy to −5°C.

SPACING: 50cm apart.

PRODUCTIVITY/EFFICIENCY: Yields vary, but expect a typical haul of around six large tubers per plant, though you may get double that.

GROWING: Little required. If leaving in open ground over winter give a thick mulch of compost or straw.

POTENTIAL PROBLEMS: Generally problem free.

HARVEST: Dig the tubers in autumn before the first frosts and store somewhere cool and dark.

127

Yacon

FRUIT AND NUTS

Almonds

130

ALMONDS
Prunus dulcis. Deciduous tree. 🌥

I've planted a fair few almonds of various varieties and they are particular – sunshine and shelter are a must if you want nuts. The more you dilute this, the less likely you are to have anything to harvest. Spring is their pinch point: get the blossom past the frosts and there's little in your way. Growing your own not only gives you really delicious almonds, but also the prospect of green almonds picked in summer, tasting of fresh peas as much as almonds. Shelled, fresh, home-grown almonds are a rare treat, and a fine beer-snack when pushed around a pan, salted, spiced and honeyed.

VARIETIES: 'Mandaline' and 'Ferragnes' are two relatively recent French varieties, which flower a little later than most, but for the greatest likelihood of success in the majority of this country I'd recommend almond/peach hybrids such as 'Ingrid' and 'Robijn' — they taste as you'd hope a superb almond would, and are hardier and earlier producing than traditional varieties. Check with your supplier to see if your chosen variety needs a pollinator.

STARTING OFF: Buy as a plant or graft your own on to 'St Julien A' or 'Myran' rootstocks.

POSITION: A sunny, sheltered spot with a moisture-retentive but well-drained soil.

SPACING: This varies with rootstock and soil type, but 6m apart is a good rule of thumb.

PRODUCTIVITY/EFFICIENCY: Almonds are self-fertile but will give you more nuts if you grow two or more varieties. Not reliable producers every year but can be heavy yielding.

GROWING: A liquid feed and/or compost/manure mulch around the base will greatly invigorate the plant and boost health and the likelihood of a harvest.

POTENTIAL PROBLEMS: Leaf curl can be a problem so protect leaves from spring rains (which bring the fungus) with a cover if possible but leave access underneath for pollinators. Almond/peach hybrids are less susceptible to leaf curl. Almonds can flower before any pollinators are around, so use a soft paintbrush to do the job yourself. Don't plant almonds near peaches as they can cross-pollinate, resulting in bitter nuts. Protect leaves of young trees from slugs and snails (see pages 364, 370).

HARVEST: In October when the green hull has split and a gentle shake of the tree causes the nuts to drop to the ground, spreading a blanket beneath the tree will ensure that you don't lose any in the grass. The nuts in the centre of the tree may take a few more days to ripen.

ALPINE STRAWBERRIES
Fragaria vesca. Hardy perennial. 🌥

If you're looking for a brilliant way of lining a path or bed, you could do far worse than alpine strawberries. As well as providing intensely flavoured berries for year after year, the plants hold their shape over winter, providing low structure to the garden – and as soon as the days lengthen and there's a whiff of heat in the air, the fruit pop out. Not the sort of thing to feed the five thousand, but perfect as garden treats or allowed to dissolve in a glass of fizz.

131

Alpine strawberries

VARIETIES: 'Mignonette' is the finest red you can grow, or try 'Yellow Wonder' or 'Pineapple Crush' for creamy yellow strawberries, which birds won't bother with quite so much.

STARTING OFF: Alpine strawberry seed is very small so it is easiest sown in trays. A February sowing under cover will give you fruit in the same year. Leave the seed on the surface and put the tray inside a plastic bag to prevent the soil drying out, and uncover as soon as germination starts. When big enough to handle, prick seedlings out into modules or small pots, planting out when the roots are showing. Sowings can be made direct from April – cover the seed with just a dusting of compost.

POSITION: Tolerant of most soils and in full sun or some shade.

SPACING: 15–30cm apart.

PRODUCTIVITY/EFFICIENCY: You will get a steady supply of alpine strawberries from May to September. They are also happy growing in containers.

GROWING: Keep watered whilst establishing. An occasional mulch of compost will give you greater yields. A fortnightly feed with comfrey tea whilst flowering will encourage yet more flowers and fruit.

POTENTIAL PROBLEMS: Relatively untroubled by pests and disease.

HARVEST: Pick when deep red (white/yellow varieties when soft to the touch) every day or two from May until September.

APPLES

Malus domestica. Deciduous tree.

There are so many choices when it comes to apples – flavour, aroma, texture, size of tree, season of eating – that you need to sit yourself down and ask yourself some serious questions before deciding. First of all, do you have room for more than one tree? If not, the vast selection becomes considerably narrowed to one of the few self-fertile varieties – 'Braeburn' or 'Sunset' for example. One of the biggest distinctions to be aware of is between early and later apples: as a rule, the earlier in season an apple is ready to pick, the less time it stores for. 'Beauty of Bath' will give you perhaps six days in August to eat it once it's left the

tree, whereas an 'Adam's Pearmain' picked in October will give you six months. It's not just about storing qualities though – you'll not find the earlies in the shops for precisely the reason that they don't store, so you open up different flavours and an early part of the season if you grow them yourself. There's no right or wrongs, just what you prefer.

VARIETIES: There are varieties for eating, cooking, juicing and cider, with some of them (such as 'Veitches Perfection') suitable for more than one of these purposes.

Apples are grafted on to a rootstock, which determines the ultimate size of tree. Several rootstocks are available. MM26 is dwarfing, MM106 semi-dwarfing, and rootstocks M25 and MM111 will make trees around 8m tall. For good pollination the

Apples

trees you choose must have compatible flowering times or be self-fertile. Check with your supplier to see if your chosen variety needs a pollinator. 'Orleans Reinette', 'Old Somerset Russet', 'Lord Lambourne' and 'Ashmead's Kernel' are delicious eaters. Try 'Annie Elizabeth' or 'Bramley's Seedling' for cookers. 'Kingston Black', 'Dabinett' and 'Brown's Apple' are very good cider apples, or try 'Veitch's Perfection' for a lovely cooker and eater.

STARTING OFF: Source grafted trees as maidens or 2–3-year-old bushes and trees.

POSITION: Rootstocks are tolerant of most soils, but MMIII and MM106 are better for heavy clay and wetter soils. A sunny spot is important for sweet apples, especially late ripening ones, although cooking apples will ripen sufficiently in some shade. Fruit set will be better with shelter from the worst of the winds.

SPACING: 2.5–9m apart, depending on rootstock.

PRODUCTIVITY/EFFICIENCY: Carefully chosen varieties can give you eating and cooking apples from late July through to March. While trained varieties such as stepovers, cordons and espaliers give you less fruit, they can be grown in spaces that otherwise wouldn't be used, e.g. along the edge of a path.

GROWING: Water in dry weather, especially in the first year and as often as required if growing in a pot. Underplant with comfrey, which is high in nitrogen and potassium, cutting it to the ground a couple of times a year and allowing the leaves to rot down. Prune bushes and trees in winter, and trained varieties in summer.

POTENTIAL PROBLEMS: Use pheromone traps if codling moth is a problem. Some varieties (such as 'Lord Derby' and 'Ellison's Orange') are resistant to scab and canker. If your tree is affected with scab, prune blistered stems and incinerate along with any leaves and fruit affected by the tell-tale blotches. For canker, remove all affected stems, cut out any affected wood on large branches and paint wounds with a wound paint.

HARVEST: In general, the later the apple ripens the longer it will store for, with earlier ripening apples best eaten within a week or so of picking. When ripe the apple should come away easily if you lift gently and give a quarter turn. Leave for longer if not.

Apricots

133

APRICOTS

Prunus armeniaca. Deciduous tree.

A home-grown apricot is a fine thing – it may not have the shoe-splattering juiciness of a peach perhaps, but it has a depth of flavour and richness, which comes only with apricots that are separated from the tree when absolutely at their ripe peak. They need sun and shelter to be at their best.

VARIETIES: 'Flavourcot' and 'Tomcot' are delicious, or try 'Moorpark' for a later variety. Try an older variety such as 'Bredase', or 'Aprigold' for a dwarf variety. Self-fertile.

STARTING OFF: Source grafted trees as maidens, 2- and 3-year-old bushes, or as trained forms.

POSITION: Sunny and sheltered in a deep soil that is moisture retentive and with good drainage.

THE NEW KITCHEN GARDEN

SPACING: Depending on type of rootstock, space up to 4.5m apart.

PRODUCTIVITY/EFFICIENCY: Mature fan-trained trees (see page 346) can give up to 14kg of fruit, and a tree up to 55kg, which is a pretty heavy harvest of a fruit that is usually expensive to buy. Apricots can begin to produce in their second year.

GROWING: Thin fruits if crowded to allow remaining ones to get to a larger size. Give an annual feed of compost of cut comfrey. Cut out diseased and dead wood during the growing season between May and September.

POTENTIAL PROBLEMS: Choose later-flowering varieties to avoid late frosts damaging apricot flowers, or plant against a sunny, south-facing wall. Newer varieties (such as 'Flavourcot'®) are less susceptible to bacterial canker. Pruning in midsummer helps minimise the risk of bacterial canker and silver leaf: any affected areas should be cut out and incinerated.

HARVEST: Between July and September. Pick when fruits are just tender, aromatic and when they separate easily from the tree with only the slightest persuasion.

134

ASIAN PEARS

Pyrus species. Also known as: apple pears or Chinese pears. Deciduous tree.

There are a few species that come under the Asian pear umbrella, but *Pyrus pyrifolia* is the one for the delicious fruit. Despite the name and a pear-like flavour, the fruit resembles a lightly-russeted apple, yet is altogether juicier and more crisp. Very popular in parts of the Middle and Far East (Korea especially), they will grow perfectly well in the UK – I'm mystified as to why they are so uncommon here.

VARIETIES: Try 'Shinsui' for an early Asian pear and 'Shinko' for a later one. 'Shin Li' has a hint of cinnamon. Asian pears are not self-fertile so you will need another variety with a compatible flowering time.

STARTING OFF: Source grafted maidens or 2-year-old trees.

POSITION: Full sun in most soils, with good drainage.

SPACING: Up to 9m apart, depending on rootstock used.

Asian pears

PRODUCTIVITY/EFFICIENCY: With careful choice of variety you can have Asian pears from July to October. Trees begin to produce fruit in years 2 or 3 with 180kg of fruit possible from a mature tree.

GROWING: Prune every 1–3 years to stimulate new growth. Thin fruit if the young crop is heavy, as allowing too heavy a crop to develop can lead to biennial cropping. Asian pears can be trained as espaliers.

POTENTIAL PROBLEMS: Some varieties of Asian pear are less susceptible to fireblight and bacterial canker.

HARVEST: Leave to ripen fully on the tree as they won't ripen further after picking. They'll leave the tree easily when ready.

AUTUMN OLIVE

Elaeagnus umbellata. Also known as: Japanese silver-berry. Deciduous shrub.

If you have a little space, this is one of the best plants you can grow. Fruitful, fast growing, nitrogen fixing and in leaf for most of the year, autumn olive feeds you and your garden equally. With leaves very similar to the olive, it catches the light beautifully and its abundant intense pink berries are a great late autumn harvest: lightly speckled and a pinker version of redcurrants to the eye, their sharp, full flavour is superb in tarts, preserves and ice creams.

VARIETIES: Try varieties 'Brilliant Rose', 'Big Red' or 'Jewel'. Self-fertile.

STARTING OFF: Source named varieties from suppliers. If growing from seed, sow in trays or modules in autumn and allow the cold to get to it. Pot on once large enough to handle, planting out when filling a 1-litre pot.

POSITION: Tolerant of most situations and soils, including some shade and exposure.

SPACING: Every 2.5m apart for hedging and 5m for individual plants.

PRODUCTIVITY/EFFICIENCY: A heavy-cropping plant, much loved by bees.

GROWING: Prune as necessary to maintain the size you want, bearing in mind it can easily reach 5m or more in height if allowed to.

POTENTIAL PROBLEMS: Generally trouble free.

HARVEST: Run your fingers down the stem to pull fruit into a waiting bag. Berries can be astringent if not fully ripe – I like them when they are still tart but not to the point of wincing; it's very much up to you and your taste buds how early or late you harvest.

Autumn olive

B

Blackberries

BLACKBERRIES

Rubus fruticosus. Deciduous shrub.

As plentiful as blackberries may be in urban hedges and rough ground as in rural, it is very much worth considering them for your garden, as garden varieties tend to be sweeter and more productive than wild blackberries. With the right varieties, you can extend the season from midsummer through well into autumn too. I don't prefer their flavour to wild blackberries – I like the sharpness and occasion of foraging for them – but in many ways I think of them as a separate fruit altogether.

VARIETIES: Growing a range of varieties will keep you in blackberries from July to the first frosts. Try early and vigorous 'Bedford Giant', compact and thornless 'Waldo', or vigorous and later ripening 'Chester Thornless'. Self-fertile.

STARTING OFF: Source named varieties from a supplier. New plants are easily made when shoot tips touch the soil.

POSITION: Tolerant of most soils and in full sun for best fruit.

SPACING: 2.5–3.5m apart, further if allowing the plant to ramble.

PRODUCTIVITY/EFFICIENCY: Heavy crops can be had from July to October from a relatively small space.

GROWING: Allow plant to ramble, or train along horizontal wires.

POTENTIAL PROBLEMS: Net against birds.

HARVEST: Ripe fruit will separate easily from the plant.

BLACKCURRANTS

Ribes nigrum. Deciduous shrub.

One of the must-have fruits, for its leaves as much as the currants. Blackcurrants are pretty indestructible, easy to grow, need minimal maintenance and give such a fine return on your investment for years. Better still, their flavour is way superior to bought currants because you can wait until they are perfectly ripe to pick them, rather than have to harvest them early and firm to withstand the journey to the shelves. The leaves too are one of my favourite flavours of the year

Blackcurrants

– pick a few for fruit tea (honestly, it's one of the few that really are worth it), or for making the very finest sorbet you can make.

VARIETIES: Any of the 'Ben' varieties are delicious as well as having good disease resistance with 'Big Ben' having very big berries. 'Titania' is an early variety with a lovely sweet/sharp balance. Self-fertile.

STARTING OFF: Source plants from a good supplier or propagate your own from hardwood cuttings in winter (see page 344). When planting (in the winter for bare root; any time for potted plants) cut all back almost to the ground and just above a bud.

POSITION: Tolerant of most soils with reasonable drainage but needs full sun.

SPACING: 1.5–2m apart.

PRODUCTIVITY/EFFICIENCY: Cropping starts after 2 years with full cropping at 4 years and they will be productive for 15 or 20 years. With careful choice of cultivars you can have blackcurrants from July to September and each plant can produce around 4kg of fruit.

GROWING: Blackcurrants are hungry and thirsty so give an annual mulch with compost or manure, watering in dry weather whilst fruits are swelling. Prune out one-third of older stems each winter.

B

POTENTIAL PROBLEMS: Net against birds, particularly in a dry summer. Spray off aphids with a jet of water. Cut off and burn any stems affected with big bud mite, which in turn should help avoid reversion disease.

HARVEST: Blackcurrants are ripe a little while after the berries have turned a deep colour.

BLUE BEAN

Decaisnea fargesii. Also known as: blue sausage fruit and dead man's fingers. Hardy deciduous shrub. 🌿

One of my favourite-looking plants: imagine electric blue broad beans hanging from a large-leaved ash and you'll be on the right lines. The pulp inside the pods is the edible bit, tasting delicately of melon. Also within the pods, a clutch of large seeds that fly rather well when spat. Mine have only recently started fruiting, so I'm still at the 'eating them by the plant as they ripen' stage, but I suspect the pulp will be very good in cocktails and fruit salads.

VARIETIES: No named varieties. Self-fertile.

STARTING OFF: I'd start with a plant as they can take a while to get established, though they can be started from seed. Best sown from fresh, ripe seed in autumn in seed trays in a greenhouse or polytunnel. They should germinate in spring after exposure to the temperature fluctuations (stratification) of winter.

POSITION: Sunny or partial shade, and sheltered from cold winds. Moist but well-drained soil.

SPACING: 4m apart.

PRODUCTIVITY/EFFICIENCY: Easy but not highly productive. Self-fertile.

GROWING: An annual mulch will be appreciated.

POTENTIAL PROBLEMS: Very cold hardy, to about -28°C, but flowers and new growth can be damaged by late frosts.

HARVEST: Plants usually start fruiting when 3–4 years old. The pods are picked when blue and soft. Split them open as you would a runner bean and scoop out the flesh with a spoon. Blue beans don't store for very long so enjoy freely when fresh.

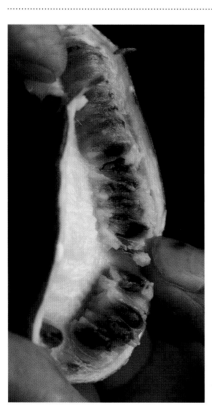
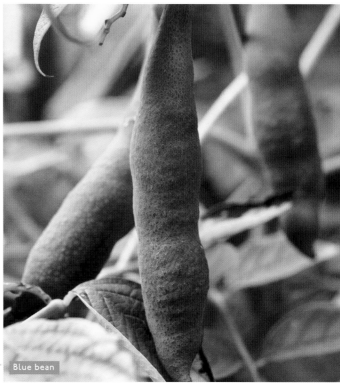

Blue bean

BLUEBERRIES

Vaccinium corymbosum. Deciduous shrub.

One of the fruits that almost everyone who grows it, grows in containers. Blueberries need very acidic soil to thrive and the easiest way to ensure they get it is to plant them in a container full of ericaceous compost. The fruit is delicious – many of the varieties available to grow at home have a more intense flavour than those in the shops where they are expensive to buy, yet easy to grow.

VARIETIES: *V. corymbosum* 'Atlantic' is a vigorous plant producing in July, 'Bluecrop' for large berries in early to mid-August, and 'Chandler' for large sweet berries in late August and September. Blueberries are partially self-fertile meaning that a single plant will produce fruit, but you will get significantly more fruit if you have two or more plants.

STARTING OFF: Source named varieties from a good supplier. Plants are easily propagated by hardwood cuttings (see page 344).

POSITION: Full sun in a soil with a pH between 4 and 5.5, and that is damp but not waterlogged. They will happily grow in large pots using ericaceous compost.

Blue honeysuckle

SPACING: 1.5m apart.

PRODUCTIVITY/EFFICIENCY: Berries ripen over a long time and the right cultivars can supply you with a steady stream of berries from July to September. Although blueberries produce early in their life, they often slowly increase in productivity until cropping fully after 6 years.

GROWING: Mulch generously each year with bark chippings, pine needles or ericaceous compost. Water with rainwater as tap water tends to be too alkaline. Prune out dead, weak and crossing branches as well as growth more than 4 years old to stimulate younger fruit-bearing growth.

POTENTIAL PROBLEMS: Generally problem free, but net against birds.

HARVEST: Pick fruits when they are soft and fully indigo blue.

BLUE HONEYSUCKLE

Lonicera caerulea. Also known as: honeyberry. Hardy deciduous shrub (see left).

Often touted as an alternative to blueberries, and I can see why – its berries are blue, after all – but they're far more worthy of our consideration than simply as an alternative to something else. Hardy, prolific in good years and fruiting very early in the season (often in May), blue honeysuckle is one of my favourites. The berries are like stretched blueberries to look at, with a good deep, honeyed (hence the name) edge to their flavour.

VARIETIES: 'Kamchatka' is particularly hardy, or you could try 'Blue Velvet' or 'Mailon' for very large fruits. You will need two different varieties for pollination.

STARTING OFF: Source plants of named varieties from a good supplier or propagate from hardwood cuttings in winter (see page 344).

POSITION: Tolerant of most soils and in full sun for good fruiting.

SPACING: 1.5m apart.

PRODUCTIVITY/EFFICIENCY: Blue honeysuckles can start producing fruit in their second year and the berries ripen over several weeks. Low maintenance and fruiting when little else is. A good early bee plant too.

B
B

139

GROWING: An occasional mulch with compost would be appreciated.

POTENTIAL PROBLEMS: Generally pest and disease free.

HARVEST: Pick fruit when a dark purple and the fruits have softened.

BOYSENBERRIES

Rubus hybrid. Deciduous shrub.

Supposedly a rather complex cross of blackberry, raspberry, dewberry and loganberry, you might expect (as I did) that boysenberries would have something of an indistinct flavour: nothing of the sort. This is one of the best flavours of the summer – full, fruity, deep and winey. The fruit look a little like long blackberries and are grown in exactly the same way, either in a low-maintenance scramble or trained into a fan.

Boysenberries

VARIETIES: No named varieties although some strains are thornless. Self-fertile.

STARTING OFF: Source bare-root plants from a good supplier.

POSITION: A sunny spot. They are tolerant of most soils except very heavy clay and are drought tolerant too.

SPACING: 2m apart.

PRODUCTIVITY/EFFICIENCY: Boysenberries are vigorous growers with heavy crops of berries.

GROWING: An occasional mulch of compost or manure.

POTENTIAL PROBLEMS: Generally pest and disease free.

HARVEST: Pick berries when a deep black colour and they come away easily from the core.

CAPE GOOSEBERRIES

Physalis peruviana. Also known as: Inca berry, Aztec berry, giant ground cherry and golden berry. Half-hardy perennial, often grown as an annual.

I've probably turned my nose up at a hundred or more of these fruits, wrapped in their papery nest – removed from the sides of cheesecakes, tarts and ice creams served at the end of pub meals of varying quality. The fruit look and taste like a golden cross between a cherry tomato and a regular gooseberry. I've not had a good one but in the spirit of adventure, this year I'm going to grow plenty and try them in all sorts of recipes that sit in that sweet/sharp territory they inhabit, and see if I can't make friends with them, as I have with its close relative, the tomatillo.

VARIETIES: The dwarf 'Pineapple' is one of the few named varieties available.

STARTING OFF: Sow seeds in modules under cover in February and March, and pot on when the roots are showing. Plant out after last frosts or grow under cover.

POSITION: Tolerant of most soils but likes reasonable drainage. It can be grown as a perennial if sheltered from frosts.

SPACING: 60cm apart.

PRODUCTIVITY/EFFICIENCY: Cape gooseberries are heavy yielding with very little input.

GROWING: Lightly spray plants with water or tap

the stems to encourage pollination. Ensure soil stays moist. Stake plants as necessary. Plants will produce more fruit and less leaf if not fed.

POTENTIAL PROBLEMS: Generally pest and disease free.

HARVEST: Collect fruit that has dropped to the ground. They are ready to eat when the fruit inside the papery husk has turned a golden yellow, which may happen a while after they have dropped. They can store for over a month if left in their husks.

CHERRIES

Prunus avium and *Prunus cerasus*. Deciduous tree.

There are some days in midsummer when there's nothing I'd rather eat than cherries. Straight from the tree, on pizza, in salads or clafoutis, they are part of almost every meal. I grow a few different varieties here and I love them all, but they can be an expensive (and heartbreaking) way of growing bird food. You can load the odds in your favour by growing them trained against a wall (easy to net) or as dwarf varieties within a fruit cage, or try the white varieties, which the birds are less interested in.

VARIETIES: So many lovely sweet varieties – 'Stella', 'Summit' or 'Kordia' among them, along with 'Vega' if you are interested in trying a white cherry. Try 'Morello' for a sour cherry or a 'Duke' type such as 'May Duke' if you fancy a cross between a sweet and sour cherry. Check with your supplier if your chosen variety requires a pollinator.

STARTING OFF: Easy and cheap bought as young plants, or graft your own on to a rootstock. Cherries can be bought partially trained if you are planning to fan train.

POSITION: Deep, fertile and well-drained soil. Full sun for sweet cherries, although 'Morello' needs less heat and will happily produce where little else will when planted against a north- or east-facing wall.

SPACING: Depends entirely on the rootstock you choose, but in general allow between 3–4m if using a Gisela rootstock, and 4.5–5m for a Colt rootstock. If you only have room for one then check that your chosen variety is self-fertile. If planting more than one then ensure that pollination groups are compatible.

Cherries

PRODUCTIVITY/EFFICIENCY: Low maintenance – just pruning (see below) – and can be very productive if the blossom escapes the frosts and the fruit stays out of beaks.

GROWING: To avoid silver leaf, prune during the growing season but wait until after harvesting. With sweet cherries, the aim is to maintain an open-centred goblet shape with a balance of wood that is at least one year old and some new replacement branches – it is largely about removing crossing, weak or diseased wood. Acid cherries such as 'Morello' fruit largely on the previous year's wood, so while a goblet shape is still the aim, acid cherries need to be pruned to maintain a balance of last year's wood and new growth to replace it. Cutting back around a quarter of newly fruited wood to a new shoot in late summer causes the tree to throw more energy into these new replacement shoots. Cut any central growth back to a good side shoot to keep the centre open.

Cherries can be trained into many shapes, but a fan offers the dual benefits of utilising a sheltered spot and ease of netting from birds. Water in dry spells as cherries are quite shallow rooting. Give an annual mulch of compost or manure.

POTENTIAL PROBLEMS: Cherries are early flowering so give them (particularly the sweet cherries) a sheltered spot. Birds will love your cherries as much as you, especially if a sweet variety. 'Duke', 'Morello' and white varieties of cherry are less troubled by the birds. Bacterial canker and silver leaf are the most common diseases encountered.

HARVEST: At the height of summer, pick and eat whilst warm from the tree.

CHILEAN GUAVA

Myrtus ugni or *Ugni molinae*. Half-hardy evergreen shrub.

Not the hefty, tropical guava familiar from the shops, but a deliciously sweet/sharp berry that's even more welcome ripening as it does in the depths of autumn. It was Queen Victoria's favourite fruit, which is saying something given she appears grumpy enough not to have many favourites of anything. Their flavour is like a raspberry and blackcurrant and blueberry combined – I tend to eat most of them straight from the bush, but they're great in muffins and fools too.

VARIETIES: Most sold as a generic Chilean guava, but you might find the variegated 'Flambeau' or yellow-leaved 'Butterball'. Self-fertile.

STARTING OFF: Source plants from good suppliers. Propagate by taking cuttings or layering (see pages 342–345), or from seed in autumn or spring.

POSITION: Naturally a woodland edge plant so tolerant of some shade. It needs shelter from cold winds and good drainage. It is hardy down to -10°C when dormant so may need taking under cover in more northerly regions. Tolerant of most soils.

SPACING: 2.5m apart.

PRODUCTIVITY/EFFICIENCY: Chilean guava will provide you with fruit in early winter and with little input.

GROWING: Just prune for shape if and when you fancy, and a handful of manure or a liquid feed now and again to boost your crop.

Chilean guava

POTENTIAL PROBLEMS: Generally pest and disease free.

HARVEST: Pick fruits as they ripen in late autumn/early winter.

CHOCOLATE VINE

Akebia quinata. Hardy evergreen climber.

A wonderful plant for growing over or along a structure to add interest throughout the year – it has glossy leaves borne in fives that cling to the plant all year. Flowers come in spring and early summer, and have a gorgeous chocolatey scent. In a good year – or under cover – these will be followed by fat pods. Pop these pods open to reveal a centre filled with a translucent pulp (that tastes mildly of cool melon) and big seeds – suck in the former and spit out the latter.

142

VARIETIES: Usually sold as its generic form. Even though Akebia plants have both male and female flowers, having two plants greatly increases the likelihood of pollination occurring.

STARTING OFF: Source plants from a specialist supplier or sow seed in modules in spring.

POSITION: Tolerant of most moist but well-drained soils. Likes full sun or partial shade.

SPACING: Can climb to 10m high and will reach 40cm wide.

PRODUCTIVITY/EFFICIENCY: A beautiful plant but a little reluctant to fruit in a cooler climate.

GROWING: Provide support — perhaps through the crown of a tree as in the wild. Prune whenever you like to keep growth at a lower level if you prefer. Makes a great hedge twining through a fence or other plants.

POTENTIAL PROBLEMS: Generally pest and disease free.

HARVEST: Young, soft shoots can be eaten throughout the growing season (steam them briefly and serve as a dressed side dish) and fruits are harvested in autumn. The soft pulp inside the fruit won't keep, so eat it straight away.

CRANBERRIES
Vaccinium macrocarpon. Evergreen shrub. 🌱

When grown commercially in the USA, cranberries are harvested by flooding. A huge bund is built around the plantation and flooded with water at harvest time – the dislodged cranberries float to the surface and are sieved off to market. It's not likely you'll grow them on that scale, or have the acidic soil conditions they need, so it's best to grow them in containers where the pH is easy to control. The berries themselves are wonderfully sharp, sour and juicy, classically cooked into a sauce in a little orange juice, and sweetened with honey or sugar, and port added once softened. They're really good too added to tarts and other puddings to punctuate with their sharpness – and once you start using them, you'll find plenty more excuses to use them.

VARIETIES: Try 'Early Black' or 'Pilgrim' for berries in August. You could also try *Vaccinium vitis-idaea*, commonly known as the lingonberry, which has similar requirements (see page 154). Self-fertile.

STARTING OFF: Source plants from specialist suppliers or layer (see page 345) established plants in spring and early autumn.

POSITION: Cranberries need an acidic soil, with a pH of 4–4.5. They will grow well in moist and boggy soils, and soils with a high peat content. They are most fruitful in poor soils. They can also be grown in containers and hanging baskets using ericaceous compost.

SPACING: 30cm apart.

PRODUCTIVITY/EFFICIENCY: A very good groundcover plant needing little attention. Plants will begin to fruit in their fourth or fifth year and can go on fruiting for up to 100 years.

GROWING: Water with rainwater. Little pruning needed other than removing damaged shoots. They dislike root disturbance.

POTENTIAL PROBLEMS: Cover to protect crops from birds.

HARVEST: Pick when fruits have a reached a deep colour.

C

143

Chocolate vine

ELDER

Sambucus species. Deciduous shrub or tree.

There are few plants that highlight the turning of the seasons as well as the elder. I can't imagine there could be spring into summer without their flowers, nor a summer into autumn without their berries. Whether you're in the city or countryside, chances are elder is not far from you – it will grow on any rough ground and can be found in field boundaries here and there. It's easy to grow in your garden too, with common, unusual and particularly ornamental varieties available.

VARIETIES: *S. nigra* is the UK's native species and 'Haschberg', 'Ina' and 'Sampo' are heavily flowering and fruiting varieties. You could also try *S. racemosa*, which makes a smaller tree and tolerates considerable shade, or *S. canadensis*, which produces a succession of flower heads from July to November.

E
F

Elderflowers

STARTING OFF: Source named varieties from a good supplier or propagate from hardwood cuttings (see page 344).

POSITION: Tolerant of most soils, although a moist rich soil is its natural preference.

SPACING: Can reach 6m wide but are easily pruned (see below) to fit a smaller space.

PRODUCTIVITY/EFFICIENCY: Valuable for its heavy crops of flowers and berries from its second year. Elder makes a very good hedge.

GROWING: Prune as and when you fancy to control size if desired.

POTENTIAL PROBLEMS: Generally pest and disease free.

HARVEST: Flowers are ready in late May/early June and are most fragrant when the sun is shining on them. Berries are ready in August and September, and are easily harvested with a harvesting comb (or failing that, a fork) into a container.

FIGS

Ficus carica. Deciduous shrub or tree.

The finest fig I've ever eaten was a couple of summers ago, not, as you might imagine, in the heat of the Mediterranean, but in the comparative cool of Tottenham, North London. Chris Achilleos has possibly the most incredible allotment I've ever seen (he opens his allotment, 94 Marsh Lane Allotments, most years under the National Gardens Scheme, see www.ngs.org.uk); a sheltered garden of edible and ornamental delights, with cricket ball-sized figs that were splitting under the burden of their own ripeness. Succulent, sweet and with the most sublime depth of flavour, these figs made me plant a couple more, in as sheltered and sunny a spot as I could find, when I got home.

VARIETIES: 'Brown Turkey', 'Brunswick' and 'White Marseilles' are reliable croppers outside in an English climate. Try 'Rouge de Bordeaux' or 'Precoce de Dalmatie' if growing in a sunny, sheltered spot. Self-fertile.

STARTING OFF: Source plants from a good supplier or propagate from hardwood cuttings (see page 344).

POSITION: Good drainage and sun. Roots will need

Figs

restricting to promote fruiting, so they're very much one to grow in containers.

SPACING: 4–5m apart.

PRODUCTIVITY/EFFICIENCY: This is a very low maintenance plant that can give 15kg of fruit in good conditions.

GROWING: Can be grown as a bush or trained against a wall as a fan. Give plants an annual mulch of compost or manure.

POTENTIAL PROBLEMS: Generally pest and disease free. Keep container-grown figs moist throughout growing season to prevent fruits from dropping.

HARVEST: Pick fruit when they soften and droop. They won't ripen further when picked.

FUCHSIA

Fuchsia species. Evergreen shrub behaving as a herbaceous perennial in colder areas. ᔟ

You won't get fruit from a fuchsia every year unless you are in the most sheltered and sunny spot, but when they come you'll be very glad of them. In a sunny summer, those awful, gaudy flowers will turn into long fruity batons, with a flavour somewhere between kiwi, strawberry and blackcurrant, with just a hint of pepper. After a few years, you can pick plenty – I'm hoping to try fuchsia ice cream next year – but early on you're unlikely to get a harvest large enough to do much with, but when they are hard to beat just eaten fresh from the bush, who cares?

Fuchsia

VARIETIES: All species are edible but *Fuchsia magellanica* is the hardiest. 'Riccartonii' is particularly hardy with scarlet-purple berries, and 'Globosa' is very productive. Self-fertile.
STARTING OFF: Source plants from a good supplier or buy semi-ripe cuttings in late summer (see page 342).
POSITION: A well-drained soil in sun or partial shade, avoiding frost pockets. They do well in coastal areas.
SPACING: 3m apart.
PRODUCTIVITY/EFFICIENCY: Very little work needed for a good crop of berries.
GROWING: In colder areas mulch around base of plants in winter. Cut out deadwood in spring.
POTENTIAL PROBLEMS: Net against birds.
HARVEST: Pick fruits when dark and softening.

GOJI BERRIES

Lycium barbarum. Also known as: wolfberries. Deciduous shrub.

Fresh goji berries are a pleasure I've yet to really appreciate, but dried, which is how most are available in the shops, they are rather fine. Be aware: gojis will grow for any fool but what they give in ease, they take in space, sprawling upwards and across with vigour. They are perfectly lovely, and perfect in a large garden, but perhaps not the first choice for container growing or for those with limited space as they want to go bonkers.

VARIETIES: There are few named cultivars; 'Crimson Star' is one that you might find. Self-fertile.
STARTING OFF: Source plants from a good supplier. You can also grow from seed or dig up new plants that are made when shoot tips touch the ground.
POSITION: Fruits best in full sun and is tolerant of most soils.
SPACING: 3m apart.
PRODUCTIVITY/EFFICIENCY: Goji berries start fruiting in year 2 or 3 and need little work.
GROWING: Cut back hard in winter if you want to control its sprawling growth, and be aware that the branches will root where they touch soil — ideal for creating new plants, but to be avoided if you don't want them to spread.

Goji berries

POTENTIAL PROBLEMS: Generally pest and disease free.
HARVEST: Goji berries ripen steadily from summer into autumn. Pick when fully coloured.

GOOSEBERRIES

Ribes uva-crispa. Deciduous shrub. ⌁

Gooseberries are the best of both worlds as far as fruit are concerned – early and sharp, late and sweet – and I love both equally. The first crop usually goes to make sharp sauces (perfect with mackerel), and pureed for knickerbocker glories and to go with the early summer elderflower; the sweeter, late picking for crumbles and ice creams. Picking half of the berries early allows the rest of the plant's energies to ripen the remaining gooseberries more easily.

VARIETIES: 'Invicta' is very productive and delicious – good for both cooking and eating fresh. You could try 'Hinnomaki Red' or 'Redeva' for lovely sweet red berries.

STARTING OFF: Source plants from a good supplier or take hardwood cuttings in winter (see page 344).

POSITION: Gooseberries can fruit in a shady spot but will produce more in the sun.

SPACING: 1.5m apart.

Gooseberries

PRODUCTIVITY/EFFICIENCY: A gooseberry can give up to 4kg of fruit in good conditions, and asks very little of you.

GROWING: An annual mulch of compost or manure will get the most out of your gooseberry. Most commonly grown as bushes, gooseberries can also be grown as cordons, standards or fan trained. For bushes and standards, prune new growth back to 5 leaves in summer to encourage fruit buds; in winter prune side shoots back to around 2 buds from the base and shorten branches by a quarter, cutting to an outward-facing bud to maintain a good framework. For cordons and fans, prune side shoots back to 5 leaves in summer and then again to 1 or 2 buds in winter.

POTENTIAL PROBLEMS: Choose resistant varieties (some, such as 'Invicta', have at least partial resistance) to avoid powdery mildew.

HARVEST: Gooseberries can be harvested in May when they're sharp, primarily for cooking, and in June and July when some can be sweet enough for eating fresh.

147

GRAPES

Vitis vinifera. Deciduous climber. ⌁

A grape vine is a mightily impressive plant. Buy one small and within a few years it'll have formed a woody framework along or over whatever you train it against, and – in most years at least – it will give you many bunches of delicious fruit. Frankly, I've very little interest in wine made from anything other than grapes – once in a while, I taste a reasonable non-grape wine but for the most part, if you want to make your own wine, grow grapes.

VARIETIES: 'Phoenix' is an excellent white variety for eating and winemaking, 'Boskoop Glory' is a reliable producer outside, with good black grapes for eating. 'Madeleine Angevine' is a late-flowering variety for winemakers in colder areas. If you have a greenhouse in a sunny spot, you could try 'Muscat Alexandria'. Self-fertile.

STARTING OFF: Source grafted plants from a good supplier.

POSITION: A very sunny spot with shelter if possible. Vines prefer a moist but well-drained soil. They can

Grapes

be grown in containers, but don't neglect feeding and watering.

SPACING: Vines are vigorous and can climb up to 30m, but they can also be pruned to fit into a small space.

PRODUCTIVITY/EFFICIENCY: The size of your crop will depend to a large extent on the space you allocate to your vine.

GROWING: Prune to keep a manageable size (see page 370). Take off leaves that shade grape bunches.

POTENTIAL PROBLEMS: Ensure good ventilation in your site choice to avoid powdery and downy mildew.

HARVEST: Fruits ripen from August to October, depending on variety. Don't forget to pick tender young leaves for eating (especially good as dolmades, stuffed with rice) before late spring/early summer. The best are those that are about three leaves down from the tip on the young shoots.

HAWTHORN
Crataegus species. Deciduous tree. 🌿

One of the most common of our hedgerow plants, and well worth adding to your own if there are none nearby to plunder. I love the flowers' perfume (though it is one of the many my wife turns her nose up at: to her it's like cat's pee) even more than the berries, but the berries are a fine autumnal treat, especially made into haw ketchup.

VARIETIES: Many hawthorns are edible and *C. ellwangeriana* and *C. schraderiana*, amongst others, have fruit that is good raw as well as cooked. All species are self-fertile.

STARTING OFF: Source grafted plants from a good supplier.

POSITION: Grafted plants will be happy in most soils and like some sun to fruit well.

SPACING: Mature trees can reach 5m high by 4m wide.

PRODUCTIVITY/EFFICIENCY: Plants usually start fruiting around year three.

GROWING: Little maintenance required, though will happily take to trimming or pruning in winter for shape.

POTENTIAL PROBLEMS: Generally pest and disease free.

HARVEST: Pick fruits as they begin to soften in September or October.

Hawthorn

Hazel

HAZEL

Corylus species. Deciduous shrub or tree. 〰
(previous page)

Hazels are fairly widespread in our hedgerows, but the very finest varieties are so much better in flavour and texture that I'd urge you to find space for one if you can. As well as fine nuts in autumn (white filberts are my very favourites), hazels provide sticks for garden supports, with their catkins lighting up their corner in the cold months.

VARIETIES: Hazelnuts are either *Corylus avellana* (hazel), *C. maxima* (filbert) or a cross between the two. Try 'Gunselbert' or 'Butler' for good flavoured and productive trees. Hazels are partially self-fertile and will produce bigger crops with cross-pollination.
STARTING OFF: Source trees from a specialist – they are usually supplied on their own rootstock.
POSITION: Hazels fruit best in full sun and need a well-drained soil. They are wind pollinated.
SPACING: Around 6m apart or half that for hedges.
PRODUCTIVITY/EFFICIENCY: Hazels are good value, with a mature tree producing around 5kg of nuts each year. It is worth coppicing hazels if you have more than one as the poles make good plant supports. Just bear in mind it will take the coppiced tree a couple of years or so to start producing nuts again.
GROWING: Hazels grown as single-stemmed trees may produce suckers and it's best to cut these out during the summer.
POTENTIAL PROBLEMS: Squirrels will need controlling if in your area.
HARVEST: Hazelnuts are ready in September. Collect them from the ground or pick from the tree. Hazelnuts usually keep for a few months in their shell; dried in a dehydrator they will keep for several years; after roasting for 15–20 minutes at 140°C or so they will keep their flavour and texture frozen for at least a year.

JAPANESE PLUMS

Prunus salicina. Deciduous tree. 〰

A really beautiful and flavoursome change from the plums we know and love, Japanese plums blossom early and ripen in July, well ahead of most tree fruit. So full of blossom and fruitfulness are they, that they haven't the spare energy to get beyond five feet or so tall, which makes them great for a small garden. The fruit is juicy, sweet and meaty – substantial and bold, and highly recommended.

VARIETIES: Try self-fertile 'Methley' for reddish-purple fruits ripening in July, or 'Shiro' for large, sweet yellow fruit in July (also self-fertile). Some Japanese plums are partially self-fertile and will produce more with another pollinator nearby. European plums don't pollinate Japanese plums.
STARTING OFF: Source grafted plants from a good supplier.
POSITION: Grow in a warm, sheltered place as this species of plum flowers early.
SPACING: 4m apart.
PRODUCTIVITY/EFFICIENCY: At full production, a Japanese plum tree can give you up to 40kg of fruit.
GROWING: Create a good, nicely spread branch structure in early years, pruning in summer after fruiting, cutting out dead and diseased wood in subsequent summers. You should also thin out fruit in the early years so that the tree isn't overly burdened. Give trees an annual mulch of compost or manure in late winter/early spring.
POTENTIAL PROBLEMS: Less affected by pests and disease than its European counterpart.
HARVEST: Pick the fruits when the aroma and flavour are well developed.

JAPANESE QUINCE

Chaenomeles species. Also known as: oriental quince. Deciduous shrub. 〰

I used to think of these as quince for anyone who hasn't the space for a normal quince tree, but the more I use them the more I think of them as their own glorious thing. The fruit, hard and unforgiving as quinces are at first, are like a slightly smaller version of their namesake, but with a spiciness and zing of their own. Whereas quinces are very much autumnal, Chaenomeles have one foot still in summer. Try them juiced, with plenty of balancing sugar and water, for a refreshing summer drink.

VARIETIES: There are many varieties bred mainly for their ornamental characteristics. 'Salmon Horizon' and 'Crimson and Gold' are both beautiful and productive. Self-fertile.

STARTING OFF: Source plants from a specialist nursery.

POSITION: Tolerant of most soils and a fair amount of shade. The flowers are quite frost tolerant too.

SPACING: 2–5m, depending on variety.

PRODUCTIVITY/EFFICIENCY: Chaenomeles will provide you with many unbuyable fruits for little maintenance.

GROWING: A little pruning for shape, if and when you fancy, is all they require.

POTENTIAL PROBLEMS: Generally disease and pest free.

HARVEST: Fruit is ready in September to October and will keep for several weeks.

Japanese quince

Japanese wineberries

J

151

JAPANESE WINEBERRIES
Rubus phoenicolasius. Deciduous shrub.

Wineberries are one of my very few desert island plants. Productive and delicious, low-maintenance and unbuyable, they also add colour and structure to the garden in the depths of winter when there's little else to catch the eye. The pink/purple-furred canes grow one year, sprouting fruiting side shoots the next, catching the winter sun when most other plants have disappeared into the cold. The fruit itself is fabulous – a fuller, winier version of a raspberry – and at its most prolific between the peaks of summer and autumn raspberries.

VARIETIES: No named varieties. Self-fertile.

STARTING OFF: Source plants from a good supplier or propagate by seed, hardwood cuttings or layering stem tips (see pages 344).

POSITION: Wineberries are happy in shade but fruit best in a sunny spot. They are tolerant of most soils.

SPACING: 2m apart.

PRODUCTIVITY/EFFICIENCY: With very little work effort on your part, wineberries will provide you with a steady supply of fruit from July to September.

GROWING: Cut old fruited stems to the ground. The odd mulch of compost or manure will be appreciated.

POTENTIAL PROBLEMS: Generally pest and disease free.

HARVEST: Pick when the protective hairy calyxes have opened out.

JOSTABERRIES

Ribes x *culverwellii*. Deciduous shrub.

A cross between a gooseberry and blackcurrant, with the best of both in its flavour, jostaberries make a great choice if you have room for only one of the others, or indeed if you've got space for all three. Get out those blackcurrant and gooseberry recipes and try them with jostaberries instead – spot on.

VARIETIES: No named varieties. Self-fertile.

STARTING OFF: Source bare-root or pot-grown plants from a good supplier. Jostaberries can also be propagated by hardwood cuttings (see page 344).

POSITION: Tolerant of most soils and some shade. Jostaberries can be grown successfully in containers.

SPACING: 2m apart.

PRODUCTIVITY/EFFICIENCY: Jostaberries are fast growers, reaching full size (2–3m) and production in 4 years or so. They will provide you with heavy yields of large fruit for around 15 years.

GROWING: Give an annual mulch of compost or manure. Prune in winter as you would blackcurrants to give a supply of new fruit-bearing wood.

POTENTIAL PROBLEMS: Good pest and disease resistance.

HARVEST: Harvest around June/July. As with the gooseberry you can harvest at various stages depending on whether you are cooking or eating fresh.

JUNEBERRY

Amelanchier species. Deciduous tree.

A beautiful shrub or tree with striking thin-petalled flowers in spring, followed by dark purple/black currant-sized berries in early summer. Allow them to ripen and soften before eating – their flavour is quite similar to blackcurrants but sweeter. They're really good as they are, and take to preserving well – making fruit leathers especially.

VARIETIES: Many of the *Amelanchier* species produce edible fruit. *A. canadensis* is the serviceberry but you could also try *A. lamarckii* 'Ballerina', or *A. alnifolia*, the large-fruited saskatoon.

STARTING OFF: Source plants from a specialist supplier.

POSITION: Sun or part-shade and happy in most soils.

SPACING: Plants can reach 6m high and 4m wide.

PRODUCTIVITY/EFFICIENCY: Trees start producing fruit in their second or third year, and fruit is ready to harvest in July. Easy and beautiful.

GROWING: Little or no maintenance required.

POTENTIAL PROBLEMS: Generally pest and disease free, but watch out for the birds when the fruit ripens — may require netting.

HARVEST: Fruit are ready to pick in July when dark purple and slightly soft.

KIWIS

Actinidia species. Deciduous climber.

The full-size kiwis most of us are familiar with need room – a single plant can reach 5m or so in each direction with little encouragement, and you need male and female plants to produce fruit. They are beautiful and, if trained properly (as you would a grape), very fruitful. A better bet for most are the dwarf varieties, aka hardy or self-fertile varieties. These dwarfs will reach only 2–3m in spread and produce plenty of grape-sized kiwis, ripening late in autumn and into winter. They are as delicious as the full-sized varieties and (weird as it may seem) you can eat them furry skin and all – it dissolves in a second.

VARIETIES: There are three species of edible kiwi: *Actinidia arguta*, *A. deliciosa* and *A. kolomikta*. Generally speaking, plants are either male or female and you will need a male plant for pollination of the female to take place. More recently, however, there are some self-fertile varieties available. *A. arguta* is very hardy and good varieties to try are the dwarf 'Issai' (self-fertile) or 'Jumbo' (long large fruits), the latter of which will need a male plant like 'Weiki' for pollination. If you have a sheltered warm spot, try

Kiwi flowers

Kiwi fruit

self-fertile dwarf *A. deliciosa* 'Jenny' or the full-size 'Hayward' with a male pollinator 'Tomuri'.

STARTING OFF: Source a self-fertile or female with male pollinator from a specialist supplier. Suppliers will tell you if and which pollinator is required.

POSITION: Tolerant of most soils, but do plant in a sheltered spot and avoid frost pockets.

SPACING: Kiwis can be trained horizontally to fit the space available to you.

PRODUCTIVITY/EFFICIENCY: Very many fruits are produced by a single plant, from September to November. Large kiwis should be up to full production in 6–8 years; dwarf/self-fertile varieties much more quickly.

GROWING: Pruning is needed to control vigour. Fruit is borne on new growth arising from older canes. Canes become less productive after 3 years so prune out one or two 4-year-old canes each year whilst the plant is dormant to stimulate fresh growth. Apply a good mulch of compost or manure each spring.

POTENTIAL PROBLEMS: Protect young plants from slugs, snails and cats, but other than that they are generally pest and disease free.

HARVEST: Pick fruits when very slightly under-ripe; left too long they become slightly alcoholic in taste and slushy in texture.

LINGONBERRIES

Vaccinium vitis-idaea. Also known as: mountain berry or cowberry. Evergreen shrub.

A popular foraged berry in Scandinavia and grown commercially in the States, the lingonberry is pretty uncommon in the UK. That will change: they are simply too good. They sit somewhere near cranberries on the taste spectrum, making excellent jams, sauces and to add zip to flapjacks and other biscuits and cakes, and they go really well in savoury dishes, with chicken especially.

VARIETIES: Try 'Ida' or 'Red Pearl'. Self-fertile.
STARTING OFF: Source from a good supplier and propagate by division or layering (see pages 342, 345).
POSITION: Moist, acidic soils and ideal for a cooler climate. Lingonberries grow well in containers with ericaceous compost.
SPACING: 50cm apart (30cm for ground cover and dwarf varieties).
PRODUCTIVITY/EFFICIENCY: These make good groundcover plants to suppress weeds. Lingonberries usually fruit in their first year and are fully productive by their third year.
GROWING: Lingonberries are drought-tolerant and need very little maintenance. Use rainwater if watering is necessary, as tap water is more alkaline.
POTENTIAL PROBLEMS: None.
HARVEST: Lingonberries flower twice. If a late frost doesn't get the first flush of flowers you will have fruit in late July and then again in late September.

MEDLAR

Mespilus germanica. Deciduous tree.

If you're after something that fruits reliably every year, requires no maintenance, and where the fruit is both unbuyable and delicious, the medlar should be on your list. Looking like an apple with a more open end, medlars have a flavour somewhere between cooking apples and dates – sharp and deep at the same time. They are best used when bletted: when the pale apple flesh begins to break down, soften and darken. Bletting draws out the deep winey side of their flavour and smooths out any sharpness. They are fabulous for jellies, jams and all manner of puddings.

VARIETIES: I've never been able to tell any varieties apart for flavour, although 'Large Russian' has larger fruit than most. 'Westerveld' and 'Nottingham' are both commonly available and excellent. Medlar 'Seedless' has slightly smaller fruits and considerably fewer seeds. Self-fertile.
STARTING OFF: Source grafted plants from a good supplier.
POSITION: Tolerant of shade, but will fruit better in full sun. Moisture-retentive but well-drained soil.
SPACING: Around 5m, depending on rootstock.
PRODUCTIVITY/EFFICIENCY: Mature medlar trees can produce up to 20kg of fruit and begin fruiting in their second or third year.
GROWING: Little maintenance required. Pruning isn't necessary.
POTENTIAL PROBLEMS: Generally pest- and disease-free.
HARVEST: Pick when softening after the first frosts. They can be picked earlier and ripened inside.

Medlars

MELONS

Cucumis melo. Half-hardy annual.

Melons are something of a gamble – they'll need a good summer and a sunny, sheltered spot, ideally under cover, to fruit. That said, what's to lose – a few seeds and a little time and compost – when the reward can be beautifully ripe, sun-warmed fruit, bursting with juice. If the year is good and my luck's in, I eat almost all of them fresh as they are, though the odd one might make it into a sorbet or cocktail.

VARIETIES: 'Minnesota Midget' and 'Queen Anne's Pocket' are flavoursome small melons, or try cantaloupe 'Sweetheart'. If you have a heated greenhouse you could try muskmelon 'Blenheim Orange' or the watermelon 'Sugar Baby'. Self-fertile.

STARTING OFF: Sow in 9cm pots under cover, about 6 weeks before the last frosts, and plant in a mound of soil to prevent the stem becoming too wet. If planting outside, warm the soil for a few weeks first using a cloche or black plastic, and harden the plant off (see pages 334–335).

POSITION: Somewhere warm and sunny, preferably under cover with a moisture-retentive, humus-rich soil with good drainage.

SPACING: 50cm apart if growing vertically, and between 1–1.5m apart if plants are scrambling.

PRODUCTIVITY/EFFICIENCY: You will get around 4 or 5 melons per plant (more for smaller varieties).

GROWING: Plants can be grown on the flat, pinching out after 5 leaves have developed and allowing 4 lateral shoots to grow. For trained melons, allow a single stem to grow and pinch out when 2m tall, and then pinch out each lateral after 5 leaves. Side shoots growing from laterals will carry the fruit. Melons suspended in the air will need supporting with netting, tights or similar. Allow only 4 or 5 melons to develop (more for varieties producing smaller melons).
Water and feed regularly with comfrey tea or similar. You may need to help pollination along by using a soft dry brush between flowers – each plant has both male and female flowers.

POTENTIAL PROBLEMS: Use a biological treatment if red spider mite is a problem. Keep soil moist to avoid powdery mildew.

HARVEST: Pick when fruits smell aromatic and leave to ripen indoors for a few more days for the best flavour.

Melons

MIRABELLE PLUMS

Prunus cerasifera. Also known as: cherry plums.
Deciduous tree. ᔕ

Mirabelles are strangely under-appreciated in the UK
while being popular on the continent. Certainly they
need a good spring with the early blossom avoiding
frosts, but once past that potential trouble time,
there's nothing between you and delicious, early
mirabelles. If you've not eaten them before, expect
small but juicy and flavoursome plums ready to pick
before most other plums.

VARIETIES: Try 'Golden Sphere' for yellow fruit
and 'Gypsy' for red, both being partially self-fertile.
'Mirabelle de Nancy' is self-fertile and produces
small sweet fruit.
STARTING OFF: Source grafted plants from a
specialist supplier.

M

156

Mirabelle plums

POSITION: Tolerant of most situations, but fruits
best in sun and with some shelter from winds.
SPACING: Between 2.5–7m, depending on
rootstock.
PRODUCTIVITY/EFFICIENCY: Mirabelle plums can
crop heavily and need little maintenance to remain
productive.
GROWING: Give plants an annual mulch of compost
or manure. Prune out only dead and crossing
branches.
POTENTIAL PROBLEMS: Prune from late spring into
summer to avoid silver leaf.
HARVEST: Pick fruits as they soften, and their flavour
and aroma develops — often as early as July, or as late
as September, depending on variety.

MULBERRIES

Morus species. Deciduous tree. ᔕ

My favourite fruit. Every year when I eat them, I'm
surprised they surpass the peaches that come in
midsummer, or the first strawberries, but every year
they do. Picked at their dark peak, their flavour is deep
and complex - raspberry, blackcurrant and blackberry,
with a little sherbet. So laden are they with deep
purple juice, that you can expect your hands and
clothes to be covered: dress appropriately. It is this
abundance of juiciness that keeps them from the
shops; it's impossible to pick them at this peak and
get them to the shops (much less to your home) with
them in one piece.

VARIETIES: Morus species include *M. alba*, *M. nigra*
and *M. rubra*. Mulberries can take many years to fruit,
but some of the quickest are from *M. alba* x *M. rubra*
crosses. Try 'Illinois Everbearing', which fruits in
2–3 years and crops over a long period, or 'Carman',
which produces white fruit from a young age. *M.
nigra* 'King James' (aka 'Chelsea') produces very big,
black mulberries. *M. alba* 'Agate' produces huge,
flavoursome, black fruits. All species are self-fertile.
STARTING OFF: Source plants from a good supplier
or propagate from semi-ripe cuttings (see page
342).
POSITION: Needs some sun and shelter, but is
tolerant of most soils. Mulberries can be grown in
large containers.

Mulberries

SPACING: Up to 10m, depending on cultivar and if allowed to grow to full size. Size can be restricted by pruning in summer.

PRODUCTIVITY/EFFICIENCY: Mulberries will crop heavily over a long period of time once established. Trees are slow-growing, so reasonable crops can take several years.

GROWING: Mulch thickly around the base for the first couple of years and water well until established. Prune out any dead or diseased wood in winter.

POTENTIAL PROBLEMS: Protect young plants from slugs and snails (see pages 364, 370).

HARVEST: Fruits are soft and don't keep. Hand-pick when deeply coloured, or spread a sheet around the base of the tree and gently shake the branches. Fruit will ripen over a long period so harvest often. *Morus alba* species have the best leaves for eating, stuffed with whatever filling you fancy.

NEPALESE RASPBERRIES

Rubus nepalensis. Also known as: Himalayan creeping bramble. Frost-tender evergreen.

A fantastic evergreen creeping fruit that colonises ground relatively quickly. The glossy, deep-green leaves and deep-red berries make for a beautiful plant that's pretty rufty-tufty too – it won't complain if you walk on it now and again. The berries come in summer and, though rarely prolific, are very good, quite raspberry-like.

VARIETIES: Available only in its generic form. Self-fertile.
STARTING OFF: Source plants from a specialist supplier. Plants can also be grown from seed by sowing in modules in autumn and left in a cold frame, or by dividing established plants in spring.
POSITION: Grows best in a frost-free, semi-shady spot. Prefers moist but well-drained soil.

Nepalese raspberries

SPACING: Plant 1m apart for relatively fast ground cover.
PRODUCTIVITY/EFFICIENCY: A low-maintenance plant that makes a good weed-suppressing groundcover, and that will also provide you with fruit in late summer.
GROWING: No maintenance required.
POTENTIAL PROBLEMS: Generally pest and disease free.
HARVEST: Berries are ready for harvesting from July to August.

OLIVES

Olea europaea. Borderline hardy tree.

Not one to grow if you're after a cast-iron guarantee of a harvest, but perhaps beautiful enough to take the gamble on. Shelter and sunshine are essentials to a healthy plant, never mind fruit; with those and a well-drained soil you may get lucky and harvest more than a few fruit in autumn. Choice of variety is very important (see below) as is ensuring that your plant hasn't spent most of its life somewhere far sunnier than where you plan for it – like you would, it'll complain long and hard if uprooted from the balmy heat of Tuscany for the chilly wilds of North Yorkshire.

VARIETIES: 'Arbequina' makes a small tree, and begins fruiting early in its life as well as ripening earlier than many other varieties. You could also try 'Frantoio', 'Leccino' and 'Maurino', which all hail from northern Italy. Olives need another variety available for pollination and are wind pollinated so need planting fairly near to each other.
STARTING OFF: Source plants from a good supplier, ensuring they are of a variety and strain suitable for your climate.
POSITION: Tolerant of a wide range of soils but free drainage is a must. Give olives the sunniest spot you have, and shelter from easterly and northerly winds. Olives are very suitable for containers.
SPACING: Olives can be pruned to fit the space available.
PRODUCTIVITY/EFFICIENCY: Varieties such as 'Arbequina' can start producing olives early in their lives, whilst others may take up to 12 years. The

size of harvest is likely to be variable in the UK, dependant on the weather and the shelter afforded to your trees.

GROWING: Undertake light, formative pruning in spring and aim for an open goblet shape. Remove all suckers from the base of the tree. If growing in a pot, feed fortnightly with a liquid seaweed or comfrey feed, and when potting on only go up slightly in size.

POTENTIAL PROBLEMS: Pruning early in the year ensures wounds heal sufficiently before winter. If your winter temperatures routinely drop below -5°C then wrap the trunk and crown of your olives in horticultural fleece in their early years. Pots will need insulating with bubble wrap too or bringing inside.

HARVEST: Harvesting will be somewhere between October and January, and when the olives are slightly soft when squeezed. They will need to be soaked and then brined before they can be eaten.

PEACHES AND NECTARINES
Prunus persica. Deciduous tree.

Both peaches and nectarines need sun and shelter, yet even with both are far from assured harvests each year, but the fruit are so special you'll be glad you took the risk when they do produce. Most peaches in the shops are picked early and firm to allow them time to be transported to the shelves and ripen at home – their texture and flavour never quite recovers from that early harvesting. Grow them yourself and you'll find it very hard to enjoy those from the shops again.

VARIETIES: 'Red Haven' and 'Rochester' peaches are delicious and reasonably resistant to leaf curl; 'Pineapple' nectarine is sweet and delicious. You could also try the dwarf nectarine 'Nectarella' or dwarf peach 'Bonanza'. Peaches and nectarines are self-fertile.

STARTING OFF: Source grafted plants from a good supplier.

POSITION: Full sun in a sheltered position, and moisture-retentive and well-drained soil. Peaches grow well in containers and will fruit well planted inside a polytunnel or greenhouse. Nectarines will fare best against a wall.

Nectarines

SPACING: Between 3–5m apart, and less for dwarf plants.

PRODUCTIVITY/EFFICIENCY: Yields may vary considerably depending on the summer, though in a good year can produce up to 35kg of fruit (14kg for a fan). Trees will begin to produce in their second or third year.

GROWING: Diseased and dead wood should be pruned out in summer after fruiting. Prune fan-trained peaches and nectarines in summer — fruit forms largely on shoots formed the previous year, so fruited wood should be replaced each year with new growth. Provide with an annual mulch of compost or manure.

POTENTIAL PROBLEMS: Leaf curl is the biggest problem in a damp climate. Grow resistant varieties such as 'Rochester' (despite claims to the contrary none are that resistant) and if possible protect plants from spring rains in particular. You may

Peaches

Pears

need to help pollination along by using a soft brush, especially if growing under cover.

HARVEST: The fruits are ready in mid- to late summer, when aromatic, soft and leave the tree with the merest gentle persuasion.

PEARS

Pyrus communis. Deciduous tree.

I'm busy planting a few more pears here this winter; we've half a dozen or so, but we eat so many it's time to have some more that produce at either end of the season – early and late – so that we can enjoy them for more of the year. For me, pears are a perfect candidate for growing as trained fruit – espaliers, stepovers and cordons in particular. Few are self-fertile, so planting cordons that take little room gives you the possibility of pears in even a small space.

VARIETIES: As with apples, there are dessert and culinary as well as perry pears (for making perry). Try the old English culinary 'Black Worcester' or old French 'Catillac'. Try the late season 'Conference' and 'Doyenne du Comice' dessert pears, which are both reliable in the UK. Or try 'Beurre Giffard' for an aromatic pear ready to eat in August.

Pears need a pollinator to bear fruit; even those that are self-fertile will bear heavier crops with a pollinator. If space is limited you could try a 'family' tree with several varieties grafted on to a single stem. Choose varieties in compatible pollination groups, but watch out for the ones that won't pollinate other specific varieties, e.g. 'Doyenne du Comice' and 'Onward' are poor partners even though they are in adjacent groups.

STARTING OFF: Source grafted plants from a good supplier.

POSITION: A sunny, sheltered position. The main rootstocks used are tolerant of a wide range of soils, with the exception of Quince C, which prefers a fertile soil.

SPACING: 2.5–8m apart, depending on rootstock.

PRODUCTIVITY/EFFICIENCY: Pears can take between 3–10 years to begin bearing fruit, and can yield between 15–100kg once fully producing, depending on rootstock.

GROWING: Pears take well to training and can be trained as fans, cordons and stepovers. Undertake formative pruning in winter. Prune trained trees in summer: any new shoots over 20cm should be cut back to three leaves above the cluster that forms at the base. Give plants an annual mulch of compost or manure, except those on a pear rootstock, which don't need it.

POTENTIAL PROBLEMS: Choose varieties resistant to canker, fireblight and scab. Cut out any limbs affected by fireblight and burn, disinfecting your saw afterwards.

HARVEST: It is important not to leave the pears for too long on the tree or they risk becoming 'sleepy' (grainy, soft and perhaps brown) in storage. Test the pears for readiness as their time for ripeness approaches by holding the bulbous end of the pear in your palm and, with your index finger on the stalk, gently tilt the fruit upwards; it will come away easily if ready. Only the earliest pears will be ready to eat from the tree. Later-ripening varieties will be ready several weeks to several months after picking, so store pears in a cool place, checking regularly for ripening. When beginning to ripen, the skin will yellow slightly and at this point bring them into the house to ripen fully.

PECANS

Carya illinoinensis. Deciduous tree.

A gorgeous tree, worth growing for its shape and leaves alone, but with good varieties, in a sheltered sunny spot, you might just get lucky and end up with delicious nuts. Don't expect much from them for a few years; mine refused to grow above ground while they sent down sturdy roots, but finally, they woke up and sprang into life, and have at least tried to catch up. I've planted mine on a high spot by the river – they originate in the river basins of the southern states of America, and they seem to like the similar conditions.

VARIETIES: For the UK and other northerly climates, your chosen varieties should be a northern type pecan, which are early-producing trees. Try 'Campbell NC4', 'Carlson 3', 'Lucas' or 'Mullahy'. Self-fertile.

STARTING OFF: Source grafted trees from a specialist supplier.

POSITION: Full sun in a sheltered place with a rich, deep but well-draining soil.

SPACING: 6–7m apart.

PRODUCTIVITY/EFFICIENCY: Pecans need a good amount of sun to fruit and are unlikely to fruit every year without it, but they require little of your time.

GROWING: Keep weed free around the base whilst the pecan is establishing its deep taproot in the first few years — it will appear not to grow during this time.

POTENTIAL PROBLEMS: Generally pest and disease free.

HARVEST: When the husks of the nuts start to split, spread a sheet on the ground under the pecan and shake its branches.

PINEAPPLE GUAVA

Acca sellowiana. Also known as: feijoa. Evergreen shrub.

A gorgeous shrub, rather like a larger leaved olive, and with one of the most beautiful of the edible flowers, and with a flavour to match – fruity, crisp, sweet and with a spicy, slightly cinnamon hint, they are superb raw. In the warmest, most sheltered spots, ideally under cover, you might coax fruit from a pineapple guava too. The fruit looks like a small avocado and tastes somewhere between a pineapple and strawberry, which should be invitation enough to grow them if you have a sunny spot.

VARIETIES: Plenty of named varieties available, including 'Mammoth' and 'Triumph', though 'Smith' is supposed to be most likely to fruit in cooler climates. Check whether the variety you are buying is self-fertile or requires a pollinator, but

Pineapple guava

again this is only necessary if you are hoping for fruit – they will produce edible flowers regardless.

STARTING OFF: Source plants from a specialist supplier.

POSITION: Tolerant of most situations, but prefers humus-rich and well-drained soil. Prefers full sun but will tolerate a little shade. If you are hoping for fruit give it the warmest spot you can — a walled garden is ideal. Pineapple guava is hardy to -12°C and suitable for the warmer parts of the UK.

SPACING: Pineapple guava can reach 2.5m in height and spread, but is easily kept smaller by pruning.

PRODUCTIVITY/EFFICIENCY: An attractive addition to your garden, but quite a large one for the return in edible flowers that you'll get. That said, it requires no maintenance.

GROWING: Prune as and if you fancy to keep this to a size you want.

POTENTIAL PROBLEMS: Generally pest- and disease-free.

HARVEST: Pick flowers throughout July. Pick fruit before the frosts set in — they may not yet be ripe but will ripen in storage.

PLUMS, DAMSONS AND GAGES

Prunus domestica and *Prunus insititia.* Deciduous tree.

Each of these three variations on a theme is very much worth considering. Although damsons tend to be more for cooking than eating fresh, variety plays a huge part – the 'Dittisham Damson' tree gives us incredibly juicy, succulent fruit that we eat fresh as much as cooked. There's such variation in flavour, texture and harvest time, that it's hard to generalise – better to spend time looking at specialist nursery catalogues, and picking the flavours and textures that take your fancy.

VARIETIES: Plums and gages are from the *Prunus domestica* species and Damsons from *P. insititia*. Try 'Czar' for an early plum, 'Merryweather' for a heavy-cropping, late-ripening damson, or 'Early Transparent' for a sweet gage.

This group of plants can be self-sterile (needing a pollinator), partially self-fertile or self-fertile, so check whether a pollinator is needed when choosing your varieties, making sure pollination groups are compatible.

STARTING OFF: Source grafted plants from a good supplier.

POSITION: There are rootstocks available to suit most soil types. Although very hardy plums and gages are late-flowering, site in a frost-free place and the sunnier the better for dessert varieties, especially the later ripening ones.

SPACING: 2.5–7m apart.

PRODUCTIVITY/EFFICIENCY: Plums, damsons and gages begin to fruit in 2–6 years, giving between 15–65kg of fruit, depending on rootstock.

GROWING: Plums, gages and damsons can easily be grown as pyramids, cordons or fans (see page

346). Once the shape is established, you only need to remove dead and diseased wood each year. Thin fruits to 8cm. Mulch annually with compost or manure.

POTENTIAL PROBLEMS: Prune between May and October to avoid silver leaf. Choose varieties with some resistance to canker, such as 'Marjorie's Seedling' plum and 'Oullins Gage'.

HARVEST: Pick when fully coloured and the fruit comes away easily.

Quince

QUINCE

Cydonia oblonga. Deciduous tree.

Now that quinces are available as very dwarfing trees – growing to 1.5m or so in height and spread – there's almost no excuse for not growing one. Beautiful twisted white/pink blossom in spring, aromatic fruit in autumn and a lazily irregular habit all year round, quinces are right up there on my list of garden trees, whether you have an acre or a balcony. Let the fruit develop on the tree into autumn – perhaps even longer than the leaves cling to the tree – then pick and bring inside. The aroma will slowly build until it fills the room, perhaps even the house. Cooking brings out their loveliness; try a slice or two in an apple pie, poach them in cider or wine then bake them with butter, dried fruit and honey, or make membrillo – a semi-firm 'cheese', which is in fact a thick, sweet paste, that goes beautifully with meats and blue cheese.

VARIETIES: I've never been able to detect a difference in flavour between varieties, but if you are in a wet location, try 'Serbian Gold' (aka 'Lezovacz') or 'Champion', which have good blight resistance. Self-fertile.

Plums

STARTING OFF: Source grafted plants of named varieties from a fruit supplier.

POSITION: A sunny, sheltered position for best fruiting. Tolerant of most soils with the right rootstock.

SPACING: 4–5m apart, depending on rootstock; 1.5m if growing the very dwarf trees.

PRODUCTIVITY/EFFICIENCY: Quince will begin fruiting between years 2–4, depending on rootstock, and will yield around 15kg of fruit.

GROWING: An annual mulch of compost or manure will be appreciated. No pruning needed.

POTENTIAL PROBLEMS: Use resistant varieties to avoid leaf blight; incinerate fallen/affected leaves and prune and incinerate dead shoots in winter.

HARVEST: Pick in October as the fruits begin to soften. They can keep for 2 months or more if stored in a cool place.

RASPBERRIES

Rubus idaeus. Deciduous shrub.

If you put a gun to my head and made me choose between raspberries and strawberries, raspberries it would be. Their depth of flavour, that winey edge, just wins for me. There are two types: summer fruiting and autumn fruiting. I grow mostly autumn varieties as they grow canes that produce fruit in the same year, so you can strim the lot to ground level every year and they'll come back to fruit the next; their longer time in the sun gives them a deeper flavour too. Summer varieties can be very good indeed, but they fruit on canes that grew last year, which means pruning out only the canes that have fruited and leaving the rest for next year; plus they fruit when there are plenty of strawberries around.

VARIETIES: Try heavy cropping 'Glen Clova' for tasty early fruit or 'Glen Magna' for late-season fruits. 'Tulameen' is a vigorous mid- to late-season raspberry with good flavour. Good autumn varieties to try are 'Autumn Bliss' and the yellow 'All Gold'. Self-fertile.

STARTING OFF: Source canes from a good fruit nursery.

POSITION: Full sun or a little shade. A fertile soil

Raspberries

with good drainage is best. They will be shorter-lived on alkaline soils and don't thrive at all on chalk.

SPACING: Space summer raspberries 35–45cm apart in double rows 1m apart. Space autumn raspberries at 50cm apart and allow them to expand into a single narrow line about 30cm across.

PRODUCTIVITY/EFFICIENCY: Plants will supply you with a steady supply of berries over several weeks. With the right choice of cultivar you can harvest raspberries from June to November. Raspberry plants tend to live for around a dozen years.

GROWING: Support all this season's growth of summer raspberries, as this will provide fruit the following year. In autumn, remove fruited wood that was tied in the previous winter. Reduce amount of new stems to around 10 per metre, taking out the weakest first. Feed plants with an annual mulch of compost or manure.

Autumn raspberries fruit on this year's growth and will usually be happy unsupported. Cut stems of autumn raspberries to the ground in late winter. Feed plants with an annual mulch of compost or manure.

POTENTIAL PROBLEMS: Don't plant where raspberries, blackberries or strawberries have previously been grown to limit the opportunities for diseases. You may need to net against birds. Cultivate the soil at the base of raspberries during the winter to deter raspberry beetle.

HARVEST: When ripe, raspberries readily come away from the plug.

RED- AND WHITE CURRANTS

Ribes rubrum. Deciduous shrub.

In many ways these two currants are under-appreciated, largely because of our love for sugar perhaps. Neither is the sweetest fruit, but both have a fine flavour and will produce well in less than the sunniest locations – fans are perfectly happy against a north-facing wall. Both make fabulous jelly to go with meat and cheese, and add a little delicious tartness to pies, tarts and crumbles.

VARIETIES: 'Jonkers van Tets' (aka 'Jonkheer van Tets') is an old early-cropping redcurrant, 'Red Lake' is mid-season and 'Rovada' is late season. 'White Versailles' and 'White Grape' are flavoursome white currants. Self-fertile.

STARTING OFF: Source plants from a fruit nursery or propagate from hardwood cuttings in winter (see page 344).

POSITION: Tolerant of most soils and will fruit well in a fair amount of shade.

SPACING: 1.2–1.5m apart if growing as bushes, around 45cm for cordons and 2m for fans.

PRODUCTIVITY/EFFICIENCY: Red- and white currants will start to fruit in their second year, and will get to full production in around 6 years. They can fruit well for 20 years, producing around 4kg each year, and are happy in semi-shade where little other fruit thrives.

White currants

R

165

Redcurrants

GROWING: Give an annual mulch of compost or manure. Formative prune main branches in winter and prune side shoots in summer.

POTENTIAL PROBLEMS: Summer pruning of side shoots to five leaves will help control blister aphid. Pick off any sawfly larvae in the spring to prevent defoliation. Net against birds.

HARVEST: Leave redcurrants for a few days after they have turned a lively red, in order to develop their sweetness. White currants will turn a creamy colour when ripe. Pinch whole trusses of fruit from the bush and use a fork to separate berries from the stalks.

RHUBARB

Rheum x *hybridum*. Hardy perennial.

One of my favourite flavours, and definitely one of the most reliable and easy to grow. Once established, expect rhubarb's huge leaves to push out early and strongly every spring – it's the delicious, fibrous, sour stalks at their centre you're after. I can't have enough of them, so I grow varieties that produce in succession and force some early. Forcing is as easy as putting a bucket (or traditional forcing pot) over an early variety and allowing the warm microclimate to hurry growth along. In the absence of light, the plant uses stored starches (rather than photosynthesis) to drive growth – some of these starches are converted into sugars in the process, resulting in pink, sweet stalks, a few weeks earlier than the first of the non-forced varieties.

VARIETIES: Try 'Timperley Early', which is one of the earliest rhubarbs, and 'Victoria', one of the latest. 'Holstein Blood Red' is an old variety with very red stems. You could try Himalayan rhubarb (*Rheum australe*) if you have the room. It is majestic and will provide you with large apple-flavoured stems when traditional rhubarb has gone over.

STARTING OFF: Source crowns from a good supplier or propagate by division in early spring, and plant whilst dormant (normally November to March). Plant with the crown at soil level, or just above if soil is on the wet side.

Forced rhubarb

R

Rhubarb

POSITION: Likes a humus-rich moist soil in full sun.

SPACING: Im apart with 2m between rows, with 2m apart for Himalayan rhubarb.

PRODUCTIVITY/EFFICIENCY: Rhubarb can produce a steady supply of stems from April (earlier if forcing) to July if you choose varieties that crop in succession, and with very little input from you.

GROWING: Allow the plant to establish for a year before harvesting. Give plants an annual mulch with compost or preferably manure. Cut off flower stalks as they detract from edible stem production. Divide plants every 5 years or so to maintain vigour.
For an early crop in January, force plants by covering with an upturned pot (holes covered), bucket or forcer, surrounded by fresh manure or straw if you have any. Leave forced plants to recover for the rest of the growing season and don't force the following year – they will be sufficiently recovered to force again the year after that.

POTENTIAL PROBLEMS: Generally pest and disease free.

HARVEST: Choose stems with good colour and leaves that have just opened, and, holding near the base, pull and twist. The leaves are poisonous so put them straight on the compost heap.

SCHISANDRA

Schisandra chinensis. Also known as: magnolia vine and five flavour berry. Deciduous vine.

I confess, I've not had much joy in getting Schisandra to fruit, but this may be ineptitude on my part: others I know find it no problem. It is a beautiful enough climber as it is, so I shall excuse its lack of productivity and pair it up with another variety in the hope that they pollinate each other and fruit a little better. The fruit hang in long racemes – strings of fruit – which look not unlike opaque redcurrants. They have a complex flavour that dominates the commercially available drink Amé; their Chinese name is wu wei zi, meaning 'fruit of five flavours'.

VARIETIES: Schisandra plants are either male or female, and both are required for pollination. However, you could try 'Eastern Prince', which is self-fertile.

STARTING OFF: Source plants from a specialist supplier or propagate established plants by division.

POSITION: A moist and preferably acid soil, although with lots of organic matter dug in it will grow in a more alkaline soil. Will tolerate some shade.

SPACING: Can reach 7m in height.

PRODUCTIVITY/EFFICIENCY: Given some support this vine can be left largely to its own devices, though it will take a few years for fruiting to begin.

GROWING: Prune in spring to reduce size if you fancy. Plants need support but this could be the canopy of a tree.

POTENTIAL PROBLEMS: Generally pest and disease free.

HARVEST: Pick the fruit in autumn when berries are bright red.

SEA BUCKTHORN

Hippophae species. Deciduous shrub.

A rough, tough, hardy shrub, which you may find naturalised in sand dunes in parts of the UK. An excellent hedging plant if keeping people or animals out/in is your aim. The fruit are rich in vitamins A and C, and abundantly borne, but might generously be described as astringent. Let this not dissuade you from investigating their loveliness - sea buckthorn's flavour is quite unique and hard to navigate via other fruit, almost more of a flavoursome aroma - but sweetened in drinks or cocktails is quite something, and sea buckthorn makes one of the most delicious ice creams I've ever eaten.

VARIETIES: There are several sea buckthorn species, but the most edible are *H. rhamnoides* and *H. salicifolia*. You will need both male and female plants for pollination.

STARTING OFF: Source plants from a specialist supplier.

POSITION: Well-drained soil in full sun. Sea buckthorns are tolerant of exposure.

SPACING: Space 5–8m apart, depending on variety. If planting as a hedge space at around Im.

PRODUCTIVITY/EFFICIENCY: Heavy crops of fruit are borne from the third year. An excellent hedging plant, ground stabiliser and bee plant.

GROWING: Cut off any suckers that appear where you don't want them.

POTENTIAL PROBLEMS: Generally pest and disease free.

HARVEST: Snip the fruit from the plant when the berries become a rich orange and soften slightly to the touch. This will be in September and October.

STRAWBERRIES

Fragaria x *ananassa*. Hardy perennial. ༄

If you can, find room for a few strawberries – even if just in a container. The flavours of the best home-grown varieties are such a league apart from those in the shops and, as is usually the case, you'll find the difference it makes is huge to pick them when fully ripe. Unless you are a keen preserver, I'd suggest having plants that ripen at different times, to give you a successional harvest rather than a glut. I eat most of my strawberries fresh, either straight from the plant or in Eton mess, knickerbocker glories and other summery desserts. Their flavour transfers well into most preserves – jams and fruit leather especially – and strawberry ice cream is so much better when made with home grown.

VARIETIES: There is a multitude to choose from, but it's possible to be in strawberries from May right through to November. Try 'Honeoye', 'Cambridge Favourite', 'Royal Sovereign' and 'Mara des Bois', along with 'everbearing' varieties such as 'Flamenco' and 'Albion' for the latest strawberries. You could also try alpine strawberries such as 'Mignonette' (see page 131). Self-fertile.

STARTING OFF: Usually available as barefoot mini-plants or in pots – they can be planted whenever they are available, but ideally in late summer/early autumn when the ground is still warm. You can also propagate them from runners.

POSITION: Full sun in moisture-retentive, well-drained soil.

SPACING: Plant strawberries 50cm apart in rows with 90cm between rows.

PRODUCTIVITY/EFFICIENCY: Plants usually produce well and with the right choice of varieties can give a long season of fruit, but not without some input: manure as a feed and straw as a mulch around the plants help give a continued high harvest. Plants tend

Strawberries

to tire after around 5 years, so replant a quarter every year after year 5.

GROWING: Suppress weeds and keep soil moist by mulching between the rows with straw when you see the first fruits are appearing. When fruiting is over, cut back the fruited stems, runners and leaves and add well-rotted manure or compost.

POTENTIAL PROBLEMS: Net against birds who want your strawberries as much as you do. Slugs and snails can be a problem in a wet year as can botrytis. Use your preferred method on the former and take care not to splash your strawberries when watering, and to keep a good airflow around plants to avoid the latter.

HARVEST: Pick when well coloured and when the sun is warm to bring out their fullest flavour.

SWEET CHESTNUTS
Castanea species. Deciduous tree.

A few years ago I turned a corner with sweet chestnuts. As with many things, pairing them with cream and chocolate brought out the best in them (they'd probably make my shoe taste good too), and as a cake, it's hard to better. Roasted over an open fire, as in the old festive song, they are fabulously nutty and sweet – but be careful not to burn them, as they turn bitter very easily. Easy to grow, increasingly reliable producers as climate change takes effect, and relatively untroubled by pests and diseases, sweet chestnuts are a fine choice for a good-sized garden or larger.

VARIETIES: Sweet chestnuts are from the *Castanea sativa* species, or are a hybrid *C. sativa* x *C. crenata*. 'Bouche de Betizac' and 'Marigoule' are hybrids that are doing well in the UK. *C. sativa* 'Belle Epine' is a good pollinator and fruiter. Generally, sweet chestnuts are not self-fertile and will need another variety to pollinate, and although some such as 'Marigoule' are partially self-fertile, they will still produce more with a pollinator.

STARTING OFF: Source grafted plants from a specialist supplier.

POSITION: A sunny spot in well-drained soil that ranges from acid to neutral.

SPACING: A full-grown tree can reach 20m high and 15m wide; however, size can be controlled by pruning or coppicing, in which case plant at around 8m apart.

PRODUCTIVITY/EFFICIENCY: A 50kg harvest of chestnuts from a 10-year-old tree is not unusual.

GROWING: If restricting the size of your chestnuts, prune lightly in winter into an open goblet shape during the first 2 or 3 years after planting, or coppice every 10 years or so. Coppiced trees will take 2 or 3 years to begin producing nuts again. If growing as a standard tree little is required.

POTENTIAL PROBLEMS: Use sticky or pheromone traps if chestnut weevil or chestnut codling moths are troublesome, although in reality damage is rarely significant from these pests.

HARVEST: Chestnuts fall to the ground when ready and at the same time as the leaves. They tend to fall

Sweet chestnuts

over a period of 2 weeks, and will need collecting every other day or so to prevent deteriorating. A nut wizard makes collecting a great deal easier. Nuts will store for a few weeks if allowed to dry in the sun or at room temperature for a couple of days, and are then stored in the fridge. They also freeze well after boiling for 5 minutes and then peeling. They will keep for several years if dehydrated.

S

171

Walnuts

WALNUTS

Juglans regia. Deciduous tree.

As with sweet chestnuts, climate change means that walnuts are likely to be ever more prolific and reliable croppers in the UK, and if you have a bit of space, they make a fine tree. Or rather trees, as while many varieties are self-fertile, they'll produce bigger crops more reliably with a pollinating partner. Growing your own means you get the tastiest varieties and the chance to pick green walnuts – harvested before the shell forms – which make a fabulous aperitif and are delicious pickled. We eat most of our walnuts fresh, often with cheese and fruit, occasionally in chicken recipes, and in endless puddings.

VARIETIES: For the UK, use late-flowering varieties that will side-step any frosts. 'Franquette' and 'Broadview' are both late flowering as well as good quality, early yielding and disease resistant. You could also try 'Corne du Perigord' and 'Fernor', which are also disease resistant. Check with your supplier whether your chosen variety requires a pollinator.
STARTING OFF: Source grafted plants from a good supplier. There are rootstocks to suit most soil types so ask your supplier.
POSITION: Tolerant of most soils but full sun is a must.
SPACING: A full-size tree can reach 20m high and 15m wide, although pruning can keep that to 8 metres or so wide.
PRODUCTIVITY/EFFICIENCY: Grafted trees can start cropping in 3–4 years, but will take around 10 years or so to produce large quantities.
GROWING: Prune lightly in winter into an open goblet shape during the first few years after planting. Thereafter, remove dead or crossing branches and prune to restrict size. Don't plant anything valuable underneath as walnuts can release chemicals that inhibit the growth of neighbours.

POTENTIAL PROBLEMS: Grow blight-resistant varieties to avoid leaf spot and walnut blight. Some plants, such as apples, will not grow well next to walnuts trees. Trap and (as is required by law) humanely kill squirrels by whichever method you find best if you don't want to share your nuts.
HARVEST: Pick walnuts green for pickling in midsummer, with the main harvest in autumn.

WORCESTERBERRIES

Ribes divaricatum. Hardy shrub.

Worcesterberries are a thorny North American relative of the gooseberry, with a touch of blackberry about them in looks and flavour. What you gain in disease resistance and productivity, you pay for a little in thorns, but the flavour is very much worth it – like a slightly blackcurranty gooseberry, that was for some time thought to be a cross between the two.

VARIETIES: Usually found only in its generic form.
STARTING OFF: Source bare-root or pot-grown plants from a good supplier, or propagate from hardwood cuttings in autumn (see page 344).
POSITION: Moist, fertile but well-drained soil. These berries will also do well on a poor soil, as long as it's not wet.
SPACING: 1.8m apart.
PRODUCTIVITY/EFFICIENCY: A very productive fruit bush.
GROWING: Prune as for gooseberries to keep to the size you prefer.
POTENTIAL PROBLEMS: Worcesterberries avoid most of the diseases that afflict blackcurrants and gooseberries, although birds can be a problem. Prune the centre of the plant to be light and airy to deter sawfly.
HARVEST: Pick berries in late July/early August when a deep black colour and just softening to the touch.

HERBS AND SPICES

Angelica

ANGELICA

Angelica archangelica. Also known as: Garden Angelica, Holy Ghost and Norwegian Angelica. Hardy biennial.

A lovely umbelliferous herb, tall and striking. Not one you'll use every day in all likelihood, but its looks may bump it up the pecking order above some others, perhaps. Its flavour is gently astringent, musky even, being one of the key ingredients in many gins. Really worthwhile investigating.

VARIETIES: There are many ornamental angelicas available, but the edible type is the ecclesiastically named *Angelica archangelica*.

STARTING OFF: Sow fresh seeds in early autumn in modules for planting out in mid-spring, or, alternatively, sow direct where they are to grow. Seeds will lose their viability quickly so do not save from one year to the next.

POSITION: Prefers at least partial shade and can do very well in deep shade. Likes a moist soil.

SPACING: 1.2m apart.

PRODUCTIVITY/EFFICIENCY: As trouble free and low maintenance as it gets, happy in shade and great looking.

GROWING: Angelica is a biennial and will die after flowering, but self-seeds freely.

POTENTIAL PROBLEMS: Slugs and snails can attack young plants.

HARVEST: Cut young leaves and stalks for crystallising in early summer. Seeds are ready to harvest from summer onwards.

ANISE HYSSOP

Agastache foeniculum. Also known as: liquorice mint. Hardy perennial.

A beautiful, aromatic and delicious herb that, I confess, I grow as much for its looks and bee-friendliness as its fine flavour. It tastes of mint and aniseed in an approximately 1:3 ratio, and has that gentle sweetening effect that sweet cicely's aniseed also brings. Use the leaves or flowers raw – more than a moment's cooking robs its flavour. Try them shredded finely with strawberries, in cocktails, or with seafood.

VARIETIES: Named varieties are hard to find.

STARTING OFF: Source plants from a specialist supplier or grow from seed under cover in spring.

POSITION: A sunny spot in well-drained and rich soil. Can be grown in a large container.

SPACING: 30–45cm apart. Can reach 1m in height.

PRODUCTIVITY/EFFICIENCY: Fresh leaves are produced throughout the growing season. It may be worth growing two plants if you want both leaves and flowers – the leaves become tougher once the plant starts to flower.

GROWING: Pick off flower heads if you want to prolong your supply of tender leaves.

POTENTIAL PROBLEMS: As with most herbs, relatively untroubled by pests and diseases.

HARVEST: Pick tender leaves and flower heads through summer as needed. Any flowers left to seed and desiccate can be picked off through winter to add their distinctive flavour to sorbets, syrups and ice creams.

Anise hyssop

Babington's leek

BABINGTON'S LEEK

Allium ampeloprasum var. *babingtonii*. A hardy, native perennial.

A fine perennial leek that would be welcome at any time of year, but flourishing as it does in the back end of winter and into spring it is all the more valuable. When everything else is shutting down, Babington's leek wakes up, being ready to harvest as the first hint of spring is in the air. Sweeter than regular leeks, and with a warm gentle hint of garlic, I like them best cut just above the base as mini leeks. Any that you don't pick do as leeks do: throw up long stems, which develop glorious seed heads. Bees love them, as do I – the florets add oniony bite scattered over salads and on pizzas.

VARIETIES: No named varieties.
STARTING OFF: Source bulbils from a good supplier and either grow on in a 1-litre pot for planting out later, or sow direct. Can be dug up, split and divided to create new plants.
POSITION: Very unfussy, and being native to our seashores is hardy and robust.
SPACING: 45cm or so apart.
PRODUCTIVITY/EFFICIENCY: A very low-maintenance plant that gives three different crops at different times of year, particularly valuable for its leeks in late winter and early spring.
GROWING: Little maintenance needed. The plant will clump up over the years if allowed, and gently self-sow.
POTENTIAL PROBLEMS: Generally pest and disease free.
HARVEST: Harvest the bulbs in late summer (these can be stored if dried like regular onions), replanting one or two for future crops. Bulbils can also be used but make sure you get them before they have formed a papery skin. During the winter, cut the stems at ground level and use as you would leeks.

BASIL

Ocimum basilicum. Half-hardy annual.

The herb everybody loves, that eaten with a sun-warm tomato straight from the vine sums up summer in a mouthful. Easy to grow, prolific and expensive to buy

African blue basil

in the shops, basil is one of the great transformers – sweet, bright and with an aniseed/liquorice flavour that even those who profess to dislike aniseed or liquorice seem to love. As well as pairing it with tomatoes and mozzarella, basil works beautifully with chicken and in ice cream (honestly). As with many annual herbs, use it raw: its flavour and aroma vanish when cooked.

VARIETIES: Try the classic 'Sweet Genovese' or 'Lettuce Leaf' with its large crinkly leaves. 'Siam Queen' has an intense liquorice flavour and aroma, with a lovely lemony edge which makes it good for Asian dishes. The bushy 'Greek' basil with its tiny leaves is a must on the window sill and perhaps my favourite for scattering through salads. Do also try 'Cinnamon' basil and 'Lime' basil.

STARTING OFF: Sow seed in modules under cover from late spring until August, planting out once the danger of frosts has passed. Make successional sowings for continuous supply throughout the summer.

POSITION: A sunny spot in rich and moist but free-draining soil. Basil will grow happily in pots but don't let it dry out.

SPACING: 15–20cm apart.

PRODUCTIVITY/EFFICIENCY: A very effective transformer. A few basil plants can provide you with all you need throughout the summer.

GROWING: Thrives in warmth, so grow at least some under cover as insurance against a UK summer if you can. Pinch out the shoots to make a bushy plant and remove the flowers to keep the best flavour.

POTENTIAL PROBLEMS: Generally pest and disease free but doesn't like cold temperatures.

HARVEST: In the height of summer, pick off individual leaves as needed — take care, as they bruise easily.

BAY

Laurus nobilis. Evergreen shrub/tree. 🍃

I'm not sure if I've had a piece of fish or a stew where bay hasn't been involved since about 1983. It has a little of so much going on, both dark and light: citrus, smoky fires, rich roses and, peculiarly, more than a hint of cola bottles, those rubbery sweets of my childhood. Give it a sheltered, sunny spot and you'll have years of sweet-savoury brightness and depth at your fingertips. As well as fish, soups and stews, bay and dairy is a match made in heaven – bay ice cream is a must-try.

VARIETIES: There are few named cultivars but you could try 'Aurea' for a yellow leaves.
STARTING OFF: Source plants from a good supplier. They can be bought as trained forms.
POSITION: Bay will be happiest out of cold winds and frost pockets. Find it a spot in sun or partial shade with free-draining soil. It will happily grow in a container.
SPACING: Bay can reach 6m in height and width, but can easily be pruned to fit within your chosen area.
PRODUCTIVITY/EFFICIENCY: A single plant will provide you with plentiful bay.
GROWING: Generally, little is required but don't allow young plants to dry out, although older ones are fairly drought tolerant.
POTENTIAL PROBLEMS: Bothered by few pests and diseases.
HARVEST: Pick leaves as needed throughout the year. Older plants in warmer areas might also produce berries – these can be used as a spice.

BERGAMOT

Monarda didyma. Also known as: bee balm, lad's love and mountain mint. Hardy perennial. 🍃

Not the bergamot that gives the citrus wham to Earl Grey tea, but a beautiful, pungent herb, somewhere at the rosemary-marjoram end of the spectrum. A bee-friendly plant that repels plenty of would-be garden nuisances, so making it a fine companion plant for pest-prone plants.

Its flavour is quite 'big' so use sparingly, at least at first. Treat it more as you might an annual herb, adding

Bergamot

B

179

it very late to cooking or just as you're serving. It pairs particularly well with squash and sweet root veg.

VARIETIES: There are a lot of ornamental varieties available. Try 'Croftway Pink' or 'Cambridge Scarlet' if you're after different colour flowers. You could also try *M. citriodora* or 'Lemon Bergamot' whose leaves are strongly lemony.
STARTING OFF: Buy plants or sow seed in modules in the spring. Seed needs warmth to germinate well.
POSITION: A rich moist soil in sun or partial shade.
SPACING: 50cm apart. Can reach up to 90cm in height.
PRODUCTIVITY/EFFICIENCY: A single plant should satisfy your culinary needs.
GROWING: Mulch to retain moisture, and water in dry weather. May need support. Remove flowers to prolong harvesting. You could grow more than one plant to allow bees to forage on those you don't cut back. The plants will need lifting and dividing every 3 years or so to maintain vigour.
POTENTIAL PROBLEMS: Generally pest and disease free.

B

Borage

HARVEST: The best flavour is just before the plant flowers. Leaves, shoot tips and flowers are all edible — the flowers raw and the leaves and shoots raw or cooked.

BORAGE

Borago officinalis. Hardy annual.

An absolute must for any garden, borage's cucumber flavour carried in its young leaves and flowers is wonderful added to salads, cocktails or with fruit such as strawberries. One of the great bee-friendly plants for the garden too. Grow it once and you are likely to find it springing up randomly in subsequent years. Borage brings life and colour unexpectedly, self-sowing readily to lift otherwise green veg beds early in the season and through into late autumn.

VARIETIES: Borage is more usually seen in its blue form but the white *B. officinalis* 'Alba' is beautiful.
STARTING OFF: Seed germinates readily sown directly in April. Sow again around midsummer for a continual supply until the autumn.
POSITION: Full sun in most soils but prefers good drainage.
SPACING: 50cm apart and will reach 60–90cm in height.
PRODUCTIVITY/EFFICIENCY: You will have a continual supply of flowers from early summer (and earlier from self-sown plants) until October with little effort on your part. Plants self-seed happily.
GROWING: Taller plants may need staking. Deadhead to keep plants flowering.
POTENTIAL PROBLEMS: Generally pest and disease free.
HARVEST: Leaves and flowers are edible. If using leaves raw then pick them young.

CARAWAY

Carum carvi. Hardy biennial, often grown as an annual.

As with fennel seed, caraway is more of a spice than a herb. I never use the leaves (though some do as a breath freshener or in place of parsley), but the seeds are a real treat. I use them with brassicas, cabbages especially, and a handful in bread dough brings a lovely nuttiness to the cooked loaf. Try caraway with fruit too: they bring a kind of mouth-freshness like freshly brushed teeth on a cold morning.

VARIETIES: Most often sold in its generic form.
STARTING OFF: The seed needs warmth to germinate, so sow seed under cover in modules in April, or direct from May to July.
POSITION: Full sun or partial shade in a moisture-retentive soil with good drainage.
SPACING: 25cm apart.
PRODUCTIVITY/EFFICIENCY: Plants will flower the year after they are sown and will occupy the ground for some time. Just a few plants will provide you with a reasonable amount of seed and may self-sow if allowed to.
GROWING: A very deep-rooting plant that doesn't like being transplanted.
POTENTIAL PROBLEMS: Generally pest and disease free.
HARVEST: Pick fresh leaves as required. If harvesting the seed then cut plant stems a few centimetres above the ground in the middle of a warm sunny day and when the heads are quite dry. Put the heads inside a paper bag and hang them upside down for a couple of weeks, after which the seed should be dry and come away easily from the plant.

Caraway

CAROLINA ALLSPICE

Calycanthus floridus. Also known as: spicebush and sweet shrub. Deciduous shrub.

A beautiful, substantial shrub with the most heady, heavily perfumed flowers I grow on the farm, but it's the woody bark that makes it to the kitchen. Dried in the sun or in a low oven, the bark can be pounded or ground into a powder that has a flavour and aroma similar to cinnamon (which won't grow in this country). Use it as you would cinnamon, with fruit, in spice blends for pork, or dust it over porridge or rice pudding. Don't eat the fruit or the flowers as they are poisonous!

VARIETIES: The variety 'Athens' is reputedly particularly fragrant. You could also try *C. occidentalis*, known as California allspice.

STARTING OFF: Source plants from a specialist nursery.

POSITION: Tolerant of most soils and in full sun for the best fragrance.

SPACING: Can reach 3m high and wide if allowed.

PRODUCTIVITY/EFFICIENCY: You will have to wait a year or two until the plant is well established before harvesting any branches, but thereafter it should provide you with all the spice you need and with little effort on your part.

GROWING: Prune to restrict size if need be whenever you wish, otherwise little maintenance required.

POTENTIAL PROBLEMS: Generally pest and disease free.

HARVEST: Cut out the drier-looking branches (which are usually stronger in taste) in July and August, peeling off the bark and drying on a window sill for storage.

Carolina allspice

CELERY LEAF

Apium graveolens var. *dulce*. Hardy biennial, mostly grown as an annual.

A close cousin of celery and celeriac, you can consider this a cut-and-come-again version of the former, ideal for adding a leafy end to soups and stews. I'm not a fan of raw celery, so am inclined to grow and use more of this. It's not a million flavour miles from lovage, but is altogether gentler; a few thinly sliced leaves in a leafy salad is far from overpowering. The leaves and seeds pair up equally well with apple and cheese.

VARIETIES: No named varieties available.
STARTING OFF: The seed is very small and easiest sown in trays and pricked out into modules. Sow under cover in early spring but don't cover the seed. Plant out as the soil warms up or direct sow when the soil is warm enough.
POSITION: A humus-rich, moist soil is preferred, as is some shade. Does well in containers if given sufficient water.
SPACING: 25cm apart, or around 10cm if growing as cut-and-come-again.
PRODUCTIVITY/EFFICIENCY: Celery leaf will give you a celery flavour over a longer period of time and for much less trouble than celery.
GROWING: Water if in danger of drying out — it likes being a little damp at all times. Cut back flower stems if you want to prolong leaf harvest.
POTENTIAL PROBLEMS: Generally pest and disease free.
HARVEST: Use leaves and stems in the plant's first year — in a sheltered spot you may have these through the winter. You can harvest leaves and stems in the second year too, but the flower stems must be cut back. Harvest the seeds in autumn of the second year, cutting stems on a dry day and hanging them upside down in a paper bag for a couple of weeks. Seed can then be easily separated from the plant.

CHERVIL

Anthriscus cerefolium. Also known as: garden chervil and hedge parsley. Hardy annual.

A fabulous, yet subtle herb that everyone should grow. Imagine a gentle, delicate parsley crossed with the faintest hint of aniseed and you'll have chervil. As well as being fine on its own (notably with eggs, fish, chicken and in salads), it has a wonderfully generous ability to catalyse other herbs, making the best of them while keeping in the background itself. Very popular around the Mediterranean, and given how easily it produces, there is little excuse for it not to be here too.

VARIETIES: No named varieties available.
STARTING OFF: Sow seed in quantity, successively from March until autumn. Start early sowings in modules or guttering under cover. Later sowings can be made direct.
POSITION: Humus-rich, moisture-retentive soil in part-shade. Chervil does well in pots.
SPACING: 20cm apart.
PRODUCTIVITY/EFFICIENCY: Chervil can be harvested 6–8 weeks after sowing, can be cut several times and will provide you with leaves over the winter.
GROWING: Keep watered in dry weather. Chervil doesn't like being transplanted, so don't be surprised if you have a few losses if not sowing direct.
POTENTIAL PROBLEMS: Chervil will quickly run to seed if too hot or if the soil dries out.
HARVEST: Cut leaves 2–3cm above the soil and it will regrow. Harvesting is possible throughout the year, even in the depths of winter if under cover.

183

CHIVES

Allium schoenoprasum. Hardy perennial.

From early in February, when the narrow tubular leaves begin to spear out of the soil, until late autumn when they retreat from the cold, chives will feature in at least one meal most days. There's very little that intense onion zap won't improve - salads, cocktails, soups, pâtés and sauces to name just a few. The flowers, too, are as delicious as they are beautiful, broken over anything from leafy salads to hearty stews to add spots of onion flavour. Easy to grow, nearly impossible to accidentally kill and productive for years, they're almost compulsory.

VARIETIES: Try the white form *A. schoenoprasum* var. *albiflorum*. You could also try garlic chives (*A. tuberosum*) or Siberian chives (*A. nutans*).

Chives

STARTING OFF: Source chive plants from a good supplier or divide established clumps.

POSITION: Tolerant of most soils and situations, but prefer sun and a moist, rich soil. Chives will grow happily in containers.

SPACING: 20–30cm apart.

PRODUCTIVITY/EFFICIENCY: For little effort after planting you can crop chives from spring through to autumn, for years.

GROWING: Watering in dry weather will keep leaf production going and hold flowering back. Give an occasional mulch of compost.

POTENTIAL PROBLEMS: Generally pest and disease free.

HARVEST: Cut leaves near to the ground. Separate flower heads into florets for use in salads and garnishes.

CORIANDER

Coriandrum sativum. Hardy annual.

I treat coriander as two very distinct crops now: growing it as microleaves for the full intense coriander leaf flavour; and letting some plants develop to full size and go to seed (like anyone can stop them), letting them be their beautiful selves before collecting the seed. As micros, the flavour has everything you want from coriander – aromatic pungency and smooth intensity, with none of the cloying soapiness that can come with more mature leaves. Sow them densely.

VARIETIES: 'Santo' and 'Leisure' are reputedly slower to bolt than most, and 'Confetti' has very finely cut foliage and a particularly sweet flavour.

STARTING OFF: Doesn't like transplanting, so sow seed in modules or guttering under cover from early April (earlier if cropping under cover). Begin sowing direct from late April and sow successively through the summer. Coriander will do well in a pot and it works well as microleaves.

POSITION: A rich, moisture-retentive soil (but not wet) and some shade are preferable to delay plants running to seed.

SPACING: 20cm apart for regular coriander growing; 50cm for large plants to go to seed; densely for microleaves.

Coriander

PRODUCTIVITY/EFFICIENCY: Coriander plants do run to seed quickly, but as the flowers and green seeds can also be eaten it is a very useful plant.

GROWING: Water in dry weather.

POTENTIAL PROBLEMS: Plants are quick to run to seed, but this can be slowed by watering in dry weather and frequently cutting the leaves back to 3cm or so above the ground.

HARVEST: Cut leaves to 3cm above soil level, pick flower heads and green seeds as desired. Seeds can also be allowed to dry on the plant. For micros, harvest (either by cutting or lifting from the compost) when just 5cm tall – a pinch of a dozen or so is all you need to brighten up salads or seafood, such is the seedlings' intensity.

DILL

Anethum graveolens. Hardy annual.

I have a bit of a love-hate relationship with dill: there's a threshold over which it shifts from a gorgeous, aromatic transformer of eggs, seafood and onions to borderline throat-catching and excessive – like smoke from a pinched candle. On the right side of the line, I love its ability to wake up a straight mayonnaise, bring cucumbers out of their shell, and lift potatoes and carrots in a completely different direction from other herbs.

VARIETIES: 'Super Dukat' reputedly has a finer flavour than the generic type.

STARTING OFF: Doesn't like transplanting so sow seed in modules from early April (earlier if cropping under cover). Begin sowing direct from late April and sow successively through the summer.

POSITION: Prefers a light soil with good drainage and some shade to hold back flowering.

SPACING: Around 30cm apart.

PRODUCTIVITY/EFFICIENCY: Easy to grow, dill will be ready to harvest in 6–8 weeks.

GROWING: Water in dry weather to stop plants running to seed and cut out any flower stems to keep leaf production going.

POTENTIAL PROBLEMS: Generally pest and disease free.

HARVEST: Cut leaves as required. If harvesting seed for storage, cut stems on a dry day and hang them upside down for 2 weeks with the heads in a paper bag. They can then be easily separated from the plant.

ENGLISH MACE

Achillea ageratum. Also known as: Sweet Nancy. Hardy perennial.

Not the mace often used to spice up curry recipes, but a leafy herb with creamy daisy-like flowers. The leaves carry a distinctive flavour and scent that is somewhere in the middle of mint and chamomile. It goes well with chicken and fish especially, and in soups and stews. Mild and fresh flavoured, I tend to use the leaves as a flavouring to infuse, as when chewed the flavour becomes stronger, leaving a slight (although not unpleasant) tingle on the tongue. A beautiful and distinctive herb.

English mace

VARIETIES: Generic.

STARTING OFF: Source plants from a specialist supplier or divide existing plants in the spring or autumn.

POSITION: Tolerant of most well-drained soils and in a sunny position.

SPACING: 30cm apart.

PRODUCTIVITY/EFFICIENCY: Leaves can be harvested throughout the growing season.

GROWING: Little maintenance is required, but cut back flower stems to promote fresh growth.

POTENTIAL PROBLEMS: Generally pest and disease free

HARVEST: Pick fresh young leaves throughout the growing season.

FENNEL

Foeniculum vulgare. Hardy annual.

Distinct from Florence fennel (grown for its bulb), though herb fennel does share some of its wonderful aniseed. The leaves (thin fronds, not unlike dill) are fabulous used sparingly to pep up a leafy salad, tomatoes and fish, with its sweet, fragrant aniseed, but it is the seeds that come in late summer that I love most. They make the finest of fudges, bring a fresh bright edge to bread and are one of the cornerstones of five spice. A reliable self-seeder, which once grown will pop up every year unless you pick all the seeds.

VARIETIES: There is a purple-leaved form, *F. vulgare* 'Pupureum', or try 'Giant Bronze'.
STARTING OFF: Source plants from a good supplier or can easily be grown from seed. Sow in modules in spring or autumn, planting out when 7–10cm tall.
POSITION: Tolerant of most soils with reasonable drainage but likes them moist and to be in the sun. Fennel has a big taproot and consequently is fairly resilient. It can be grown in a container, if the pot is deep enough.
SPACING: 50cm–1m apart. Plants can reach 2.5m in height.
PRODUCTIVITY/EFFICIENCY: Will come back year on year with no effort on your part, with edible leaves from early spring until autumn.
GROWING: Cut any flower stems back to the ground to encourage leafy growth and grow more than one if you want to harvest seeds as well as leaves. Replace plants every few years.
POTENTIAL PROBLEMS: Fennel seeds very freely, so cut back flower stems before seed is ripe if you want to limit its spread.
HARVEST: Cut leaves as desired. Harvest the seed anytime, either when green for use fresh, or brown for further drying and storage.

F

187

Fennel

FENUGREEK

Trigonella foenum-graecum. Half-hardy annual with some frost resistance. ✑

With its gentle curry flavour, fenugreek lifts and warms salads and soups, and is easy to grow. I grow most of ours as microleaves or sprouts – the volume may be small but the flavour is intense and clean. It's also very good left to grow into larger plants and the leaves and seeds picked for the kitchen.

VARIETIES: Fenugreek is found in white- and yellow-flowered forms. The white-flowered form has slightly larger leaves and will not regrow after cutting. The yellow-flowered form is the hardier of the two and can be cut several times.

STARTING OFF: Fenugreek doesn't like being transplanted so sow direct between April and August, or grow as microleaves or sprouts by sowing reasonably thickly into a seed tray or guttering on your window sill.

POSITION: Full sun and good drainage.

SPACING: Sow in drills 20cm apart and thin to 5cm apart within the row. Alternatively, broadcast sparingly.

PRODUCTIVITY/EFFICIENCY: Leaves are ready to be harvested around 6 weeks from sowing. If you only want to make one sowing in the year then grow the yellow-flowered form, which will regrow after

cutting. Fenugreek can also act as a green manure (see pages 356–360) by fixing nitrogen in the soil.

GROWING: Cut back any flower stems to encourage fresh leafy growth.

POTENTIAL PROBLEMS: Generally pest and disease free.

HARVEST: Cut microleaves when they are 3–4cm tall, before they become bitter. Harvest fenugreek leaves when the plant is 25cm or so tall. If harvesting the seed, cut flower stems on a dry day when the pods are yellow and before they have split. Hang them upside down in a paper bag to dry for around 2 weeks.

FRENCH TARRAGON

Artemisia dracunculus. Half-hardy perennial. ✑

Yet another bright and breezy herb with aniseed at its heart, yet manages to be very much its distinctive self. It's hard to conjure up a finer roast chicken recipe than one with French tarragon – they were born to be together. As a partner to chervil, parsley and chives it makes up *fines herbes* – a handful of which in an omelette is a fine lunch indeed. Tarragon mayo, vinegar and béarnaise sauce are, if you need them, three other fabulous reasons to grow this excellent herb. It is really trouble-free when given heat, light and a well-drained soil.

VARIETIES: Sold in its generic form, but you could also try the annual Mexican tarragon. Russian tarragon (*A. dracunculus dracunculoides*) is hardy and can be grown from seed, but its flavour is inferior to French tarragon.

STARTING OFF: Source plants from a good supplier or propagate using runners from established plants.

POSITION: Full sun or partial shade in well-drained soil. French tarragon is particularly suited to a pot as you can move it inside when frosts and cold weather threaten.

SPACING: 45cm apart.

PRODUCTIVITY/EFFICIENCY: French tarragon can be harvested from late spring and through the summer months.

GROWING: Replace plants after a couple of years with younger ones propagated from runners, as tarragon loses its flavour with age.

French tarragon

POTENTIAL PROBLEMS: Generally pest and disease free.

HARVEST: Pick leaves and stems throughout the growing season.

HORSERADISH

Armoracia rusticana. Hardy perennial. ☙

Like mint, nettles and willow, horseradish is pretty hard to kill off, making it a must-have if you are convinced that you have been born uniquely incapable of keeping any plant alive. The nose-twitching heat of its root can be difficult to source, and when it's so easy to grow, why not start your own supply? As a partner to beef it is unrivalled, used sparingly it adds punch to a dressing for coleslaw or greens and, heresy though it might be, I like it with cold lamb. Horseradish is one of those harvests that is so much better if grown yourself: the aroma (which complements the heat beautifully) fades quickly after grating, so ready-made sauces can never bridge the gap.

VARIETIES: Generic.

STARTING OFF: Source young plants from a good supplier and plant in spring or propagate from root cuttings in winter.

POSITION: Any moist soil will do, as horseradish is fairly indestructible. It can be grown in a container as long as it is deep.

SPACING: 45cm apart.

PRODUCTIVITY/EFFICIENCY: A no-maintenance flavouring for harvesting during the winter months.

GROWING: The flip side of its indestructibility is that its invasive nature is hard to combat. Either dig up what you don't need if it expands, or grow it in a container to limit spread. Water in dry weather while establishing.

POTENTIAL PROBLEMS: Generally pest and disease free.

HARVEST: Roots are very deep so break off the top 10–20cm. These will keep for a while in the fridge if wrapped in paper. Harvest liberally to check its spread. The leaves are also edible – hot when raw, mild when cooked. Try them shredded with bacon or in bubble and squeak.

HYSSOP

Hyssopus officinalis. Hardy perennial. ☙ (overleaf)

A gorgeous marriage of citrus and deep rosemary is carried in the leaves' flavour, complementing fish, red meat, cheese, soups and stews equally well. Don't let a garden nibble persuade you otherwise – it can (like lemon) seem rather too bitter when eaten raw, but when cooked, contrasting with salty dishes or softened by dairy ingredients, it comes into its own. It is also a beautiful plant for the garden, available in white-, blue- or pink-flowering versions.

VARIETIES: Generic.

STARTING OFF: Source young plants from a good supplier or start from seed in modules in spring.

POSITION: Likes a free-draining soil in full sun.

SPACING: 60cm apart, or 30cm if using as hedging.

PRODUCTIVITY/EFFICIENCY: A single plant will provide you with ample flavouring from spring to autumn.

GROWING: Deadheading flowers will encourage new leaves. Cut back hard in spring to promote new growth and a bushier plant. An occasional mulch of compost would be appreciated.

POTENTIAL PROBLEMS: Generally pest and disease free.

HARVEST: Pick leaves as required.

H

189

Horseradish

H

190

Hyssop

JAPANESE PARSLEY

Cryptotaenia japonica. Also known as: mitsuba. A perennial hardy to -10°C that can also be treated as an annual. ❧

This clumpy perennial has leaves that resemble flat-leaved parsley and carry much of the same flavour, softened with celery and a hint of bright angelica. Use it where you might parsley, in Japanese recipes that call for mitsuba and try it with fish.

VARIETIES: Generic.
STARTING OFF: Sow seed in spring or autumn in modules under cover. Sow direct from April.
POSITION: Prefers moist soil and a shady place, turning yellow if grown in full sun.
SPACING: 20cm apart if using as ground cover; 10cm if growing as a cut-and-come-again crop.
PRODUCTIVITY/EFFICIENCY: Takes little space for a punchy harvest, and needs no attention to produce it.
GROWING: Little maintenance required.
POTENTIAL PROBLEMS: Protect young plants and new spring growth from slugs and snails.
HARVEST: Cut leaves and stems as desired throughout the growing season and lightly through the winter. The seeds carry a similar flavour and can be used fresh or dried.

LAVENDER

Lavandula species. Hardy evergreen perennial. ❧

As if you need a reason beyond its looks and perfume to grow lavender, but used sparingly it is a wonderful thing to add to your palate of culinary herbs. It's certainly something that is easy to overdo, but a little used in custard, biscuits, ice cream or in place of rosemary with roast lamb shows it off at its best. Easy to grow, as long as it has full sun and a well-drained, sheltered spot.

VARIETIES: *Lavandula angustifolia* varieties are the best for culinary purposes. You could try 'Hidcote' for its intense blue colour, 'Alba' for white flowers or 'Munstead' for purple blooms. *Lavandula* x *intermedia* 'Provence' is also highly rated for its flavour.
STARTING OFF: Source plants of named varieties from a good supplier or grow *L. angustifolia* from seed

in spring. You can also propagate, taking softwood cuttings in early summer or hardwood cuttings in autumn (see page 344).
POSITION: Full sun in free-draining soil. Lavender is very happy in a container.
SPACING: 30–90cm apart depending on if you are growing as a low hedge or a single plant.
PRODUCTIVITY/EFFICIENCY: Plants provide plentiful leaves and flowers throughout the growing season, need little attention and have few potential problems. Do avoid damp spots though, as root rots can occur. Should rosemary beetle appear, shake them off and remove.

Lavender

J
L

191

GROWING: Water whilst establishing. Trim to a neat domed shape in spring and cut back after flowering in August taking care not to cut back into old wood as new growth rarely springs from it.

POTENTIAL PROBLEMS: Generally pest and disease free.

HARVEST: Pick leaves and flowers as required. The flowers are at their best just before they open.

LEMON BALM

Melissa officinalis. Hardy perennial.

One I grew for its unspectacular loveliness covering the ground, drawing in insects and adding a soft green/yellow to the forest garden (see pages 319—323) before discovering its fine partnership with mint in a herb tea. And I'm not a fan of most herb teas. If you want a lemony flavour for cooking, I'd look no further than lemon verbena or lemongrass, but neither of those flourishes in most positions outside in Britain, while lemon balm gives you the option, and is a great all-rounder in the garden.

VARIETIES: You could try *M. officinalis* 'Aurea' or 'All Gold' for a yellow-leaved lemon balm. 'Quedlinburger Niederliegende' has a stronger flavour.

STARTING OFF: Grows easily from seed or divide established plants in spring or autumn.

POSITION: Relatively unfussy about soil type but likes decent drainage. Lemon balm is happy in sun or part-shade and will do very well in a container.

SPACING: 45cm apart.

PRODUCTIVITY/EFFICIENCY: A herb that will provide you with plentiful leaves throughout the growing season and with very little effort on your part.

POTENTIAL PROBLEMS: None.

GROWING: Cut back a proportion of the flowering stems to maintain a supply of flavoursome, young leaves and if you want to keep self-seeding to a minimum. Bees will appreciate it if you leave a few flower stems for them.

HARVEST: Fresh, young leaves throughout the growing season, or dry by gathering young stems just before flowering and laying them on a tray in the airing cupboard.

LEMONGRASS

Cymbopogon citratus. Tender perennial.

The sweet aromatic herb that lends its spicy lemon flavour and fragrance to so many of the Southeast Asian dishes we know. Although the stems are increasingly available in the shops, growing lemongrass means you can use the leaves too. Both carry that bright, fresh lemon taste that works so well in fragrant curries, soups, and with fish, as well as when poaching fruit.

VARIETIES: Usually sold in its generic form.

STARTING OFF: Source plants from a specialist nursery or sow seed in modules in spring (it needs warmth to germinate), potting on when the roots are showing. You can also propagate by dividing established plants or you could even try rooting shop-bought lemongrass by putting in a glass of water.

POSITION: Lemongrass is most suitable for growing in a pot so that it can be brought indoors over the winter. It will appreciate as much heat as you can give it during the spring and summer but keep soil moist.

SPACING: 30cm apart.

PRODUCTIVITY/EFFICIENCY: Little effort required in return for fresh, flavoursome stems. Plants are ready to harvest from their first year.

GROWING: Ensure compost is kept moist especially during spring and autumn, and a monthly feed from spring into autumn will be appreciated.

POTENTIAL PROBLEMS: Generally pest and disease free.

HARVEST: Cut stems as required through summer. Younger leaves can also be used as a flavouring.

LEMON VERBENA

Aloysia triphylla (syn. *A. citriodora*). Half-hardy perennial.

Give me three herbs to take to a desert island and this would be one of them; limit me to just one, and it still might make it. It has everything you'd want from a lemon but with a uniquely sherbety fizz. Pam the Jam, of River Cottage fame, has a bedroom window-high plant growing against her house, protected from the worst of the winds and enjoying the heat reflected from the wall; it flourishes outside and I envy her every centimetre of it. For the rest of us, this is one to grow under cover or in a pot to bring indoors through the coldest months. The leaves are used as you might bay – for the infused flavouring rather than actually eating them. I use it most in cocktails (fruit and alcohol) and in ice creams, though in summer I'm inclined to put it in cakes, make a syrup of it (infuse a fistful of leaves with equal amounts of simmering water and sugar) and put it through a grinder with sugar to add bright zip. A must-have.

Lemon verbena

VARIETIES: Generic.
STARTING OFF: Source plants from a good supplier or propagate from softwood cuttings (see page 342).
POSITION: Drainage and a bit of extra warmth are key for the survival of lemon verbena. Grow in a tunnel or at the base of a wall in a warm sheltered spot. Lemon verbena will do well in a container.

SPACING: Can reach 2.5m in height and width.
PRODUCTIVITY/EFFICIENCY: A true transformer, giving huge flavour from little volume. You can harvest leaves throughout the growing season and even pick desiccated leaves from the plant in winter. A great herb for container growing.
GROWING: Responds well to a good prune in spring. Bring under cover in winter as they can suffer if the temperatures drop low.
POTENTIAL PROBLEMS: Generally pest and disease free.
HARVEST: Pick fresh leaves as required from mid-spring into autumn.

LOVAGE
Levisticum officinale. Hardy perennial. ∽ (overleaf)

I can find no better way of describing lovage than how I always do: like the best vegetable stock, in leaf form. You don't need much – a leaf or two is usually plenty – which makes a joke of its size (see Spacing below). It's rather lovely in its green, leafy way – when established, it is visually a cross between rhubarb and flat-leaved parsley. Try the seeds late in the season too: they're similarly savoury and really good sparingly used in a loaf or in soups and stews.

VARIETIES: No named varieties available.
STARTING OFF: Source young plants from a good supplier or sow seed in modules in spring, planting out when a few centimetres tall. Plants can also be propagated by division in spring or autumn.
POSITION: Sun or partial shade in a moist soil with reasonable drainage.
SPACING: If growing more than one, space 1m or so apart. Left alone, lovage will reach 2m in height.
PRODUCTIVITY/EFFICIENCY: A little goes a long way with lovage and a single plant should provide you with plenty, with little required on your part.
GROWING: Cutting plants back hard in June will promote fresh new growth.
POTENTIAL PROBLEMS: Generally pest and disease free.
HARVEST: Pick leaves as required from early spring until early winter, with seeds ready in late summer and autumn.

L

193

MARIGOLD

Calendula officinalis. Also known as: pot marigold and common marigold. Hardy annual. ᘓ

I'm not a huge fan of orange flowers but marigolds are an exception I can't help but make. Cheery without being gaudy, the bright flowers of the marigold break easily into their constituent narrow petals, which I use most to add a flourish to salads of all kinds. Their flavour is gentle – a faint pepperiness is all – but with their splash of colour, it's plenty. A handful of petals leach their orange readily when warmed through in olive oil, adding colour and a hint of pepper to dressings or in dishes such as paella. The leaves, while less striking, carry more of that peppery fresh flavour – superb in a leafy salad.

Lovage seed

Marigold

VARIETIES: Try 'Indian Prince' for purple-backed flowers and 'Sunset Buff' for a soft apricot-coloured flower.

STARTING OFF: Seed is quite big so sow in 9cm pots in spring or autumn, planting out when the roots are showing. Calendula is hardy and can also be sown direct outside where they are to flower.

POSITION: Likes a sunny spot but is quite unfussy about soil.

SPACING: 20cm or so apart.

PRODUCTIVITY/EFFICIENCY: As easy as anything. Not likely to be something you'll harvest frequently, but a sensory pleasure through the summer months and, once grown, it'll often seed itself year on year, saving you the trouble. A great companion plant, deterring asparagus beetle and drawing in aphid-eaters such as hoverflies.

GROWING: Water whilst establishing and deadhead to encourage more flowers to appear.

POTENTIAL PROBLEMS: Generally trouble-free. Even slugs aren't that interested, though you may want to protect newly planted-out seedlings. If blackfly are bothersome wipe off or cut out affected parts.

HARVEST: Pick young tender leaves as needed through late spring and summer, and flowers when fully open. Keep them in water in the kitchen until you are ready for them.

MARJORAM AND OREGANO

Origanum majorana. Also known as: sweet marjoram and garden marjoram. Half-hardy perennial. ༄

O. vulgare. Also known as: pot marjoram and wild marjoram. Hardy perennial. ༄

Two of my favourite herbs, which, while distinct, are closely related and share a warm spiciness. Sweet marjoram is perhaps my favourite. It smells like the first evening I had in Corsica, a teenager's dream of the Mediterranean: hot, spicy and utterly exotic. While I treat sweet marjoram as I would a delicate herb such as chervil (using it to brighten tomato salads and so on, giving it no more than a moment's heat if that), oregano is altogether richer, weightier and adds savoury depth when cooked with beans, lamb, tomatoes or squash. That said, the smallest new leaves of either, cast

Marjoram

sparingly into a salad or more generously strewn over a pizza before cooking, are hard to rival.

VARIETIES: You could also try *O. vulgare* 'Hot & Spicy' for a stronger flavour.

STARTING OFF: Source plants of both species from a good supplier or lift and divide established plants. If starting from seed, sow oregano in modules in spring or autumn, potting on once before planting out. Sow seed of sweet marjoram in spring.

POSITION: Likes a sheltered, warm, sunny spot in well-drained soil. The flavour will be more intense the dryer the conditions. Both species will do well in a pot. If growing sweet marjoram as a perennial, plant it somewhere very sheltered or in a pot that can be brought under cover over winter.

SPACING: 30cm apart.

PRODUCTIVITY/EFFICIENCY: Plentiful leaves from two or three plants over the growing season, with *O. vulgare* appearing year after year.

GROWING: Bring sweet marjoram pots inside over winter. Cut back flowering stems once they have gone over.

POTENTIAL PROBLEMS: Generally pest and disease free.

HARVEST: Harvest tender flower buds and leaves as required.

M

Mint

MINT

Mentha species. Hardy perennial.

I could write a book about mint. The varieties are too numerous and varied to do it justice in a few paragraphs, but I hope to stir up enough inquisitiveness that you investigate more than a standard garden mint, good as it may be. If you grow only one, make it Moroccan mint - it is the best for tea, and a fine all-rounder. Chocolate mint, too, makes a refreshingly different tea, a fine ice cream, and is my favourite for adding to poaching liquid for fruit (peaches, especially).

VARIETIES: Try Moroccan mint for teas. Apple mint has a wonderfully soft flavour and is the most readily expansive, covering ground rapidly. Spearmint 'Kentucky Colonel' is traditionally used in mint juleps and mojitos. You could also try Bowles mint for jellies and sauces.

STARTING OFF: Source plants from a good supplier or propagate from established plants by digging up a section of root that has some stalk attached, and potting up.

POSITION: Mints like a very moist soil and sun or partial shade. They grow well in deep containers, which will also keep their spreading growth in check.

SPACING: Plants spread irregularly.

PRODUCTIVITY/EFFICIENCY: Effortless: once planted, you'll never be without it.

GROWING: Cut back to the ground in winter and give an occasional mulch of compost or manure. Don't grow different mints next to each other, as they lose their distinctiveness if their roots intertwine.

POTENTIAL PROBLEMS: Generally pest and disease free.

HARVEST: Pick stems and leaves as required throughout the growing season.

MYRTLE

Myrtus communis. Also known as: common myrtle. Half-hardy evergreen.

A fantastic herb that produces well all year round (I find it especially useful in winter) and with wonderful berries that I use in place of juniper. Its scent and flavour are fairly similar to juniper but there is also some of the bright generosity of bay. And, as with both juniper and bay, myrtle imparts itself beautifully when burned on the barbecue or in a smoker. Myrtle and meat - red or white - were made for each other.

VARIETIES: You could also try the small-leaved *M. communis* subsp. *tarentina*.

STARTING OFF: Source plants from a good nursery.

POSITION: Although half-hardy it will grow very well in a sunny, sheltered, free-draining spot. Growing in a pot is ideal as you can bring it indoors for the winter.

SPACING: Can reach 3m in width, though usually stays smaller.

PRODUCTIVITY/EFFICIENCY: A small evergreen shrub with plentiful leaves, requiring little input.

GROWING: Very little required apart from the occasional mulch with compost.

POTENTIAL PROBLEMS: Generally pest and disease free.

HARVEST: Pick new leaves from spring through to autumn, and pick not too heavily over winter or dry some leaves in midsummer to use through the cold months. Fruit can be harvested in autumn.

Nasturtiums

NASTURTIUM

Tropaeolum majus. Half-hardy annual. ✑ (previous page)

I can't think of a single reason why any garden would be without nasturtiums. Their fabulously fairy tale flowers are abundantly borne throughout the growing season, looking a treat, drawing in bees, and they are one of the finest edible flowers available. If you've yet to experience them, pop one in your mouth whole: their first flavour is of rocket, becoming more honeyed as you reach the nectar, ending in a flourish of pepper. The young leaves are similarly fine – a fresh brassica flavour with gentle pepper, superb in salads or as the base for a risotto. As fast-growing ground cover, an effective companion plant and a weed-suppressing self-sower, it will be a hard-working part of your garden too.

VARIETIES: Try the dark foliage of 'Empress of India' or the deep red flowers of 'Black Velvet'. 'Moonlight' has pretty primrose-coloured flowers and 'Alaska' has variegated leaves.
STARTING OFF: Sow seed in modules under cover from April and plant out after the last frosts.
POSITION: Nasturtiums flower best in poor soil but like some moisture. Ideal for containers.
SPACING: 15–30cm apart.
PRODUCTIVITY/EFFICIENCY: A very productive crop over the summer and early autumn months, with leaves, flowers and young seed pods all being edible. Self-seeds if allowed.
GROWING: Water whilst establishing.
POTENTIAL PROBLEMS: Pinch out parts affected by blackfly.
HARVEST: Pick young leaves, flowers and seed as required.

PARSLEY

Petroselinum crispum and *P. crispum* var. *neapolit-anum.* Also known as: garden parsley, and Italian and flat-leaved parsley respectively. Hardy biennial, grown as an annual. ✑

I use parsley more days than not, but heavens above: let me not see it ever again as an unwanted 'garnish' on anything from a cooked breakfast to a beef Wellington. Parsley is simply too good to become the ubiquitous, undervalued 'bit of greenery'. I'll take a pesto of parsley over basil any day, and gremolata (a blend of garlic, lemon zest and parsley) brings out the best in fish, prawns, potatoes and lamb. I tend to use the curly, slightly coarser, bolder parsley when adding it late to cooking, and the flat-leaved variety for using raw. Try a handful of small leaves in a mixed salad.

VARIETIES: Few named varieties available.
STARTING OFF: A sowing in spring and in mid- and late summer should last you year-long. Sow seed in modules under cover, planting out when the roots are showing.
POSITION: A sunny spot with rich, moist soil. It will also do well in containers.
SPACING: 20cm apart.
PRODUCTIVITY/EFFICIENCY: With three sowings you can have year-round parsley for very little effort – a very productive cut-and-come-again herb.

Parsley

GROWING: Keep soil moist during dry weather. Protect winter plants with a cloche or fleece.

POTENTIAL PROBLEMS: Plant near onions and garlic to deter carrot fly.

HARVEST: Pick leaves as required but only use them in the first year – those in the plant's second year won't be so good as it gets ready to flower.

PERILLA

Perilla frutescens. Also known as: shiso. Half-hardy annual.

A peculiarly, inexplicably unknown herb with a flavour just left of the centre of cumin and mint. Shredded and added late to soups, pasta and fish dishes it brings a little of both of those fine flavours, but I think I love it most when it is more upfront, in pesto and to bring out the best in aubergines. Perilla comes in green and deep purple varieties, equally beautiful, and with a floppy-leaved habit, a little like a lazy, crinkle-edged mint.

Perilla

VARIETIES: There are green and purple forms of perilla.

STARTING OFF: Sow seed in modules under cover in April and again in June or July. Pot on and plant out after the danger of frosts has passed.

POSITION: A sunny spot in moist, rich soil. Perilla will also grow well in pots.

SPACING: 30cm apart.

PRODUCTIVITY/EFFICIENCY: Perilla makes bushy plants with lots of leaves for use throughout the summer and early autumn.

GROWING: Keep soil moist and pinch out tips to make bushy plants.

POTENTIAL PROBLEMS: Generally pest and disease free.

HARVEST: Pick leaves as needed, and use the flowers as a lively garnish or tossed through salads.

ROSE
HEDGEROW ROSE

Rosa rugosa. Also known as: apple rose. Hardy perennial shrub.

Many roses are good for eating in one form or another, but to my mind *Rosa rugosa* tops the lot. A great hedging plant, it also works well when allowed to form a relaxed clump in the corner of the garden. *R. rugosa* is the rose for syrups, jellies and fruit salads, being full of scent and flavour. Its large, loose, informal petals waft about in the lightest breeze, easily separating from the plant with a gentle pull. My eight-year-old daughter likes me to throw a handful into her running bath water to fill it with scent and colour. The hips make a fine jelly and a fabulous jam. But perhaps most pleasingly, a handful or two of petals in a jar filled with vodka makes the most amazing infusion.

VARIETIES: You could try 'Rubra' for its magenta flowers or 'Alba' for its white ones. 'Scabrosa' reputedly has larger flowers and fruit.

STARTING OFF: Source plants from a good supplier or propagate from suckers.

POSITION: Happy in most soils including poor ones. Plant in sun or partial shade.

SPACING: Can reach 1.5m high and wide. Space at 60cm–1m if planting as an edible hedge.

P / R

199

Hedgerow rose

R

200

PRODUCTIVITY/EFFICIENCY: *Rosa rugosa* flowers generously throughout the summer and autumn, followed by large hips that can also be harvested over a long period. Once planted it can be left to fend for itself.

GROWING: An occasional mulch of compost will be appreciated but is by no means essential.

POTENTIAL PROBLEMS: One of the most disease-resistant roses. They are generally pest free too.

HARVEST: Pick petals when the flowers are fully open, and hips when orangey red and just beginning to soften.

ROSEMARY

Rosmarinus officinalis. Hardy evergreen.

Lamb and potatoes, roasted, are almost impossible to imagine without the resinous loveliness of rosemary to colour them with flavour. This essentially woody herb needs a well-drained soil to be at its best – give it that and a sunny spot and it'll throw long sprigs (think a sparsely leaved Christmas tree branch) upwards all year round. A deep, warming, homely scent and flavour that's as good with fish and roasted vegetables as it is with lamb.

Rosemary

VARIETIES: Try 'Miss Jessop's Upright', which does as it says, or 'Alba' for white flowers. You could also try 'Corsica Prostratus' whose creeping habit can cause it to cascade down the side of a raised bed.

STARTING OFF: Source plants of named varieties from a good supplier or propagate from semi-ripe cuttings in late summer (see page 342).

POSITION: Full sun and shelter in a soil with very good drainage.

SPACING: 1.5m apart.

PRODUCTIVITY/EFFICIENCY: Once established, rosemary makes a maintenance-free plant which will provide you with a year-round harvest.

GROWING: Water whilst establishing and avoid picking while it reaches a nice size. Over-picking means the plant never gets a chance to reach a good productive size.

POTENTIAL PROBLEMS: If you find the beautiful rosemary beetle, hold an upturned umbrella beneath the plant and give the branches a shake, disposing of the beetles as you will. Generally disease free.

HARVEST: Snip stems off as required throughout the year.

SAGE

Salvia officinalis. Hardy evergreen perennial.

One of the 'love it or loathe it' herbs that seems to split a room. I'm in the 'love it' camp: though I don't use it often, I wouldn't be without it. Its lively camphorous, warming spiciness was made to go with pork, squash and veal. It is also a worthy addition to beans and, somewhat weirdly, apples, too. A great herb for drying – just cut and hang in the kitchen to use when suits.

VARIETIES: Purple 'Purpurascens' is beautiful and no less delicious than the traditional green variety, or try 'Icterina' for a variegated form.

STARTING OFF: Source plants of named varieties from a good supplier or propagate from softwood cuttings in spring or semi-hardwood cuttings in late summer (see page 342). The generic form and 'Purpurascens' can both be raised from seed. Sow seed in spring in modules under cover, potting on once before planting out.

POSITION: Full sun or part-shade in soil with good

Variegated sage

Sage

S

201

drainage. Some shelter would be appreciated and plants will happily grow in pots.

SPACING: Can reach 1m in width and height.

PRODUCTIVITY/EFFICIENCY: A maintenance-free plant that will provide you with year-round sage.

GROWING: Cut back hard in spring to encourage fresh young leaves. Replace plants every 5 years or so when they become woody and sparse.

POTENTIAL PROBLEMS: Generally untroubled by pests and diseases.

HARVEST: Harvest leaves as required. Also pick the flowers in early summer for adding to a salad.

SALAD BURNET

Sanguisorba minor. Also known as: garden burnet. Hardy perennial.

A herb that's crept up on me over the last couple of years, I now find I'm looking for excuses to use it at any opportunity. A hardy, year-round feature in the garden, salad burnet's oval, shark tooth-edged leaves carry the same cool, fresh flavour as cucumber. In spring, the young new growth is succulent enough to take its place in a leafy salad, acting more as a herb as the leaves become less tender in the summer. A handful in a jug of water lends it glorious refreshment – and it should be compulsory for all lovers of Pimm's.

VARIETIES: Usually sold in its generic form.

STARTING OFF: Source plants or sow seed in modules in spring or autumn, potting on once before planting out. You can also divide established plants.

POSITION: Full sun or partial shade in well-drained soil. It does very well in containers.

SPACING: 30cm apart.

PRODUCTIVITY/EFFICIENCY: Fresh young leaves can be picked throughout the growing season (and sometimes through the winter) year on year and with little maintenance.

GROWING: Cut back flower stems to promote fresh leafy growth.

POTENTIAL PROBLEMS: Generally pest and disease free.

HARVEST: Pick young leaves for eating raw before flowering. Coarser leaves can be picked for cooking.

Scented pelargoniums

SCENTED PELARGONIUMS

Pelargonium species. Half-hardy perennial.

I can't be doing with regular geraniums – I find their scent really off-putting – but scented pelargoniums (call them 'geraniums' and expect a brolly around the head from specialist growers) are something else entirely. If all you do is take a handful of leaves from 'Attar of Roses' and make a syrup for drizzling over cakes, ice cream and cocktails, you'll be convinced enough to grow them every year. Its fragrance and flavour are a must for home-made Turkish delight too. There are many different flavours and scents to try – lime, orange and chocolate amongst them.

VARIETIES: There are many and with a range of scents. Some that stand out are 'Attar of Roses' with its Turkish delight rose scent; 'Orange Fizz' with a lemon sherbet/orange scent, pretty flowers and an upright habit; and 'Pink Capitatum' with lime-scented leaves and fabulous mauve/pink flowers.

STARTING OFF: Source plants of a named variety from a specialist supplier (remembering to call them 'scented pelargoniums') or take cuttings in late summer.

POSITION: They need sun and a free-draining soil. Being tender, they are best grown in pots so they can be brought indoors for the winter.

SPACING: Grow in a roomy container.

PRODUCTIVITY/EFFICIENCY: Easy to grow and full of flavour and scent, perfect for container growing and adaptable to many recipes. In leaf from spring to early autumn. One established plant of each variety is usually plenty, as leaves replenish quickly.

GROWING: Feed every couple of weeks with a comfrey tea or tomato feed. One for growing in containers, so you can bring plants indoors over winter as they are vulnerable to the cold.

POTENTIAL PROBLEMS: Generally pest and disease free.

HARVEST: Pick leaves as required from mid-spring into autumn.

SUMMER SAVORY

Satureja hortensis. Hardy annual.

A very under-appreciated herb with a flavour and fragrance like a slightly minty, piney oregano. Substantial but not heavy, its flavour works beautifully with dairy, chicken and fish and with most vegetables, especially when cooking tomatoes. I tend to use the leaves and stems during cooking, but when the leaves are fresh and light, they work equally well added as you might parsley.

VARIETIES: Generic.

STARTING OFF: Sow seed in modules from spring, planting out when roots are showing. Make several sowings for a continual supply.

POSITION: Full sun in a well-drained soil and will do well in a container.

SPACING: 20cm apart.

PRODUCTIVITY/EFFICIENCY: A low-maintenance, hardy herb that's big on flavour.

GROWING: Cut back flowering stems to encourage leafy growth and prolong its productive life.

POTENTIAL PROBLEMS: Generally pest and disease free.

HARVEST: Pick leaves and stems as required between May and September.

SWEET CICELY

Myrrhis odorata. Also known as: anise and garden myrrh. Hardy perennial.

I am rather overly attached to sweet cicely. It comes out bright and thrusting in early spring with leaves of the sweetest aniseed, perfectly timed to accompany its natural partner, the early rhubarb. The gentle aniseed lessens the sharpness of the rhubarb, which means you can use less sugar than you might otherwise, and it brings out the flavour of the stalks beautifully. The seeds, often formed as early as late spring, are delicious too – try them in biscuits, stir-fries and spice mixes. It grows happily in a pot and is one of those very handy plants that loves half-shade and will tolerate fairly full-on shade.

VARIETIES: Generic.

STARTING OFF: Source plants from a good supplier or grow from seed. Seed need a prolonged period of cold to germinate so are best sown in situ in autumn. You could also try mixing them with damp compost in a plastic bag and placing in the fridge for several weeks before sowing in pots in spring. Seed is only viable for a year, so ensure it is fresh.

POSITION: Likes a partially shady spot in rich, moist but well-draining soil. It has deep taproots so won't do well in a pot.

SPACING: 40cm apart.

PRODUCTIVITY/EFFICIENCY: Sweet cicely will give you fresh leaves for a good part of the year and the roots and seeds can also be eaten. It is worth having more than one plant if you wish to use both fresh leaves and seeds.

GROWING: Cut back after flowering to increase fresh leaf production.

POTENTIAL PROBLEMS: Generally untroubled by pests and diseases.

203

HARVEST: Leaves can be harvested throughout the growing season. Collect seeds whilst still green to use fresh. Roots can be dug up in winter to eat and will store well in sand for several months, but I tend to leave them in situ and harvest just seeds and leaves.

Sweet cicely

S

204

SZECHUAN PEPPER
Zanthoxylum species. Deciduous shrub.

My desert island spice, without question. The harshly pink/red peppercorns in autumn are full of both peppery wallop and a peculiar tingly numbing sensation that affects the tongue and lips, as well as causing a rush of salivation and hunger. It is quite something. The combination of pepperiness and its numbing qualities makes it the core ingredient in Chinese five spice and a real treat with anything hot and salty – squid, chips or onion rings are my favourite. The leaves carry much of the scent and flavour but without the tingle; I pick them in spring while they are tiny for salads, and later to work their way into mayonnaise and sauces. Picked early, while still green, the peppercorns are perhaps even livelier, though they dry less well at this stage and so should be used fresh.

VARIETIES: *Z. schinifolium* and *Z. simulans* but you could also try *Z. armatum* (a Nepalese pepper) and *Z. piperitum* (a Japanese pepper). Self-fertile but may give heavier yields with another bush for pollination.
STARTING OFF: Source plants from a specialist supplier, as germination from seed is tricky and erratic.
POSITION: Happy in most soils but likes the sun.
SPACING: Over time can reach many metres in height and spread if allowed to, but can be pruned to a smaller size and for container growing.
PRODUCTIVITY/EFFICIENCY: Szechuan peppers begin to bear fruit in their third or fourth year and quickly become very productive. The very young leaves are really good in early spring salads. Once established, they'll ask for none of your attention.
GROWING: Little maintenance required, just pruning for size whenever you feel the need.
POTENTIAL PROBLEMS: Generally pest and disease free, although keep away from citrus trees as Szechuan peppers can (though rarely do) carry a hard-to-treat canker that affects citrus plants.
HARVEST: Pick entire heads when the outer shells begin to split revealing the dark seed inside. This can be anytime from October to December depending on the weather. Dry for a few days in the warmth and remove the stems before storing. Peppercorns freeze well too, keeping their flavour for longer.

Szechuan pepper

TASMANIAN MOUNTAIN PEPPER

Drimys lanceolata (syn. *Tasmannia lanceolata*). Also known as: Australian pepper and Cornish pepper leaf. Evergreen shrub.

An evergreen that is borderline hardy, so therefore needs a sheltered, sunny spot to thrive and produce its lively berries that can be dried and used as pepper. Given its requirements, this is a great plant for growing in an urban situation where the microclimate is likely to suit it well compared with more exposed situations. They're very happy to be clipped to form a hedge if required.

VARIETIES: Male and female flowers are borne on separate plants so you will need one of each for the female to produce berries.

STARTING OFF: Source plants from a specialist supplier.
POSITION: Fertile, moist and well-drained soil. Happy in sun or part-shade but needs shelter to do well.
SPACING: 2.5m wide and 4m high.
PRODUCTIVITY/EFFICIENCY: Its peppery seeds are produced in generous quantities and the plant needs little attention to produce year after year.
GROWING: Prune for shape as required.
POTENTIAL PROBLEMS: Generally pest and disease free.
HARVEST: Berries are ready in autumn, and the leaves can be picked for tea all year. Use fresh or spread out to dry in a greenhouse or polytunnel for a few days.

THYME

Thymus vulgaris. Hardy evergreen perennial.

I need to have quite a few plants of this on the go, to keep up with my consumption, lending its fragrant, smoky intensity to red and white meat, fish, soups too numerous to mention and roasted vegetables. If you haven't the space to grow enough for your needs, buy it, as the plants suffer when over-cropped – you can always dedicate the space to lemon and orange thyme. Both are truly splendid, adding their citrus vim to the thyme's depth. I use both in cocktails, fruit salads, on pizza, and in milk puddings – crème brûlée infused with either is heaven.

VARIETIES: Broad-leaved thyme (*T. pulegioides*) is one of the best culinary thymes. Also try lemon thyme (*T. citriodorus*) or orange thyme ('Fragrantissimus').
STARTING OFF: Source plants from a good supplier. Some thymes, such as *T. vulgaris* and 'Fragrantissimus', can also be started by seed. Sow seed in modules in spring and pot on until large enough to be planted outside.
POSITION: Thrives in poor, free-draining soil and is ideal for growing in pots.
SPACING: Up to 50cm apart, depending on variety.
PRODUCTIVITY/EFFICIENCY: As an evergreen, thyme can be harvested for use throughout the year. Grow more than one so you don't cut back too much into

T

Tasmanian mountain pepper

Flowering thyme

Broad-leaved thyme

hardwood, as thyme, like lavender, doesn't like this.

GROWING: Cut back after flowering — not too far into old wood — to encourage fresh growth.

POTENTIAL PROBLEMS: Generally pest and disease free but can be short-lived in the UK's wet weather.

HARVEST: Pick tender young stems and flowers for use in spring and summer, and tougher stems in winter for use in stocks and stews.

TURKISH ROCKET

Bunias orientalis. Also known as: warty cabbage. Hardy perennial.

A really flavoursome perennial vegetable despite its rather unappetising alternative name. Don't let it put you off. It resembles a vast dandelion crossed with cime di rapa. The leaves and miniature broccoli heads both carry a punchy, mustard greens flavour that is superb treated as a spicy green vegetable or used raw, early in the season when it is tender.

VARIETIES: Usually available only in its generic form.

Turkish rocket

STARTING OFF: Source plants from a specialist supplier, propagate by division in spring or start from seed. Sow seed in March or April in modules under cover. Pot on once and plant out once the roots are showing.

POSITION: Full sun or part-shade in most reasonably drained soils.

SPACING: 45cm apart.

PRODUCTIVITY/EFFICIENCY: A vigorous and resilient plant that provides you with crops from late winter/early spring until autumn.

GROWING: Hardy, drought resistant and reliable, with little maintenance required.

POTENTIAL PROBLEMS: Slugs like the young growth but it usually grows quickly enough to outgrow their attentions.

HARVEST: Pick young leaves in early spring for eating raw, and older leaves throughout the growing season for cooking as you would spinach. You can also eat the flower stems and broccoli-like flower buds, which appear in summer, raw or lightly cooked.

WATERCRESS

Nasturtium officinale. Hardy perennial.

A wonderfully punchy, peppery leaf that has been popular here since Roman times. It is usually commercially grown in running water, but will thrive in a good deep soil instead. Rich in vitamins and minerals, watercress is delicious as a salad leaf or when cooked.

VARIETIES: Usually available only in its generic form.

STARTING OFF: Source plants or seed from a specialist supplier. Sow seed in pots or trays that are then immersed to half their depth in water. Pot on once before planting out.

POSITION: Likes slow-flowing, clean water or moist soil. Equally happy planted in the shallows of a pond or in a pot. Happy in sun or a reasonable amount of shade.

SPACING: Has a spreading habit, and tends to knit together into a fine edible ground cover when planted at around 10–20cm apart.

PRODUCTIVITY/EFFICIENCY: Watercress has a long cropping season and needs little attention once established.

GROWING: Little maintenance needed, other than maintaining a moist environment.

POTENTIAL PROBLEMS: Generally pest and disease free.

HARVEST: Pick leaves and stems throughout the growing season.

WELSH ONION

Allium fistulosum. Also known as: Japanese bunching onion. Hardy perennial.

A really striking, handsome onion that in many ways is more like chives. The hollow stems can grow wide and substantial if allowed, but if regularly cut they stay just slightly larger than most chives. Left to grow, they'll produce flower heads, somewhere between chives and leeks in size and flavour. All parts are delicious raw or cooked, used in recipes as you would chives or leeks.

VARIETIES: This is a multiplier type of onion and is available in its generic form.

STARTING OFF: Source plants from a good supplier or propagate by dividing established clumps. Welsh onions also grow easily from seed. Sow in modules under cover in spring, and plant out when the roots are showing, or sow direct from April.

POSITION: Full sun or partial shade in a good, well-drained soil.

SPACING: 50cm apart.

PRODUCTIVITY/EFFICIENCY: Stems, leaves and flowers are all edible in this traditional cottage garden plant. It is of particular use when storage onions have come to an end and new-season onions are not yet ready.

GROWING: Allow plants to establish before harvesting stems and leaves. Cut back to the ground after flowering to encourage fresh new growth.

POTENTIAL PROBLEMS: Generally pest and disease free.

HARVEST: Leaves grow back quickly and you can make several cuttings so use the leaves as you would spring onions during the growing season. You can also lift whole stems throughout the growing season. While the plants are flowering, the stems won't be good to eat but the flowers themselves are edible.

Welsh onion

Wild garlic

WILD GARLIC

Allium ursinum. Also known as: ramson and wood garlic. Hardy perennial.

Living in the South West, wild garlic pops its nose up earlier than in most parts of the country, perhaps by mid-February, although we usually wait until March to start taking the first leaves. Check your nearest woods, as it loves the dappled shade and moist conditions of beech trees, though some grows on the riverbank that runs around our smallholding too. If there's no local source, it's easy to grow in your garden. Try to replicate its favoured shady, damp conditions to get it at its best. Risottos, ravioli, pesto, omelettes and breakfast scrambled eggs are all likely to be lifted by its gentle garlicky presence throughout the spring.

VARIETIES: Available in its generic form only. You could also try the three-cornered leek (*A. triquetrum*) or daffodil garlic (*A. neapolitanum*), both of which complement wild garlic by producing edible leaves from autumn to spring.
STARTING OFF: Buy young plants from a good supplier or sow seed directly in a damp, shady spot from June to autumn.
POSITION: A damp, humus-rich soil in a shady spot.
SPACING: 30cm apart.
PRODUCTIVITY/EFFICIENCY: Happiest in the shady damp where few plants thrive, it can produce an abundant crop for around 3 months of the year. Can be left completely to its own devices.
GROWING: No maintenance required other than weeding if growing in the garden.
POTENTIAL PROBLEMS: Generally pest and disease free.
HARVEST: Pick leaves from March to May as well as flowers.

WINTER SAVORY

Satureja montana. Hardy semi-evergreen perennial.

Not a million miles away in flavour and fragrance from its summer relative, winter savory has perhaps more menthol, thyme and pepperiness to it. It packs an altogether more powerful punch, perfect for winter recipes that require a bit of presence – just go easy though, as it can dominate.

VARIETIES: Generic.
STARTING OFF: Source plants from a good supplier or grow from seed. Sow seed in modules in early spring but don't cover, as the seed needs light to germinate.
POSITION: Tolerant of most soils but must have good drainage and full sun. Winter savory grows well in a pot.
SPACING: 50cm apart.
PRODUCTIVITY/EFFICIENCY: Particularly valuable in the garden in warmer parts of the country where it can remain evergreen, offering structure during winter as well as its wonderful flavour.
GROWING: Cut back after flowering to promote fresh new growth.
POTENTIAL PROBLEMS: Generally pest and disease free.
HARVEST: Cuts stems and leaves as required in the growing season and more conservatively in winter.

211

WHAT TO GROW

VEGETABLES

	TRANSFORMERS	MULTIS	SECONDARY PLEASURES	EXPENSIVE TO BUY	EASY	STAPLES	FADERS	UNBUYABLES	UNCERTAINTIES	QUICK RETURNS	PERENNIAL	REPEAT HARVEST
AGRETTI				●	●		●	●		●		●
ASPARAGUS				●	●		●				●	●
AUBERGINES				●			●					
BAMBOO		●			●						●	●
BEETROOT		●			●	●						
BORLOTTI BEANS			●	●	●			●				●
BROAD BEANS		●	●	●	●		●			●		●
BRUSSELS SPROUTS		●		●	●							
BUCK'S HORN PLANTAIN	●	●			●		●	●			●	●
CABBAGE					●	●						
CALABRESE				●			●					
CALLALOO	●	●	●		●	●	●	●		●		●
CARDOONS			●		●			●			●	●
CARROTS					●	●				●		
CAULIFLOWER				●	●							
CELERIAC		●			●							
CELERY	●											
CHARD & PERPETUAL SPINACH					●	●				●		●

USE THE TABLE in conjunction with Choosing What To Grow to help prioritise what makes it into your kitchen garden. The year-long guide gives an idea of when to expect to harvest each food.

	JAN	FEB	MAR	APR	MAY	JUN	JUL	AUG	SEP	OCT	NOV	DEC
AGRETTI				■	■	■	■	■	■	■		
ASPARAGUS				■	■							
AUBERGINES								■	■	■		
BAMBOO				■	■	■	■	■	■	■		
BEETROOT							■	■	■	■		
BORLOTTI BEANS								■	■	■		
BROAD BEANS				■	■	■	■	■				
BRUSSELS SPROUTS	■	■	■	■						■	■	■
BUCK'S HORN PLANTAIN				■	■	■						
CABBAGE	■	■	■	■	■	■	■	■		■	■	■
CALABRESE						■	■	■				
CALLALOO						■	■	■				
CARDOONS										■		
CARROTS				■	■	■	■	■	■	■		
CAULIFLOWER	■	■	■	■	■	■			■	■		
CELERIAC	■	■	■						■	■	■	■
CELERY							■	■	■	■		
CHARD & PERPETUAL SPINACH	■	■	■	■	■	■	■	■	■	■	■	■

	TRANSFORMERS	MULTIS	SECONDARY PLEASURES	EXPENSIVE TO BUY	EASY	STAPLES	FADERS	UNBUYABLES	UNCERTAINTIES	QUICK RETURNS	PERENNIAL	REPEAT HARVEST
CHERVIL & PARSLEY ROOT					●			●				
CHICORY	●			●	●		●					●
CHILLI PEPPERS	●			●								●
CHINESE ARTICHOKE					●			●			●	
CHINESE CEDAR	●		●		●		●	●			●	●
CHOP SUEY GREENS		●	●		●		●	●				●
CIME DI RAPA					●		●	●		●		●
COURGETTES (inc. flowers)		●			●	●	●					●
CUCAMELONS					●		●	●				●
CUCUMBERS & GHERKINS				●								●
DAUBENTON'S KALE		●			●	●		●			●	●
DAYLILIES	●	●	●		●		●	●			●	●
EARTH CHESTNUT	●	●	●					●		●	●	●
EGYPTIAN WALKING ONION	●	●	●		●			●		●	●	●
ENDIVE	●			●			●					●
FLORENCE FENNEL	●	●		●	●							●
FRENCH BEANS					●		●					●
GARLIC	●	●			●							
GARLIC CRESS	●				●		●	●		●	●	●
GARLIC MUSTARD	●		●		●			●		●	●	●

	JANUARY	FEBRUARY	MARCH	APRIL	MAY	JUNE	JULY	AUGUST	SEPTEMBER	OCTOBER	NOVEMBER	DECEMBER
CHERVIL & PARSLEY ROOT	■	■	■	■	■	■	■	■	■	■	■	■
CHICORY	■									■	■	■
CHILLI PEPPERS								■	■	■		
CHINESE ARTICHOKE	■	■								■	■	■
CHINESE CEDAR				■	■	■	■					
CHOP SUEY GREENS					■	■	■	■	■			
CIME DI RAPA					■	■	■	■	■			
COURGETTES (inc. flowers)						■	■	■	■			
CUCAMELONS							■	■	■			
CUCUMBERS & GHERKINS						■	■	■	■	■		
DAUBENTON'S KALE	■	■	■	■	■	■	■	■	■	■		■
DAYLILIES					■	■	■	■				
EARTH CHESTNUT						■	■	■	■	■		
EGYPTIAN WALKING ONION	■	■	■	■	■	■	■	■	■			■
ENDIVE	■	■	■					■	■	■		■
FLORENCE FENNEL							■	■	■	■		
FRENCH BEANS						■	■	■	■			
GARLIC				■	■	■	■					
GARLIC CRESS	■	■	■	■					■	■	■	■
GARLIC MUSTARD				■	■	■	■	■				

215

	TRANSFORMERS	MULTIS	SECONDARY PLEASURES	EXPENSIVE TO BUY	EASY	STAPLES	FADERS	UNBUYABLES	UNCERTAINTIES	QUICK RETURNS	PERENNIAL	REPEAT HARVEST
GLOBE ARTICHOKES			●	●	●						●	●
GOOD KING HENRY		●			●		●	●			●	●
GROUND NUT		●	●		●			●				
HOPS		●	●	●	●			●		●	●	●
HOSTA		●	●		●			●				
JERUSALEM ARTICHOKES		●			●			●		●	●	
KAI LAN		●			●	●						
KALE		●			●	●						●
KOHLRABI												
LEEKS	●	●	●		●							
LETTUCE				●	●	●	●			●		●
MASHUA		●	●		●	●	●	●			●	●
MEXICAN TREE SPINACH			●		●		●	●				●
MIBUNA				●	●		●	●		●		●
MICROLEAVES	●				●		●	●				
MIZUNA				●	●		●			●		●
MOOLI	●				●			●				
MUSHROOMS	●		●	●	●		●				●	●
NEW ZEALAND SPINACH					●		●	●		●		●
OCA					●			●			●	

	JANUARY	FEBRUARY	MARCH	APRIL	MAY	JUNE	JULY	AUGUST	SEPTEMBER	OCTOBER	NOVEMBER	DECEMBER
GLOBE ARTICHOKES					■	■	■	■				
GOOD KING HENRY			■	■	■	■	■	■	■			
GROUND NUT	■	■								■	■	■
HOPS			■	■	■					■	■	
HOSTA			■	■								
JERUSALEM ARTICHOKES	■	■								■	■	■
KAI LAN					■	■		■	■	■		
KALE	■	■				■	■	■		■	■	■
KOHLRABI						■	■	■				
LEEKS	■	■	■	■	■				■			■
LETTUCE	■	■	■	■	■	■	■	■	■			■
MASHUA						■	■	■	■			■
MEXICAN TREE SPINACH			■	■	■	■	■					
MIBUNA	■	■	■	■	■	■	■	■	■			■
MICROLEAVES	■	■	■	■	■	■	■	■	■	■	■	■
MIZUNA	■	■	■	■	■	■	■	■	■			■
MOOLI								■	■		■	
MUSHROOMS	■	■	■	■	■	■	■	■	■	■		■
NEW ZEALAND SPINACH			■	■	■	■	■	■				
OCA										■	■	

	TRANSFORMERS	MULTIS	SECONDARY PLEASURES	EXPENSIVE TO BUY	EASY	STAPLES	FADERS	UNBUYABLES	UNCERTAINTIES	QUICK RETURNS	PERENNIAL	REPEAT HARVEST
ONIONS	●				●	●						
OSTRICH FERN			●		●		●	●			●	●
PARSNIPS					●	●						
PEAS		●		●	●		●			●		●
POTATOES (non-maincrop)				●	●		●			●		
POTATOES (maincrop)					●	●						
PURSLANE (winter & summer)	●				●		●	●		●		●
QUINOA			●	●	●	●						
RADISH	●	●			●			●		●		
RED VALERIAN			●		●		●			●	●	●
ROCKET	●	●		●	●		●			●		
ROMANESCO			●	●	●							
RUNNER BEANS					●		●					●
SALSIFY & SCORZONERA					●				●			
SEA KALE		●	●		●		●	●		●	●	●
SHALLOTS	●			●	●							
SIBERIAN PEA TREE			●		●			●			●	●
SMALL-LEAVED LIME	●		●		●		●			●	●	●
SOCIETY GARLIC	●		●		●		●	●		●		●
SOLOMON'S SEAL			●		●		●			●		●

	JANUARY	FEBRUARY	MARCH	APRIL	MAY	JUNE	JULY	AUGUST	SEPTEMBER	OCTOBER	NOVEMBER	DECEMBER
ONIONS					X	X	X	X				
OSTRICH FERN			X	X	X							
PARSNIPS	X	X	X					X	X	X	X	X
PEAS					X	X	X	X				
POTATOES (non-maincrop)					X	X	X					
POTATOES (maincrop)								X	X	X		
PURSLANE (winter & summer)	X	X	X	X	X	X	X	X			X	X
QUINOA									X	X		
RADISH			X	X	X	X	X	X	X	X		
RED VALERIAN	X	X	X	X						X	X	X
ROCKET		X	X	X	X	X	X					
ROMANESCO	X							X	X	X	X	X
RUNNER BEANS						X	X	X	X			
SALSIFY & SCORZONERA	X	X								X	X	X
SEA KALE	X	X	X	X	X					X	X	
SHALLOTS							X	X				
SIBERIAN PEA TREE						X	X					
SMALL-LEAVED LIME			X	X	X							
SOCIETY GARLIC					X	X	X	X	X			
SOLOMON'S SEAL			X	X								

219

	TRANSFORMERS	MULTIS	SECONDARY PLEASURES	EXPENSIVE TO BUY	EASY	STAPLES	FADERS	UNBUYABLES	UNCERTAINTIES	QUICK RETURNS	PERENNIAL	REPEAT HARVEST
SORREL	●				●		●	●		●		●
SPINACH			●		●	●	●			●		●
SPRING ONIONS	●				●		●			●		
SPROUTING BROCCOLI			●		●		●					
SQUASH			●		●	●						
STINGING NETTLES			●		●		●	●		●	●	●
SWEDE					●							
SWEETCORN				●			●					
SWEET PEPPERS				●								
SWEET POTATO				●		●	●		●			
TOMATILLOS								●				
TOMATOES				●			●					●
TURNIPS					●			●				
VIOLA 'HEARTSEASE'	●		●		●		●	●		●		●
YACON			●					●			●	

FRUIT & NUTS

	TRANSFORMERS	MULTIS	SECONDARY PLEASURES	EXPENSIVE TO BUY	EASY	STAPLES	FADERS	UNBUYABLES	UNCERTAINTIES	QUICK RETURNS	PERENNIAL	REPEAT HARVEST
ALMONDS		●	●	●	●					●	●	
ALPINE STRAWBERRIES	●				●		●	●		●	●	●
APPLES			●		●	●					●	
APRICOTS				●	●				●		●	

220

	JAN	FEB	MAR	APR	MAY	JUN	JUL	AUG	SEP	OCT	NOV	DEC
SORREL					●	●	●	●	●	●	●	
SPINACH	●	●	●	●	●	●	●	●	●	●		●
SPRING ONIONS			●	●	●	●	●	●	●	●		
SPROUTING BROCCOLI	●	●	●	●								
SQUASH									●	●		
STINGING NETTLES			●	●	●							
SWEDE									●	●	●	●
SWEETCORN						●	●	●	●			
SWEET PEPPERS						●	●	●	●			
SWEET POTATO										●	●	●
TOMATILLOS						●	●	●	●			
TOMATOES						●	●	●	●			
TURNIPS					●	●	●	●	●		●	
VIOLA 'HEARTSEASE'				●	●	●	●	●	●			
YACON									●	●		

	JAN	FEB	MAR	APR	MAY	JUN	JUL	AUG	SEP	OCT	NOV	DEC
ALMONDS					●	●				●	●	
ALPINE STRAWBERRIES					●	●	●	●	●			
APPLES							●	●	●	●	●	●
APRICOTS							●	●	●			

	TRANSFORMERS	MULTIS	SECONDARY PLEASURES	EXPENSIVE TO BUY	EASY	STAPLES	FADERS	UNBUYABLES	UNCERTAINTIES	QUICK RETURNS	PERENNIAL	REPEAT HARVEST
ASIAN PEARS			●		●			●			●	
AUTUMN OLIVE			●		●			●		●	●	
BLACKBERRIES					●		●			●	●	●
BLACKCURRANTS	●	●		●	●		●				●	
BLUE BEAN			●		●			●	●			
BLUEBERRIES					●						●	
BLUE HONEYSUCKLE			●		●			●	●		●	
BOYSENBERRIES							●	●		●	●	●
CAPE GOOSEBERRIES				●			●		●			●
CHERRIES			●	●	●		●		●	●	●	
CHILEAN GUAVA					●			●		●	●	
CHOCOLATE VINE	●	●	●		●			●		●	●	
CRANBERRIES	●			●	●						●	
ELDER	●	●	●		●			●		●	●	●
FIGS		●			●	●			●		●	
FUCHSIA			●		●		●	●		●	●	●
GOJI BERRIES				●	●					●	●	●
GOOSEBERRIES				●	●					●	●	
GRAPES (inc. leaves)		●	●	●	●							
HAWTHORN			●		●		●	●				

	JANUARY	FEBRUARY	MARCH	APRIL	MAY	JUNE	JULY	AUGUST	SEPTEMBER	OCTOBER	NOVEMBER	DECEMBER
ASIAN PEARS							■	■	■	■		
AUTUMN OLIVE									■	■	■	
BLACKBERRIES							■	■	■	■		
BLACKCURRANTS						■	■	■	■			
BLUE BEAN									■	■		
BLUEBERRIES							■	■	■			
BLUE HONEYSUCKLE					■	■						
BOYSENBERRIES							■	■	■			
CAPE GOOSEBERRIES								■	■	■	■	
CHERRIES						■	■	■				
CHILEAN GUAVA										■	■	
CHOCOLATE VINE									■			
CRANBERRIES								■	■			
ELDER					■	■	■	■	■	■	■	
FIGS								■	■			
FUCHSIA							■	■	■			
GOJI BERRIES							■	■	■	■		
GOOSEBERRIES					■	■	■					
GRAPES (inc. leaves)						■	■	■		■		
HAWTHORN									■	■		

223

	TRANSFORMERS	MULTIS	SECONDARY PLEASURES	EXPENSIVE TO BUY	EASY	STAPLES	FADERS	UNBUYABLES	UNCERTAINTIES	QUICK RETURNS	PERENNIAL	REPEAT HARVEST
HAZEL			●	●	●	●					●	
JAPANESE PLUMS			●		●			●			●	
JAPANESE QUINCE			●		●			●			●	●
JAPANESE WINEBERRIES					●			●		●	●	●
JOSTABERRY					●			●		●	●	
JUNEBERRY			●		●		●				●	
KIWIS			●	●	●				●			
LINGONBERRY					●			●		●		
MEDLAR			●	●	●			●			●	
MELONS				●					●			
MIRABELLE PLUMS			●		●			●			●	
MULBERRIES (inc. leaves)		●	●				●	●			●	
NEPALESE RASPBERRIES			●		●			●			●	●
OLIVES	●		●	●					●			
PEACHES & NECTARINES			●	●	●		●			●	●	
PEARS			●		●						●	
PECANS			●	●	●				●		●	
PINEAPPLE GUAVA	●	●	●		●		●	●			●	
PLUMS, DAMSONS & GAGES			●	●	●							
QUINCE	●		●	●	●			●			●	

	JANUARY	FEBRUARY	MARCH	APRIL	MAY	JUNE	JULY	AUGUST	SEPTEMBER	OCTOBER	NOVEMBER	DECEMBER
HAZEL									■	■	■	■
JAPANESE PLUMS							■					
JAPANESE QUINCE									■	■	■	
JAPANESE WINEBERRIES							■	■	■			
JOSTABERRY						■	■					
JUNEBERRY						■	■					
KIWIS									■	■	■	■
LINGONBERRY							■	■	■			
MEDLAR										■	■	
MELONS								■	■			
MIRABELLE PLUMS							■	■	■			
MULBERRIES (inc. leaves)								■	■			
NEPALESE RASPBERRIES							■	■				
OLIVES	■									■	■	■
PEACHES & NECTARINES							■	■				
PEARS								■	■	■	■	
PECANS										■	■	
PINEAPPLE GUAVA							■		■	■		
PLUMS, DAMSONS & GAGES							■	■	■			
QUINCE										■		

	TRANSFORMERS	MULTIS	SECONDARY PLEASURES	EXPENSIVE TO BUY	EASY	STAPLES	FADERS	UNBUYABLES	UNCERTAINTIES	QUICK RETURNS	PERENNIAL	REPEAT HARVEST
RASPBERRIES			●	●	●		●			●	●	●
REDCURRANTS & WHITE CURRANTS			●	●	●					●	●	
RHUBARB (inc. forced)			●	●	●		●	●			●	●
SCHISANDRA	●		●				●	●	●		●	
SEA BUCKTHORN	●		●		●			●			●	
STRAWBERRIES			●	●	●		●			●	●	●
SWEET CHESTNUTS				●						●	●	
WALNUTS (inc. green walnuts)		●	●	●					●		●	
WORCESTERBERRIES			●		●			●		●	●	

HERBS & SPICES

	TRANSFORMERS	MULTIS	SECONDARY PLEASURES	EXPENSIVE TO BUY	EASY	STAPLES	FADERS	UNBUYABLES	UNCERTAINTIES	QUICK RETURNS	PERENNIAL	REPEAT HARVEST
ANGELICA					●			●		●	●	●
ANISE HYSSOP	●		●		●			●		●	●	●
BABINGTON'S LEEK	●				●			●		●	●	●
BASIL	●			●	●					●	●	●
BAY	●			●	●					●	●	●
BERGAMOT	●		●		●			●		●	●	●
BORAGE	●	●	●		●		●	●		●	●	●
CARAWAY	●			●	●					●		●
CAROLINA ALLSPICE	●		●					●		●	●	●
CELERY LEAF	●				●			●		●		●

	JANUARY	FEBRUARY	MARCH	APRIL	MAY	JUNE	JULY	AUGUST	SEPTEMBER	OCTOBER	NOVEMBER	DECEMBER
RASPBERRIES							X	X	X	X	X	
REDCURRANTS & WHITE CURRANTS							X	X				
RHUBARB (inc. forced)	X	X	X	X	X	X						
SCHISANDRA								X	X			
SEA BUCKTHORN								X	X	X		
STRAWBERRIES					X	X	X	X	X	X	X	
SWEET CHESTNUTS										X	X	
WALNUTS (inc. green walnuts)						X	X		X	X	X	
WORCESTERBERRIES							X	X				

	JANUARY	FEBRUARY	MARCH	APRIL	MAY	JUNE	JULY	AUGUST	SEPTEMBER	OCTOBER	NOVEMBER	DECEMBER
ANGELICA						X		X	X			
ANISE HYSSOP					X	X		X	X			
BABINGTON'S LEEK	X	X	X					X			X	X
BASIL						X	X	X	X			
BAY	X	X	X	X	X	X	X	X	X	X	X	X
BERGAMOT					X	X	X	X	X			
BORAGE					X	X	X	X		X		
CARAWAY					X	X		X				
CAROLINA ALLSPICE							X	X				
CELERY LEAF	X	X	X	X	X	X	X	X	X	X	X	X

227

	TRANSFORMERS	MULTIS	SECONDARY PLEASURES	EXPENSIVE TO BUY	EASY	STAPLES	FADERS	UNBUYABLES	UNCERTAINTIES	QUICK RETURNS	PERENNIAL	REPEAT HARVEST
CHERVIL	●			●	●		●			●		●
CHIVES	●	●	●	●	●					●	●	●
CORIANDER	●	●	●	●	●		●			●	●	●
DILL	●			●	●					●		●
ENGLISH MACE	●	●	●		●			●		●	●	●
FENNEL	●	●	●		●		●			●	●	●
FENUGREEK	●				●		●			●		
FRENCH TARRAGON	●			●	●					●	●	●
HORSERADISH	●				●			●			●	●
HYSSOP	●		●		●						●	
JAPANESE PARSLEY		●	●		●			●		●	●	●
LAVENDER	●		●		●			●		●	●	●
LEMON BALM	●		●		●			●		●	●	●
LEMON VERBENA	●		●		●			●		●	●	●
LEMONGRASS			●		●			●	●	●	●	●
LOVAGE	●	●			●			●		●	●	●
MARIGOLD	●	●	●		●		●	●		●	●	●
MARJORAM & OREGANO	●		●	●	●		●			●	●	●
MINT	●		●	●	●					●		●
MYRTLE	●	●	●		●			●			●	●

	JANUARY	FEBRUARY	MARCH	APRIL	MAY	JUNE	JULY	AUGUST	SEPTEMBER	OCTOBER	NOVEMBER	DECEMBER
CHERVIL	■	■	■	■	■	■	■	■	■		■	■
CHIVES				■	■	■	■	■	■	■		
CORIANDER					■	■	■	■	■	■		
DILL					■	■	■	■	■	■		
ENGLISH MACE				■	■	■	■	■	■			
FENNEL					■	■	■	■	■	■		
FENUGREEK					■	■	■	■				
FRENCH TARRAGON					■	■	■	■	■	■		
HORSERADISH	■	■	■	■	■	■	■	■	■	■		■
HYSSOP	■	■	■	■	■	■	■	■	■	■	■	■
JAPANESE PARSLEY	■	■	■	■	■	■	■	■	■	■	■	■
LAVENDER						■	■					
LEMON BALM				■	■	■	■	■	■			
LEMON VERBENA					■	■	■	■	■	■		
LEMONGRASS					■	■	■	■	■	■		
LOVAGE				■	■	■	■	■	■	■	■	
MARIGOLD					■	■	■	■	■			
MARJORAM & OREGANO					■	■	■	■	■	■		
MINT				■	■	■	■	■	■			
MYRTLE	■	■	■	■	■	■	■	■	■	■		■

	TRANSFORMERS	MULTIS	SECONDARY PLEASURES	EXPENSIVE TO BUY	EASY	STAPLES	FADERS	UNBUYABLES	UNCERTAINTIES	QUICK RETURNS	PERENNIAL	REPEAT HARVEST
NASTURTIUM	●	●	●		●		●	●		●		●
PARSLEY	●			●	●		●			●		●
PERILLA	●	●	●		●		●	●		●		●
ROSE (HEDGEROW)	●		●		●		●	●		●	●	●
ROSEMARY	●		●	●	●					●	●	●
SAGE	●		●		●					●	●	●
SALAD BURNET	●	●	●		●		●	●		●	●	●
SCENTED PELARGONIUMS	●		●		●			●		●	●	●
SUMMER SAVORY	●		●		●			●		●		●
SWEET CICELY	●	●	●					●		●	●	●
SZECHUAN PEPPER	●	●	●	●				●			●	
TASMANIAN MOUNTAIN PEPPER	●	●	●	●				●			●	
THYME	●		●	●	●					●	●	●
TURKISH ROCKET	●	●			●					●	●	●
WATERCRESS	●				●	●	●				●	●
WELSH ONION	●	●			●		●	●			●	●
WILD GARLIC	●	●	●		●		●	●		●	●	●
WINTER SAVORY	●		●		●			●		●	●	●

	JAN	FEB	MAR	APR	MAY	JUN	JUL	AUG	SEP	OCT	NOV	DEC
NASTURTIUM					X	X	X	X	X			
PARSLEY					X	X	X	X	X	X	X	X
PERILLA					X	X	X	X	X			
ROSE (HEDGEROW)						X	X	X	X	X		
ROSEMARY	X	X	X	X	X	X	X	X	X	X	X	X
SAGE	X	X	X	X	X	X	X	X	X	X	X	X
SALAD BURNET	X	X	X	X	X	X	X	X	X	X		
SCENTED PELARGONIUMS					X	X	X	X	X			
SUMMER SAVORY					X	X	X	X	X			
SWEET CICELY				X	X	X	X	X	X			
SZECHUAN PEPPER				X	X			X	X	X	X	X
TASMANIAN MOUNTAIN PEPPER	X	X	X	X	X	X	X	X	X	X	X	X
THYME	X	X	X	X	X	X	X	X	X	X	X	X
TURKISH ROCKET				X	X	X	X	X	X	X	X	X
WATERCRESS					X	X	X	X	X	X	X	X
WELSH ONION	X	X	X	X	X	X	X	X	X	X	X	X
WILD GARLIC	X	X	X	X	X	X	X	X	X	X	X	X
WINTER SAVORY	X	X	X	X	X	X	X	X	X	X	X	X

RATHER THAN SUGGEST different ways of growing or describe each potential way of growing, I want to let some brilliant, innovative gardeners show you what works for them.

Here is a collection of incredible, productive gardens, their gates flung open by those who have created them, their methods and thinking laid out, along with plans and planting suggestions.

I found every one inspiring in its own way. Each has given me hints and ideas that have made my own kitchen garden richer. There's always another fence to look over, another great idea to adopt and adapt.

While you can take the idea that grabs you the most and make it your own, don't feel limited to recreating these gardens. Replicate what you love; blend, tweak and embellish as you like.

CHAPTER 4

OPEN GARDENS

Saumarez Park Walled Garden, *Guernsey*

I LOVE WALLED GARDENS. Whatever their condition, the walls create something magical, a peculiar sense of both history and potential with the tensions of life outside suspended. This garden is particularly special though, in that it is so obviously the characterful creation of many. Under the care of one or two paid gardeners, walled gardens can look impressive but they often seem to miss a certain something: not here. Dozens of hands, minds and partnerships build personality and charm into the garden, and in allowing people responsibility for their own area, expertise and specialisms develop and are expressed in what becomes a patchwork of personalities.

Having fallen into disrepair, the Victorian kitchen garden found its way into the warm hands of The Guernsey Botanical Trust in 2006. Founded by noted clematis expert Raymond Evison, the charitable and voluntary project set out to return the gardens to their former glory. Ivan Le Tissier, pictured overleaf, a retired professional grower, has been quite a force in driving the project forwards since then.

The transformation is striking. In a few short years, the extensive glasshouses have been beautifully rebuilt and restored, the head gardener's office remade, the garden cleared and paths and beds reinstated.

Heritage varieties dominate, partly to stay true to the kitchen garden's Victorian origins, but also serving to conserve and promote

235

many varieties that have been almost lost to more commercial produce in recent years.

The garden now has the hallmarks of what you'd expect from a beautiful walled garden, yet it is the work of a community of volunteers, managing the growing areas in a very distinctive way. The beds are divided into sections, with a pair of 'Gardians' assigned to each one – where possible, a knowledgeable mentor works with someone less experienced. It gives the garden a very distinctive feel and ensures that every person's efforts are reflected within the overall impression, rather than being lost within it.

The garden is also at the centre of the community. Or perhaps that should be communities? It is open to the public and whether it's a sunny June day, as when I visited, or chilly in winter, the paths and seats within the walls are busy.

Ivan Le Tissier: 'It was a real tip when we came here, and for a couple of years there really wasn't much gardening to be done, it was all about clearing the undergrowth and debris. It's still early days in many ways, but it's changed quite a bit.

'I like our system of "Gardians", in pairs, taking care of small areas. Having responsibility for a particular plant group or area gives you something focused to get to grips with, to make yours, to experiment with and build up expertise in, which can be shared with anyone who's

238

interested. It also creates a sense of pride: not only are you doing something that's part of the whole, your efforts are very much given chance to shine for everyone who visits to see. It makes the garden so much more than the sum of everyone's efforts.

'There is a huge community of visitors, made up of those from the island and also tourists. In the height of summer, it can seem a completely different place from one week to the next because there is so much growing, and once they've visited, people from the island return time and again, through the seasons. There's always a steady stream of parents with children, gardeners looking for inspiration, and friends who find the garden a stimulating backdrop when meeting up.

'As a community resource, the garden does amazing things for those who take part. Walk around and chat to people and it becomes pretty apparent that many have walked through the door in need of something. One lady found peace and purpose after the unexpected death of her husband; there's a man whose once full-on life was abruptly slowed by illness; a few who just relish the opportunity to meet new people; and some who simply want to give their time and energies to something of public value. It is a place where, under the guise of gardening, people are quietly healed or fulfilled in the creation of something extraordinary, where interesting people who have gone through or are going through difficult times can find some sanctuary. That is pretty much all of us at one time or another.'

TERRACE & CREWROOM

PLOT 1

PLOT 3

PLOT 5

PLOT 7

PLOT 9

PLOT 11

CENTRE PATH

YARD & TOOL ROOM / WORKSHOP

PLOT 2

PLOT 4

PLOT 6

PLOT 8

PLOT 10

PLOT 12

KEY

- BRASSICAS, PEAS AND BEANS
- SALADS AND ORIENTAL VEGETABLES
- ROOT VEG
- PERENNIAL VEG
- HERBS
- FRUIT
- CUTTING FLOWERS
- CUCURBITS AND SWEETCORN

Main features

- A large Victorian kitchen garden
- Four main beds, with narrow beds against all the walls
- Reinstated glasshouses
- A beautiful, productive herb garden
- Volunteer-led operation
- Classic four-bed rotation in the main beds, with fruit and flowers dominating the narrow beds against the walls
- Main beds are divided into subsections, each managed by a pair of 'Gardians'
- Flowers integrated throughout
- Largely heritage varieties
- Open to the public, free of charge
- Community-centred

Particular plants and why

- Globe artichokes – a perennial classic for their expensive-to-buy artichokes and architectural beauty
- Borage – for edible leaves (when young) and flowers and for its beauty and ability to attract beneficial insects to the garden
- Chard – easy to grow, with a long season of productivity
- Lavender – for its beauty, ability to attract beneficial insects and for harvesting
- Climbing beans – productive over a long season, they take up little ground and add height to the garden
- Rows of broad beans – for their beans and also (along with the other peas and beans) for enriching the soil with nitrogen for the subsequent crop
- A mix of salad leaves – lettuce, chicories, endives and oriental leaves
- Melons and grapes – both of which thrive in the heat of the glasshouse

Tresillian House, *Cornwall*

THE GARDEN AT TRESILLIAN is, as most walled gardens are, beautifully organised and laid out, with a fullness few could fail to admire. But this garden has something beyond that. The rows and blocks of vegetables, fruit, herbs and flowers are hugely abundant, full of vitality and entirely without gap or obvious disease. And there are hoverflies, butterflies and bees in almost ridiculous preponderance.

Gardener John Harris has carried out his fine work here for many years, and puts the abundance and ecological richness down to his years of experience working in tune with the moon's cycle. As we walk, talk and taste, I soon run out of superlatives: the flavours are incredible, from the most recognisable of carrot varieties to less familiar cultivars.

When I visited in early summer, the walls of peas were hugely impressive, especially the red-flowered purple-podded pea. No one is quite sure what the true variety is: they came to John a decade ago when a family in Somerset asked him to be their custodian. The little that is known is that they date from 1830 and were kept going from a few pods found in the tunic of a family member returning from WWI. I'm determined to track down the variety because these are, with no close rivals, the most delicious peas I have ever eaten. And I'm old and fussy.

Flowers are everywhere. Partly for their in situ beauty and for cutting, but their ability to attract pollinators and predators for potential pests is also crucial for keeping the garden in perfect ecological balance. Calendula, planted in swathes by the carrots, ensures that carrot fly isn't able to pick up the scent of its favourite food and do its damage. Similarly, scented geraniums help keep the maggot away from the parsnip.

As with the edible peas, the sweet peas are immaculate. A mix of 'Henry Eckford' heritage varieties and newer cultivars are chosen for scent – you can smell 'Kings High Scent' from yards away. They are all sown in monthly lines between November and February, in the appropriate phase of the moon, giving a long succession of picking from the middle of May onwards.

The dahlias, sunflowers and other cut flowers are in similar fine fettle, with short varieties grown around the edge and tall in the middle, creating a block that's balanced on the eye and easy to access.

John Harris: 'I owe much of the garden's success to the moon. When I was young I was taken under the wing of a head gardener who taught me the fundamentals of moon gardening. Years later I struck up a conversation about it with someone at the RHS Chelsea Flower Show who was a distant relative of a Sioux Indian. We started talking about moon gardening and the way the native North Americans did things. I came away a wiser person. I then started researching the Incas, Maoris, Greeks, Romans, Aborigines and native North Americans, and how they all worked in harmony with nature. The moon seemed to be central to everything.

'The core of moon gardening is very simple. The moon has a 29-day cycle made up of two halves: waxing (when the moon is growing) and waning (as it fades away). That cycle is also split into four quarters: the new moon, the first quarter, full moon and the last quarter. Each has its own powerful characteristics and influences. The tides are highest at the new and full moon, and with the moisture rising that's when we plant everything that produces crops underground – the root vegetables and potatoes, etc. In the first quarter, we plant everything that produces a crop above the ground – the corns, flowers, legumes and the rest. Full moon is when there is maximum moisture in the soil, and the living plant is abstracting as much out of the ground as possible. This gives you the best taste, and better keeping quality. It's the ideal time to pick. In the last quarter, when the water table is dropping to its lowest, we do all our digging and manuring, taking cuttings and pruning hedges.

247

'How often do you buy something from the supermarket and it tastes like cardboard? Some of that is due to variety but most is due to picking it out of cycle with nature. Of course, if you plant in a way that's totally alien to what I do, you will still get a crop and think what's all the fuss about? But you'll get such a better crop if you follow the moon. If you want the best, this is the way.

'You won't always be able to get it spot on. The heavens may open and you're left with the choice of waiting a month or doing it next week. Well, you have to make a judgement and perhaps accept that it may not be absolutely perfect. Nothing in life is an exact science, but it is about the bigger picture, getting your priorities right and doing what you can within that framework. I'm always looking to next year and how I can improve, but I aim for contentment rather than perfection.

'Success is due to a combination of everything. You draw on all your experience and plan ahead and get a feel for things, but it's mostly down to feeding the soil, companion planting and doing things in tune with the movements of the moon. Of course, it's more subtle than that, but these are the core principles around which I work. To the unconvinced, I say take a sit down on the beach and watch: if the moon can move oceans, why not a little water in your garden? The pull of the moon's gravity affects it all.

'Moon gardening is not about doing more work; it's about doing the right work. It's all about the core principles, taking a step back now and again, and learning from what you see. Moon gardening makes you more thoughtful and observant in general. And if you are prepared to see it, a garden will always tell you what you need to know.'

Main features

- An enclosed, walled garden offering shelter and a range of microclimates to the plants
- Planting, sowing, harvesting and maintenance undertaken in tune with the moon's cycle
- Companion planting throughout
- Classic four-bed rotation in the main beds
- Fruit and flowers dominating the narrow beds against the walls
- A central herb garden, dominated by perennial herbs
- Successional sweet peas

Particular plants and why

- A wall of purple-podded peas – deliciously productive over a long season
- Scented pelargoniums – a fantastic companion plant for parsnips and fabulous flavours for making syrups
- Walls of sweet peas – not edible, but bring beauty, scent and beneficial insects to the garden
- Calendula – a companion plant for root crops, especially carrots
- A large block of sweetcorn – just-picked sweetcorn is so much better than those in the shops, and being wind pollinated, it is best grown in blocks
- Narrow lines of climbing beans – high productivity over a long season, without taking up much ground space
- Courgettes – for flowers and fruit and their easy productivity
- Currants – red, white and blackcurrants produce beautifully flavoursome fruit over a long season in the Cornish climate

251

International Solidarity Centre,
Reading

THE READING INTERNATIONAL SOLIDARITY CENTRE cafe lies a hop and a skip from the main shopping streets of the city. The coffee's great, but up above, through the skylight, there's a hint of something even more extraordinary: a rooftop garden quite unlike any I've seen.

Designed and planted in 2002 by renowned nurseryman and designer Paul Barney, the roof garden is an edible jungle in the sky. It is a food forest dominated by perennial herbaceous plants, shrubs, trees and climbers planted in layers to mimic a natural woodland.

The garden is even more of a marvel when you consider its limitations: as well as the site being a couple of floors up, the building's structure can only handle a thin growing medium. At 32m x 6m, the space suits a road more than a garden.

These weren't the only constraints. In keeping with the charity's aims, the RISC garden had to function as an outdoor classroom and demonstration space, as well as complement the charity's aim of raising awareness of global issues.

Happily, Paul's design skills married perfectly with Garden Education Coordinator and leader of the RISC team Dave Richards' vision. Now well established, the garden is a glorious sight. Within the lower tiers, there are generous swathes to lend structure, but diversity is very apparent too — there are definite themes but great variety within. If you mentally clear away what's there and look at the reality of the space, this garden is a truly incredible achievement.

Paul Barney: 'I had to come up with a design that would give the impression of increasing the surface area — the width especially. We incorporated a hierarchy of sinuous paths and there's no axis running down the middle. Instead, views hint at what's beyond without giving you too long a perspective. This also creates ecological niches for plants that thrive in forest edge conditions.

'This was 12 years ago and much of the planting was experimental — no one had really tried this on a roof before and many of the plants were marginal. We had little idea of whether they'd thrive or even survive up here. And we grew plenty of plants that people hadn't eaten much before, so there was a lot to discover, which was all part of fulfilling the education remit.'

Dave Richards: 'The limitations were considerable. Structural engineers informed us that we wouldn't have to retro-strengthen the roof as long as we kept the growing substrate to 30cm — that's only a foot of soil! Add to that the challenges of a flat roof with skylights that had to be kept clear and fan ducts to be maintained and there was quite a bit for Paul to wrestle with.

'In many ways, the garden is a giant hanging basket. For the plants to thrive we need to irrigate and keep nutrient levels high, as there is no reserve of either up here. We use compost made from the waste from the cafe downstairs, which in turn provides food for the cafe. We've also taken advantage of the gentle fall in the flat roof for our water harvesting system, which redistributes the water through a drip irrigation system powered by a small wind turbine and solar panels.

'The hard landscaping is similarly thought through. It is a combination of reused and recycled materials, including rescued bricks destined for landfill, woodchip paths edged with cordwood (tree surgeons' waste material), and with fencing and raised beds made from locally coppiced hazel and willow.'

Paul: 'A dozen years down the line, the garden is pretty much as I'd imagined it might be, although I had no idea that everything would get quite so large. We weren't sure if a tree could survive on 30cm of substrate and the answer is "yes!", although we had to cut the top off the tallest trees to keep them at 6m or so. No big trees or shrubs have died, but there have been some smaller losses. For some reason, currants don't do well up here, while wineberries thrive. We had no idea how everything would do in these conditions but it's reached

a natural balance very quickly and started to look like a real garden within just a couple of years.'

Dave: 'The garden is always evolving. As plants have matured, the shade has increased from dappled to heavy in places, which has meant some plants – three-cornered leek and wild garlic, for example – have thrived and expanded their coverage, whereas others have dwindled. We are reducing shade here and there, thinning where needed. It's something that characterised Robert Hart's seminal forest garden. It's too densely planted, not thanks to Paul's design but to us adding since. We've been greedy and wanted to have more in the garden to make it an educational space, so the original 120 species have increased to 200 or so, and that means it needs a little more management.

'The garden has more than fulfilled the education side of the brief. Interestingly, the more the garden develops over time, the more stories it contains. It illuminates issues and cultures, and the plants help you tell stories that make connections between people and places, as well as different cultures. It's also a great way of understanding and communicating the history of plants and colonisation, which is something I'm very interested in. The global diversity here — there are plants from every continent except the Arctics — makes it a very valuable resource. It's somewhere to show how we exploit people, plants and places for money or for more noble causes.'

Paul: 'I also like seeing plants that have matured from seeds or a cutting I took on plant hunts abroad. One or two have a stranger tale to tell: the Nepalese pepper, an unusual evergreen grinding pepper, comes from a visit to Montmartre in Paris. I saw this shrub in a spot where the drunks throw their bottles from Sacré Coeur, and took a cutting from it. It can be tricky to grow but this one is thriving.'

Dave: 'We opened up as part of the National Gardens Scheme after only two years, as there was already enough to impress the NGS committee. That proved to be a big move, as we have reached a far wider audience — people who perhaps might not come to the RISC cafe or the fair trade shop. We have unusual plants for those into plants for their own sake, a garden for those interested in whatever dimension of that they like, and it has broadened our community.

'Perhaps most satisfyingly, the garden has far exceeded the original brief as a garden that would appeal to children. It seems they love that windiness, the hidden areas — they're in a jungle, it's at a scale that works well for them and they can graze as they like.

'The combination of children and free food just works! The long-lost and unfamiliar flavours and plants are avenues for discovery for them. I've got kids who are eating Japanese wineberries, who are eating all parts of nasturtiums and going home and introducing their parents to them. It's become part of the school culture in places which is really exciting, and beyond the original vision.

'This garden satisfies people's hunger, their curiosities and it is a place of shared skills and enthusiasm. In appealing to all sorts of people, old and young, the garden has been instrumental in building a growing community of gardeners and food activists in Reading. And this feels very much just part of an ongoing journey. Who knows what else is to come?'

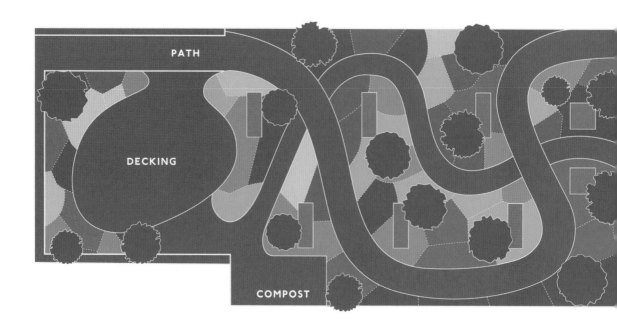

PATH

DECKING

COMPOST

KEY

■ FRUIT TREES / SOFT FRUIT
Including: Apples, pears, figs, quince, redcurrant, Nepalese raspberry, chokeberry, jostaberry, blue honeysuckle, chocolate vine, mulberry, medlar

■ SHOOTS
Including: Bamboo, udo, Solomon's seal, Good King Henry, quamash, hops, sea kale, asparagus

■ HERBS
Including: Japanese parsley, lovage, lemon balm, Vietnamese coriander, sage, rosemary, sweet cicely, lemon verbena, thyme, winter savory

■ ROOTS
Including: Earth chestnut, yacon, oca, broadleaf toothwort, liquorice

■ LEAVES AND EDIBLE FLOWERS
Including: Daylilies, sorrel, dandelion, land cress, pokeweed, sweet violet

■ INEDIBLE / OTHERS
Including: Marsh marigold, Jack in the pulpit, Russian comfrey, Japanese banana, Indian physic, purple coneflower

■ GARLIC AND ONIONS
Including: Babington's leek, Egyptian Walking onion, chives, serpent garlic, Welsh onion

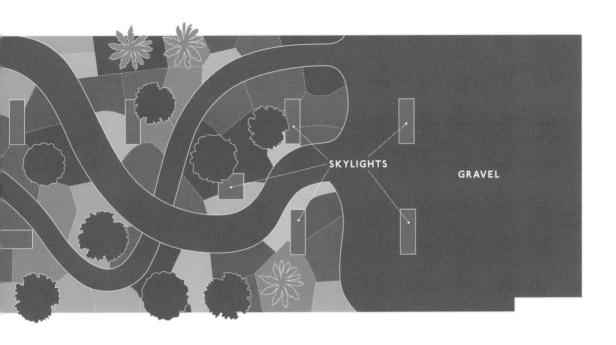

SKYLIGHTS

GRAVEL

Main features

- A garden modelled on a natural woodland, planted in tiers, from trees to groundcover
- Very limited soil depth
- Sinuous, winding paths to promote a sense of discovery and give the impression of greater width
- Good signage/labelling to fit the educational remit
- Community seating areas
- Rainwater-fed irrigation system

Particular plants and why

- Medlars – a late-season, unbuyable fruit, harvested when most of the leaves have left deciduous plants
- Creeping raspberries – for fruit and as easy groundcover
- Blue bean (*Decaisnea*) – electric blue, broad bean-like pods filled with a melon-flavoured pulp. The plant goes in that mid-tier between the herbaceous and small tree layers
- Japanese wineberries – a low-maintenance, hardy, unbuyable and delicious fruit
- Bamboo – for edible shoots and canes for support
- Szechuan pepper – aromatic peppercorns
- Sweet cicely – a perennial herb, with fabulous aniseed flavour and aroma carried in its leaves and seeds. Emerges very early in spring and does well in partial shade

Chris Achilleos' Allotment, *London*

WE ARE ALL familiar with allotments, those fabulously productive patches that form often large community resources in urban areas. Most follow a broadly similar pattern of four-bed rotation: in effect, a classic kitchen garden in miniature. Chris Achilleos' allotment couldn't be more different from that stereotype. Located bang in the heart of Tottenham, north London, Chris' urban oasis is just about the best example of what you can do with an allotment as I've ever seen.

The allotment already seems established beyond its six years: this is not, as a lot of allotments are, a collection of plants; it is a proper garden. Chris has used the edible plants as powerfully visually as he has the ornamentals, and created a space that's as abundant in wildlife as it is in flowers and food. The plants are big and flourishing; it is as beautiful as it is productive and it is from here that I had the finest figs I've ever eaten. After my first visit, I left with a couple of figs picked from one of Chris' home-raised trees. Each fruit was as large as my hand, dripping juice under the weight of their own gorgeous ripeness, I'm sorry to say as much over the train's upholstery as in my mouth, as I left White Hart Lane.

Much of Chris' success has come from having a basic design that he's allowed himself to embellish as he's found inspiration from things that have just occurred, unanticipated. It's a garden part planned, part evolved and part happy accident.

One element contributing a lot to making this quite the abundant garden it is, are the four 'walls' that surround it. Chris has inventively grown climbers and other plants against and within these boundaries, adding shelter, privacy and creating a semi-protected environment within, where even marginal plants thrive.

Chris Achilleos: 'Gardening was always a hobby; I've always liked growing plants from seed and learning how to take cuttings. As a child I watched my mother, and evolved from there. Now, whenever I'm abroad, I always bring back cuttings, and the garden keeps changing as a result.

'I'm over the moon that integrating edibles and ornamentals has worked out so well. There are no strict guidelines that say you should grow them separately. You need an eye — or at least the confidence — to try combinations and not be afraid of getting it wrong: you can always move things and try other pairings. I think it's not something you can be taught — you have to give things a try and learn from yourself as well as taking ideas from others.

'When I came here, there was a wall on one edge, so I added fences to the other sides to create privacy and a sense of it being a special world away from the rest of life. That enclosure and shelter also really helps many of the plants flourish. It enables many of the more delicate or marginal plants to do well away from strong winds. Some tropical plants even thrive as long as I keep them dry and, in some cases, bring them under the roofed area for winter. Even after this short time people say the garden seems like it's been here forever. It established so quickly. That, at least in part, is due to the shelter.

'You enter the allotment into a roofed area which is very much part of the garden. I took the side off from what was a homemade greenhouse to create a covered area that protects vulnerable plants through the winter and that also acts as a veranda for guests.

'There's never any significant problem with pests or diseases — the blend of edible and ornamentals keeps things in an easy natural balance. The ladybirds take care of any upsurge in aphid populations; the small pond I created adds to the diversity, and the frogs slip out of the pond and head for my strawberry patch every evening, gorging on the slugs and protecting my fruit, and so on.

'The garden wasn't planned too heavily. I designed the shape of the beds and where I wanted fruit and so there are triangular beds at the top for a mini-orchard, with more ornamentals towards the other end. The rest evolves and changes as I get ideas either from what happens within the boundaries here or from other people and places.

'Mulching is the key to everything I do here. Just the effort of that keeps everything low maintenance. Barked pathways and pea shingle ensure great walkways and growing closely cropped plants underneath, along with compost as a mulch, minimises the weeds and the work that comes with them.

'As far as edibles go, I have lots of fruit bushes and trees — they make me happy — and inbetween I have climbers such as peas, kiwi, passion fruit, Stauntonia, chocolate vine and grapes, which colonise the fences as well as up and over other garden structures. There are also trailing tomatoes, standard tomatoes, aubergines, kohlrabi and other favourite vegetables around the fruit trees, along with plants like daylilies and nasturtiums that straddle the boundary of edible and ornamental. I share the excess with friends — it's something I love to do — as well as picking up recipes from other people on the allotment.

'It's now become my profession. I used to be a hairdresser but after studying for three years I changed my career to horticulture. Studying and working on other people's gardens has really helped me add to my own ideas and create something special here.

'There's no limit to what you can do, even in a small space. If you take some time and research well you can usually find a way of growing whatever takes your fancy. And it always tastes so much better, whether it's a plum or a tomato.'

266

Main features

- An abundant allotment
- Fences and walls offer privacy and shelter
- Marriage of edibles and ornamentals
- Marginals and even tropical plants grow well
- Open shelter – a combination of plant shelter and veranda, created from a preexisting greenhouse
- Rich in wildlife: bees, butterflies, dragonflies and other pollinators
- A small pond adds to the diversity

Particular plants and why

- Figs – they grow easily from cuttings, and with the heat and shelter here plants grow the most fabulous figs you can imagine
- Quince tree – prolific, reminding Chris of where he comes from in Cyprus and the fruit is used to make syrupy petit fours
- Stauntonia – a rambling climber that covers structures beautifully, with edible berries
- Early plums – for midsummer fruit
- Apricots – the shelter and warmth mean a reliable apricot crop every summer
- Grapes – allowed to ramble across and over structures to add architectural presence and to partially shade the under-cover area
- Lavender – for its looks, scent, the insects it attracts and to use as a herb

CHRIS SMITH'S METRE² BEDS,
Somerset

CHRIS SMITH SPENDS most days working at his nursery, Pennard Plants. After a day up to his elbows in plants, he doesn't have the time — nor possibly the inclination — to come home to a full-on veg patch.

Instead, he's created three raised beds, each just one-metre square, in which he grows delicious, unbuyable, low-maintenance vegetables and herbs.

Perennials dominate one bed: red oca, yacon and ulluco, along with a tripod of 'Crystal Lemon' yellow cucumbers.

A second bed is more diverse, with wild rocket, strawberry mint, 'Bulgarian Carrot' chilli, 'Good King Henry' spinach, 'Hooker's' onion, broadleaved sage, lemon thyme, broad-leaved thyme and 'Everlasting' onion providing small volume yet strongly flavoured harvests.

The third bed is all about low-maintenance, repeat-harvesting beans: 'Lazy Housewife', 'Cosse Violette', 'Cherokee Trail of Tears', haricot 'Aramis' and the runner bean 'Enorma'. Two plants of each create a dense, abundant tower of beans that give a long season of repeat picking.

Chris Smith: 'I'm away a lot at horticultural shows so, while I want a productive garden, it has to be low maintenance. These three beds give me exactly that, with each performing a very distinct function.

'The first bed is pretty much permanent, and dominated by three underground crops of replant-perennials. Oca, yacon and ulluco are all from South America and are resistant to the usual blight that hits all but the early potatoes and they are very tasty. Oca comes in a few colours – I grow red oca and, like the other two tubers, it tends to swell as the days shorten. All three are lifted after the first frosts hit the leaves, giving me end-of-season harvests. Some of those I eat and some I store to replant next year. Oca's sorrel-like lemon flavour sweetens if they are kept a while in the sun, and they are superb raw or cooked, especially roasted.

'None of the beds requires weeding. I've planted closely so that there are few gaps, which naturally mulches the beds and keeps watering to a minimum. Where there was space beneath the beans when they were first planted out, I interplanted with sweet Williams, which not only looks beautiful but also draws in the beneficial insects.

'Growing in containers – and these raised beds are essentially large containers – is all about maintaining fertility. Each of these

raised beds was filled with a mix of mushroom compost, garden compost, manure and a little bark as an initial mulch. As the season progresses, I water a little in dry spells and once the plants are growing well I give them the odd feed of liquid seaweed fertiliser. The first year is generally trouble free as the growing medium is still fresh, but this winter and in subsequent years I'll be adding more compost, manure and seaweed both to refresh the growing medium with nutrients and because compaction usually takes place over time and the level settles down.

'Even though the space is far from vast, having the three beds planted as they are gives me great variety. The "flavours" bed gives something for most of the year; the beans are harvested over a long period; and then late on in autumn the bed dominated by the perennials comes into its own.

'Yacon is a fantastic plant. It is a South American tuber (like the potato) that grows to 1–1.2m, producing large, fleshy, beautiful leaves above ground and tubers beneath. In a sunny summer, you get small yellow flowers at the apex of each stem. It's grown quite like a dahlia. I wait to harvest until after the frosts hit the leaves but before any big freeze is forecast. Of the tubers lifted, the largest are left in the sun (weather permitting) to sweeten before eating, while the smallest are stored with a little shoot of top growth still attached in a dry, frost-free spot (paper bags are fine) and replanted the following spring. Their fresh green apple flavour ripens to something pear-like, and it is very good in a fruit salad. I also roast or curry yacon (as I do oca and ulluco) and it takes on other flavours beautifully.

'Ulluco is the third of the South American tubers in the bed, still very rare in the UK, and so suffers none of the diseases, not even blight, that can affect potatoes. They come in a variety of colours — mine are reds, greens, purples — and they give me a great late-season crop, very much like a good potato.

'It's year one of trialling these beds, and I'm happy with how it's gone. The metre-square approach is a great way of creating a low-cost, low-maintenance garden and making a patch of otherwise unused space outside the house productive. And perhaps the genius of it lies in the garden being three distinct beds, which helps focus and organise your thinking about what to grow.'

Particular plants and why

- Perennial onions – 'Hooker's' onion, which is a broadleaved, hardy, Indian onion, and 'Everlasting' onion, from which you can break off pieces like spring onions or harvest like Chinese chives
- Ulluco – a nutty, potato-like Andean tuber that is easy to grow and perennial
- Oca – a trouble-free perennial tuber that looks like a knobbly 'Pink Fir Apple' potato. It is superb raw or cooked
- Yacon – a disease-free tuber that tastes of mild pears
- 'Good King Henry' spinach – it doesn't like pots but grows well in a raised bed
- 'Malabar' spinach – delicious, unbuyable, grows all year round and is low maintenance
- 'Crystal Lemon' cucumber – almost spherical yellow cucumbers, with a fresh flavour and a cool, crisp texture
- Climbing French beans and runner beans – providing a huge harvest for the floor space used
- Strawberry mint – a fresh, fruity mint with fabulous flowers that insects love. Superb in cocktails and fruit salads
- Broadleaved sage – with large leaves for easy kitchen use
- Lemon, orange and broadleaved thyme – a selection to complement fish, meat and even fruit salads

273

Main features

- Three Im² beds
- Each space with its own purpose and identity
- Predominantly unbuyable crops
- Low maintenance
- A largely perennial bed, with unbuyable, disease-resistant tubers
- A 'flavours' bed, dominated by transforming flavours rather than bulky harvests
- A highly productive bed dedicated to repeat-harvest beans

LUCINDA'S FOOD FOREST,
London

GARDEN 6

LUCINDA JOHNSON'S GARDEN in Islington, north London, is a unique marriage of food forest and ornamental garden in the middle of the city. The principle of forest gardening, with its tiered approach to growing, is beautifully adapted to work in an urban situation. It keeps some order by incorporating themed areas within beds, rather than dedicating the whole space to being a food forest (as with the RISC garden on page 253). Productivity is important, but with beauty and flavour to the fore rather than just volume. Flowering plants provide aesthetic pleasure and cut flowers for the house, while attracting pollinators and predators for would-be pests.

The canopy layer that is uppermost in a classic forest garden is absent here so as to create space for other plants and allow light through to more of the garden. But there are plenty of trees on dwarfing rootstocks or trained as fans, cordons, espaliers and pleaches. This allows a wide range of fruit and nuts to be planted, without restricting the amount of light reaching the lower layers.

Beneath the trees are smaller shrubs, a herbaceous layer, groundcover plants, subterranean harvests and climbers that scramble through plants and over structures.

Intermingled between the edible plants, flourish other plants in supporting roles. Nitrogen fixers, including yellow trefoil and autumn olive, nourish the soil by taking nitrogen from the air and making it available to other plants through their root systems and/ or leaf fall. Mineral accumulators, including comfrey, drive their roots deep into the soil, bringing nutrients and other trace elements from low in the soil up to the topsoil when their leaves are cut. The combination of accumulators and nitrogen fixers helps to naturally maintain fertility, while many — trefoil and comfrey among them — draw in pollinators and other beneficial insects.

In Lucinda's full and flowing garden there is no bare soil, minimising the need for watering and weeding. The widespread use of herbs in the underplanting means that the beds remain productive for much of the year while being strikingly beautiful.

Although the garden is very new (it was planted in 2013) plants are already starting to knit together, to make relationships with each other that will become even stronger over the years. It is a low-maintenance garden: in time, the work will predominantly be about controlling the spread and desire of some to dominate and allowing others to breathe.

From a distance it can look like a bit of a jumble, but when viewed up close the order, pattern and identity of the distinctly different areas becomes apparent. Microclimates have been taken advantage of, exploiting the mix of dappled shade, deep shade and very light areas — for example, there are Mediterranean herbs planted underneath the large olive tree in the sunniest, most well-drained spot. It's a garden that serves many needs and desires.

Lucinda Johnson: 'We wanted the garden to feel quite natural, not to be too ordered for the most part. It looks a little crazy, like it'd be an adventure to walk around discovering flavours, scents and beauty — and it is. The first thing we do every morning is to come and look around. As it's so new, we've forgotten what we've planted here and there to some degree, so there are some very welcome surprises.

'Martin (my husband) and I have always been very interested in growing as much as we can that we can eat or cut and put in a vase for the house. The mix very much reflects those flavours and plants we know and love but we also wanted to have things from the places we love: plants the city allows us to grow that somewhere less urban might not. We've experimented with olives and some other great flavours that are relatively new to us, like perilla and Vietnamese coriander, which are fabulous yet not very common. This garden has opened up a new larder of flavours and has a balance of flowers that suits us both.

'We'd been thinking about having a garden together for a long time and so we started with a very long list. We wanted to plant a really big variety of the things we loved so it was nice to find a way to put in as much as we can into the space.

'It's a young garden — barely a year old — and it's been a tough first year with a hot summer and little rainfall. This has made it particularly hard with our predominantly sandy soil, but most plants seem to have flourished and it is already establishing well. It feels like it's been here for longer than it has and it already seems like a place rather than just a collection of plants.

'There have been some great results already. Many potentially marginal plants, such as peaches, have flourished, which has given us encouragement for pushing the boundary a little more: apricots are next. I can already see that this is a great exercise in experimental growing, where the garden keeps moving forward depending on the results. But as much as anything the pleasure has been in enjoying the best of the familiar. The flavour, freshness and vitality in peas, courgettes and other veg you can take for granted have been extraordinary. Picking them at their best rather than putting up with what the shops have has been a repeating joy. Add to that the new flavours and recipes — even down to a whole range of new delicious herb teas, picked and enjoyed at peak freshness — and it is hard to beat.'

Main features

- A productive garden of beds, based on forest garden principles
- Dominated by low-maintenance, perennial plants
- Pollinator friendly
- Provides many of the nutrients required within the ecosystem
- High side-planting maximises privacy
- Provides drinks, food and cut flowers for the house
- Driven by flavour more than yield
- Pleached pears
- Large specimens, including olive, grapes and Szechuan pepper
- A dense swathe of underplanting, dominated by herbs such as lavender, anise hyssop and red valerian
- Areas dominated by colour combinations and microclimates, such as a predominantly red area comprising red daylilies, bergamot and white chives beneath wineberries, Japanese quince and Carolina allspice

Particular plants and why

- A large standard grape – for instant productivity, but equally to provide structure and presence in such a young garden
- Trained fruit against the walls – using the heat from the walls to encourage a good harvest while taking up little space
- Mexican tree spinach – self-sowing salad leaves in unexpected places through the year, with beautiful pink and green leaves
- Chocolate vine, using existing trees as a scaffold – chocolate-scented flowers, followed (in a good summer) by pods filled with melon-flavoured pulp
- Nasturtiums and sweet cicely – for their leaves, seeds and flowers, and as insect-friendly groundcover in partial shade
- Salad burnet and alpine strawberries – sharing a spot with good sun for part of the day, harvested together for cocktails
- Globe artichokes – for their expensive-to-buy artichokes but also for structure and inhabiting the space between fruit trees, herbs and groundcover layers
- Kale and other brassicas – grown beneath the trained fruit, shading the roots and mulching out weeds

281

Charles Dowding's No-Dig Garden, *Somerset*

CHARLES' GARDEN IS one of the most quietly impressive I know. There is nothing seemingly out of the ordinary, few unusual or physically impressive specimens, but everything is immaculate, abundant and productive. It is a veg patch running at peak performance. Although he grows a wide range of vegetables outside and under cover, salad leaves dominate, forming the core of his production for customers.

Working without cultivating the ground, Charles adds layers of compost to feed and mulch the soil. It is a method so effective that, while some struggle to make a large farm viable, Charles' one-fifth of an acre provides a flourishing business growing vegetables for local outlets and families.

Charles' no-dig approach has at its heart the idea that well-cared-for soil develops a perfectly healthy profile of its own; a balance that is temporarily upset when dug or rotovated. Most of his energies are focused on feeding the soil with compost once a year to keep both organic matter and nutrient status in good heart and to act as a mulch.

Instead of engaging, as most traditional growers do, in an ongoing battle with weeds, the no-dig approach front-loads the effort, concentrating on eradicating existing weeds and exhausting or smothering out the seed bank that remains. The benefits are many.

In combination with allowing the soil structure to remain undisturbed, the annual application of organic matter builds fertility in a way that mimics nature, minimises ongoing weeds and encourages a soil ecology that's beneficial to healthy crops of all kinds. Water and nutrient availability is maximised thanks to worms and soil fauna in the undisturbed soil. This increased subterranean ecological activity also benefits soil bacteria and fungi, helping roots acquire nutrients.

The approach is hugely adaptable: it works on all soils — even clay — overcoming the limitations of inherent conditions through repeated applications of compost. And, as Charles' garden demonstrates, it works on a small commercial scale as well as for the home.

Charles Dowding: 'Starting out is the crucial stage; get this right and it makes life so much simpler than when perennial weeds are allowed to continue growing. Taking care of the weeds is what it's all about.

'If your potential growing space is full of perennial weeds — couch grass, buttercup and dandelion, etc. — I would advocate digging up and covering the space in black plastic for a year. Clean soil results and abundance awaits. If you can't bear to wait that long, you can always cover three-quarters of it and crop the rest. It sounds tedious to wait — we are all impatient — but if you intend to grow for more than a year or two the benefits are enormous.

'If your space is just lawn, without perennial weeds, starting off is simple: put 10cm of compost on the surface and start growing. Annual weeds and grasses will quietly die under the compost. Use cardboard for your paths, which otherwise are a reservoir for weeds, grass and slugs — all of which will seek to colonise your growing space. If you have a small space and/or just one bed, then wooden sides are worth erecting as they allow you to increase the amount of compost you use and up the fertility, which rewards you in produce. The extra investment is worth it. On a bigger, allotment scale, wooden sides can often harbour too many pests — slugs, woodlice and ants — hence I have mostly open beds.

'Once you've won your big battle with weeds up front, then the rest of the work is very much in harmony with the soil. It's not about an ongoing fight or gaining an upper hand on nature; it's about creating a different kind of environment that works with gentle but continual involvement. In that respect it has some parallels with forest gardening.

'Compost is essential. After an initial application of around 10cm, I spread 3–5cm once a year — even an inch will make things more productive. It can go on at any time, but autumn is probably best. It's when nature is dropping organic matter on the ground. It will not

only increase fertility, but act as a mulch to protect the soil against the weather. I have large loads of community compost delivered, but on a smaller scale you can either make your own or buy it in bags. This may seem expensive but not if you are operating at the right scale for your needs. This is crucial. If you are growing for yourself and family or you are a beginner, start small. Allotments are huge, so it's worth sharing one if you can.

'Two 1.5m x 5m beds will produce over 80kg of vegetables a year — a vast amount, largely thanks to the increased fertility and lack of weed competition inherent in the no-dig approach. Also because I replant in summer after early harvests. This approach means you can focus your time and energy on a small space, do it well, and really get enormous quantities of produce in proportion to the compost used. Even if you buy sacks of compost from the garden centre, the produce still makes it good value.

'The feeling is good, as you are constantly improving the ecosystem and growing conditions so the results are always improving. It builds confidence and momentum; you get drawn in. Weeding, which for most conventional gardeners is debilitating and dull, is very limited in no-dig. It is important though. Weeds come every year in compost and manure and the key to dealing with them is to get on the case early in mid-March to mid-April. Get out there with your hoe or rake as soon as you see that first hint of light green on the bare soil on a sunny morning. In this way, thousands of weeds can be eliminated. Once a week, I spend a moment walking through the beds pulling out weeds. This is the opposite experience to regular allotment weeding: it's light but effective.

'Yes, it requires you to commit to this way of growing, but then so does "normal" vegetable growing, which is very much stepping on a treadmill.

'If at all possible, invest in a propagating space, even if it is small. It is comparatively simple to look after a few square feet of young plants while they become established, rather than protect a whole plot of direct-sown seedlings. It means you can garden and start things off whatever the weather, and it keeps the vulnerable plants away from the dangers of pests, especially slugs.

'For maximum value from salad plants, I advocate cut-and-come-again harvesting. Taking off the outer leaves keeps the parent plant going for a long time. If you love salad, this is where you make the biggest difference. High-value salad leaves, produced over a long season, give you the best return on seeds and the time spent starting them off — and it keeps your patch more productive.'

Main features

- The initial phase concentrates on creating a weed-free growing area
- The soil is never dug, with a layer of compost added annually to build up fertility
- Beds are any width, from 1m–1.5m, allowing access from either side, with paths giving access for a wheelbarrow
- Highly productive from reduced effort
- Most plants are started off under cover where they can best be nurtured, then planted out when established, minimising unproductive periods
- Weekly weeding is light and easily achieved
- Good moisture retention
- Rather than pick whole lettuces or cutting rows of thickly sown seedlings, Charles takes a cut-and-come-again approach to salad harvesting

Particular plants and why

- 'Taunton Deane' or 'Daubenton's' perennial kale – has superb flavour and rarely sets seed, producing leaves almost all year round, for five or six years before the plants lose vigour
- 'Czar' runner beans – Charles leaves them unpicked until the pods dry on the plant, then harvests and shells what have become butterbeans. They are so delicious. Climbing borlotti beans are great too, for a dry harvest in autumn
- 'Uchiki (Red) Kuri' squash – a reliable harvest even in wet summers because they mature earlier than most butternuts and taste equally good

- 'Sungold' and 'Sweet Aperitif' tomatoes – two very different yet superb varieties. 'Sungold' is a balance of sweet and acid; 'Sweet Aperitif' is very much on the sweet side. 'Sungold' is early to crop – a great asset in Britain
- 'Boltardy' beetroot – so reliable from sowings at any time from February (under cover) to early July. Ideal for a second crop after harvests in early summer
- 'Lettuce Red Grenoble' for winter, and 'Maravilla di Verano' for summer – both Batavian varieties with pretty bronze leaves, firm texture and good flavour
- 'Red Baron' onions – grown from seed under cover in February reduces the risk of bolting. Having an abundance of red onions is a great feeling as winter approaches
- 'Medania' spinach – dark green leaves and hardy plants, it is especially good for summer sowing to overwinter, so you can enjoy abundant pickings in early spring
- 'Prinz' celeriac – sow under cover in March, watering well in a dry summer, then by October you will have large roots for use all winter. Does best in heavy soil for the moisture retention
- 'Solent Wight' garlic – small yields but exceptional flavour. Charles likes it raw for breakfast. . .

Anni Kelsey's Perennial Garden, *Wales*

GROWING 1000 FEET UP on the side of the Long Mountain in Powys, with rock beneath your feet and exposure to the elements as keen as the view, may not strike everyone as the perfect spot to create a garden. But Anni Kelsey hasn't let that impede her.

Colonising a patch of lawn, Anni has taken some of the principles of forest gardening and permaculture to create a productive, diverse and rather beautiful edible garden.

Idleness is very much part of the ethos of the garden: the endless interventions of growing annual vegetables aren't for Anni. Using predominantly perennial vegetables, fruit and herbs, along with a no-dig philosophy, mulches and companion planting, work and expense are kept to a bare minimum.

There are numerous replant-perennials (plants that require lifting over winter and storing in the dry, in shoeboxes or newspaper in the garage or attic) to reduce the impact of both extreme cold and over-exposure to moisture. Oca, yacon and dahlias are all lifted in the autumn, when their underground tubers are at their peak for eating, with some retained for replanting the following spring.

Alongside the obvious food plants, other unlikely suspects are allowed to flourish: dandelions are welcomed for their ability to accumulate minerals, thanks to their taproot, for drawing in beneficial insects, and for their edible leaves. Similarly, nettles are allowed to stay for their plant-feeding nitrogen and other minerals, while Anni harvests their seeds to make a good herbal tonic for the adrenal glands, and which are apparently superb sprinkled on porridge.

Anni Kelsey: 'I had an allotment a long time ago, but it was too much hard work, especially with the demands and pleasures of a family. I couldn't help but think there must be another way, and that's when I discovered perennials.

'Annuals are such a palaver to grow, and while this garden may not produce as much in volume as the equivalent, the flavours are wonderful, interesting and it is very low work.

'I came up with this idea for an integrated garden, a polyculture — but not a particularly planned one. Creating a mini-ecosystem was the aim, using plants from my old garden and others that took my fancy.

'The location is far from ideal for growing: the ground is solid clay and shale – completely un-trowelable! The creation was really driven by that. I took off the top layer of turf and turned it over to kill off the grass and planted into that. It is a great way of colonising unsuitable ground and even makes a low-energy method for perfectly good soil. As long as you pair it up with mulching to suppress the weeds and other unwanted growth.

'I use whatever's to hand: lawn mowings, hedge clippings, sticks and twigs. Nothing goes to the tip and I use the quickest method to get the material to the garden. If I can lay it on direct rather than compost it, I will. Either way, I refuse to export fertility as it is unsustainable and creates more work and expense in the long term. Other than a little time mulching (and the grass cuttings have to be tipped somewhere, so it's not extra work), the little ongoing maintenance is pretty much restricted to deadheading flowers and getting rid of the odd buttercup that pops up from the upturned turf.

'Mulching also helps retain water. Nothing here gets anything other than an initial watering when planted, apart from the Jerusalem artichokes which can flop in an extended summer dry spell.

'In the same way as an annual vegetable garden can look unimpressive early in the season, a perennial garden can be slow to start in its first year. This looked semi-empty in its first June, but full and abundant by July. And, once established, perennials typically grow quickly and early in the season, having an established root system that is ready to drive growth above ground.

'I like to plant as many edibles as I can whenever there's an opportunity that I spot. I'm planting oca, daylilies, figs, currants, wild marjoram, land cress, golden hops, wild strawberries and runner beans into the old hedge that borders our property to go with the existing wild rose, hazel, blackthorn, elder, hawthorn and damson. It extends the productivity of our patch and leaves more space in the garden.

'My partner, Pat, has also taken on the principles and has created a polyculture pot: a mix of perennials and annuals including oca, skirret, lettuce, tomato, Welsh onion and wild rocket. She did it to prove that it works on a small scale, with some things – oca, especially – thriving in the container conditions.

'My approach is playful and inquisitive rather than serious. The focus is very much on experimenting and easiness. It is a garden for people who have only so much time they can or want to give.'

PLANTING KEY

1. SQUASH
2. FIELD BEANS
3. APPLE
4. COURGETTES
5. MARIGOLDS
6. RUNNER BEANS
7. PEAS
8. POTATOES
9. MOOLI
10. DAHLIA
11. BUNCHING ONIONS
12. SHALLOTS
13. WELSH ONIONS
14. GROUND NUT
15. SUNFLOWERS
16. JERUSALEM ARTICHOKES
17. OCA
18. MASHUA
19. CHARD
20. RADISHES
21. BURDOCK
22. FENNEL
23. CARROTS
24. COSMOS
25. YACON
26. TOAD FLAX
27. BLACKCURRANT
28. WILD KALE
29. SKIRRET
30. BORAGE
31. PURPLE SPROUTING BROCCOLI
32. BUCKWHEAT
33. WILD MARJORAM
34. WILD ROCKET
35. LETTUCE
36. LEMON BALM

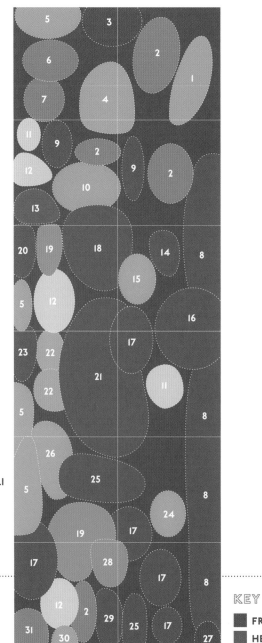

KEY

FRUIT
HERBS
ROOTS
ONIONS
FLOWERS
PEAS, BEANS, BRASSICAS
LEAVES
SUMMER VEGETABLES

Main features

- A no-dig, low-maintenance garden
- An integrated polyculture of largely perennial plants
- Interplanted mineral accumulators, nitrogen fixers and insect attractors
- Experimental and constantly evolving
- Colonising ground otherwise unsuitable for growing vegetables
- Fertility maintained from onsite
- Adaptable to even smaller spaces

Particular plants and why

- Oca – a delicious, perennial tuber from South America that experiences none of the usual potato troubles
- Yacon – another trouble-free perennial tuber from South America. It tastes of early apples or pears
- Dahlias – grown for their edible roots (as well as their ornamental flowers) and used to make rosti
- Welsh onion – a perennial onion from China (go figure), that can be grown in bunches and harvested as shallot-like onions or spring onions. Dies down in winter but reappears in early spring
- Kales – allowed to perennialise
- Skirret – in looks and flavour it is a cross between carrots and parsnip. Once popular, grown for centuries and making a comeback
- Radishes – some are allowed to go to seed, with Anni using the pods in ratatouille, and saving some for sowing in winter for micros
- Shallots and onions – some are harvested in season, while others are permitted to flower to provide next year's seed
- Burdock, grown for its root – an experiment to investigate its flavour and uses
- Some annuals, such as courgette and squash – large-leaved, repeat-cropping annual vegetables that mulch the ground with their leaves
- Fennel and carrots – for their gorgeous flowers and to attract insects. Anni replants the tops of harvested carrots, and allows them to flower

299

Le Manoir Heritage Garden, *Oxfordshire*

VISITING THE NEW HERITAGE GARDEN at the Belmond Le Manoir aux Quat'Saisons is something of a pilgrimage for food lovers, and especially for me. When we got together, my now-wife was always in the garden. I grew vegetables in the hope of seeing her occasionally. Thankfully, I had the good sense to source some from Garden Organic's Heritage Seed Library: that first summer's harvest may have been grown with little skill but the difference in flavour between what I harvested and what I used to buy from the shops was like squash and juice. I was hooked.

Le Manoir Heritage Garden shows off these varieties to the full. Although little larger than the average allotment, it is home to almost 150 vegetable varieties, almost all of which are over a hundred years old. A few, such as 'Painted Lady' runner beans and the appropriately named 'Merveille des Quatre Saisons', are widely available. Others had to be sourced from specialist seed suppliers, including 'Cherokee Trail of Tears', which was originally grown by native North Americans driven out of their homelands in the early 1800s to make room for European settlers. Although most were chosen either as existing favourites at Le Manoir or for their reputation for fine flavour, the odd one was chosen for very different reasons. '"Fat Lazy Blonde" lettuce is just too perfectly named not to try!' says Le Manoir's head gardener of thirty years, Anne-Marie Owens.

I know from my own garden that some heritage varieties are perfectly ordinary, but these are far outweighed by the many that are head and shoulders above the widely available commercial varieties, where uniformity and disease resistance are prioritised over flavour. Scarcity of seed is an issue for many heritage varieties, and the garden team is growing some in an attempt to multiply the seed reserve of those most at risk of disappearing. This also helps promote the value for domestic gardeners in saving seed: not only do you have free seed for the next growing season, but using seed produced from the best plants in your garden helps build up resistance to disease and resilience to the particularities of your microclimate.

As with all the vegetables, herbs and fruit at Le Manoir, flavour is the overriding consideration. Everything is strictly blind taste-tested by the chefs and garden team, with the best grown the following year, and perhaps finding their way into larger scale production in the main garden.

Although less than a year old, the Heritage Garden is thriving and slips easily into the immaculate gardens of Le Manoir. It is a sparkling collaboration between the Le Manoir team led by Raymond Blanc, Garden Organic, Hartley Botanic (whose impressive glasshouse provides the garden's backdrop and the home of a new gardening school) and Anne Keenan, who won the Society of Garden Designers competition to design the garden.

Anne-Marie Owens: 'Everything here is always moving forwards and pushing the boundaries. The connection between the chefs and gardeners means whatever we grow is tested in blind tastings which we all take part in. A new variety of potato will be boiled, steamed, roasted, puréed, sautéed — whatever we can try to see how it is at its best. Each year, we will grow whatever comes out best in these tests and trial whichever other heritage varieties grab our attention.'

The splendidly named David Love Cameron won a scholarship to Le Manoir, specifically to be involved in the Heritage Garden: 'Before coming here, I read about "Carruthers' Purple Podded" pea, grown on the shores of County Down — where I'm from — for over a hundred years. I lay my hands on some thanks to a radio appeal. An 86-year-old man who had become too frail to garden passed them on to me. In this summer's pea taste test they came out top, yet could easily have been lost if we and the Heritage Seed Library weren't growing them.'

This ongoing search for excellence doesn't make for an easy life for

the gardeners. Anna Greenland, Head Vegetable Gardener: 'Working for Raymond is challenging. We have to produce the finest vegetables for the kitchen while keeping the garden immaculate for guests, and on top of that he has so many ideas. Your work is never done, but it is hugely stimulating. He always asks that extra question – reaching for excellence rather than being critical. He's very knowledgeable yet respects the team's thoughts, and ensures that we are all part of the same ethos, where we are all learning so much every day.'

And the garden clearly has a special place in Raymond's heart too: 'The first thing I did when I came to Le Manoir was to create the garden, to make it as important a part of what we were hoping to build as the kitchen, to create a centre of excellence, with the garden at its heart. The Heritage Garden is particularly precious to me. It encapsulates the purity and the nobility of food, and of seeds and the importance of conserving them. The best of the heritage varieties have a unique flavour, and growing them helps us all move away from the hold commercial agriculture has over the food we enjoy. What the Heritage Seed Library and this garden do is open up a world of flavours, of varieties that have complexity and a more satisfying layering of flavours than most in the shops. Heritage varieties can help us to re-educate our palates away from valuing solely sweetness, by which our modern diet is so dominated. Food is about way more than the kitchen though; it connects with everything: the love we share around the table, what kind of town or village we will have tomorrow … what kind of food our children will eat, the seasons, the terroir, the joy of the harvest. Our horticultural and culinary heritage is central to this and I hope this garden inspires others to explore it and the unique flavours that any of us can grow and eat.'

307

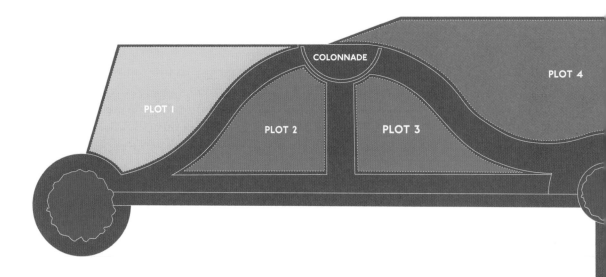

Main features

- A beautiful stand-alone garden within the wider garden of Le Manoir
- A garden of heritage varieties of vegetables and herbs
- Raising awareness about the issues of seed/ genetic diversity
- Promoting seed saving
- Growing some varieties to increase the seed bank of those varieties
- Varieties chosen for flavour
- Involvement of both chefs and garden team
- Evolving yearly as new varieties are chosen

Particular plants and why

- 'Carruthers' Purple Podded' pea – brought to Le Manoir from its home in Northern Ireland and winner of the pea taste test. Grown along with 'Black Badger' and 'Carouby de Maussane' to save for seed and increase the seed bank as well as for eating
- 'De Croissy' turnips – a delicious white-fleshed variety, Raymond's favourite and winner of the taste test

- 'Chioggia', 'Golden' and 'Cheltenham Green Top' beetroots – each superb and different colour as well as flavour
- A variety of climbing beans that produce over a long season – including 'Cherokee Trail of Tears' and 'Painted Lady'
- A sea of chard – including 'Flamingo' and 'Fordhook Giant' (which is over 250 years old) for cut-and-come-again leaves
- 'Empress of India' nasturtium – delicious flowers and leaves, and a fine companion plant, especially for brassicas
- Squash – including 'Pattison Blanc' and 'Tromboncino', a climbing variety
- 'Golden Bantam', 'Rainbow Sweet Inca' and 'Bloody Butcher' sweetcorn – for a balanced flavour rather than just full-on sweetness
- 'Sweet Florence' fennel – with an earliest record dating to 1667, it is the oldest known variety grown in the garden

KEY

- SQUASH
- CABBAGE, KALE, SPROUTS, CLIMBING BEANS
- COURGETTES, CHARD, SWEETCORN, BROAD BEANS, FRENCH BEANS
- LETTUCE, CELERIAC, BEETROOT, FENNEL
- ONIONS, CARROTS, LEEKS
- RADISH, TURNIPS, SPINACH, CHICORY

NELL DIACONO'S STEP GARDEN, *Devon*

ON THE STEPS leading from the back door up into the garden, and out into the fields of Otter Farm, my nine-year-old daughter, Nell, has created her own container garden. Pots of highly flavoured herbs and spices are pushed to the sides of each step, leaving just enough room for her parents to sidestep by without too much risk of injury.

Almost everything in these twenty or so pots is perennial and falls into the collection of plants I think of as transformers: those harvests that are high on flavour, small in volume and that lend their intensity to plainer staples (see page 32).

Szechuan pepper, scented pelargoniums, lemon verbena, three varieties of mint, perilla and tarragon are among the plants growing, and each is there because at some point over the last year or two, Nell has enjoyed their flavour in the food we've cooked. They've now become an avenue for her own adventures in the kitchen.

I've had very little involvement in Nell's choice of plants, but if I had I would have recommended she went very much down this road as they suit the way she likes to grow. The plants are predominantly perennial, so there's no need to start most off each spring, and they become productive very early in the season, which pairs up their availability with her springtime enthusiasm for growing and cooking.

Nell Diacono: 'Being on the steps is really good. I can sit here and read a book with a snack after school and smell the plants if I want to.

And if I want a cup of tea I can just take a few leaves off the mint or lemon verbena without having to walk further.

'The strawberry mint is exactly what its name says. It smells and tastes of strawberries and mint at the same time. I like sitting and rubbing the leaves, even if I'm not going to pick any. It makes fruit drinks and smoothies more interesting and I know Dad likes it in some cocktails.

'Basil mint is good too. I think that's the best one in salads but you have to cut the leaves up or pick the smallest ones, as the big leaves can be chewy and a bit too strong in one go.

'Moroccan mint is my favourite one for making tea. Dad said it was the best for that and I think he was right. It's even better when mixed in with lemon verbena leaves as it makes it sweeter. There's a big patch of Moroccan mint out in the field but having a pot near the house means I use it more as I don't always want to walk that far, especially if I'm in a hurry or a bit tired after school.

'I like the smell of scented geraniums and I've three on the steps. One smells of oranges, one of limes and the other is like Turkish delight. They all smell nice but I've only used the Turkish delight one. I made a syrup to have on ice cream.

'We grow lots of Szechuan peppers on the farm, but this one is mine. The leaves and the peppercorns are quite strong but I like spicy things. Watch out, as the peppercorns can make your lips and tongue tingle!

'I get lots of smells and flavours from quite a small space and I don't have to do much to look after them; just some watering once in a while.

'The garlic flowers (*Tulbaghia*) are really good. Mum grows garlic, which takes a long time to get ready to pick. I like it but these garlic flowers are ready really early and it keeps making new flowers all summer and into autumn. You shouldn't actually cook them but they are very good on salads. They don't make everything taste of garlic; you just get a big taste of garlic once in a while.

'Tarragon is not very nice on its own but I like to put it in the chicken before it's cooked. I don't rub and smell that one much but I like the flavour in cooking.

'I like having everything in pots because then I don't have to do any weeding. I can also change the order around if I get a bit bored of them as they are. And best of all, they go into the polytunnel when it starts to get cold, which means I can still pick some of them through the winter. Some of them die back but being indoors means they are still alive under the surface and they grow again in spring. And if I want to have my garden at the end of the main garden or nearer to the back door, then I can.

'I've got lots of ideas for next year. I think it'd be good to have basil, which I like a lot. We have had that a lot this summer, mostly in salads and with tomatoes and I'd like to have some of my own growing. I think lavender would be good too. There is some in the garden already, but I like the flowers and bees seem to too. I like chocolate mint as well. It makes a tea that tastes like chocolates and mint and Dad poaches peaches with it and it's really good.'

316

Main features

- A garden of around 20 containers on the garden steps
- Aromatic when rubbed or used
- All are transformers – herbs and spices
- Largely perennials
- Unbuyables
- Most are overwintered under cover
- Close to the house for easy kitchen access
- Low maintenance

Particular plants and why

- Strawberry mint – one of the few fruit-mints that smells and tastes as you'd hope
- Moroccan mint – the best for tea
- Scented geraniums (pelargoniums) – a variety of beautiful scents
- Szechuan pepper – spicy peppercorns and peppery leaves to rub and use in the kitchen
- Society garlic – punchy garlic-flavoured flowers that produce over a long season
- Tarragon – not Nell's favourite in itself, but likes it with roast chicken
- Perilla – a spicy herb that tastes and smells somewhere between cumin and mint
- Lemon verbena – smells of sherbet lemons
- Basil mint – another mint that is the flavour and aroma promised by its name

OTTER FARM,
Devon

SEVENTEEN ACRES MAY seem like a scale so large as to be irrelevant to most people. Yet many of the principles and thought processes apply whether you have a farm or a handkerchief of a garden.

Otter Farm is all about flavour. The starting point is in the kitchen, as well as the ending. What grows here is the answer to the question, 'What do I most want to eat?', and that is just about the finest recipe to a happy edible garden as I can think of, whatever the size.

Having spent a couple of years growing vegetables, a few herbs and a little fruit, I couldn't shake the feeling that there might be a better way. Good though the harvests were, I suspected the flavours could be more delicious and that there might be another way of growing them.

When we moved here, I made a conscious decision to start with a clean slate. Arriving at the start of winter gave me time to think before the growing season began – not necessarily a good thing in my case.

After much agonising and many abandoned scribbles, the penny dropped: I made a list of flavours rather than plants. Then I read like crazy. Gradually a picture formed. Out went the plants that weren't viable in our climate, and the remainder fell into three distinct groups: the best of the familiar veg, fruit and herbs I'd already grown; flavours that had, for one reason or another, fallen out of favour; and some marginal plants that might produce in the conditions we will experience in the climate change we are already committed to.

So, how to organise everything from this flavoursome list.

I wanted to grow some in sufficient quantities to give either sellable harvests (such as the vineyard) or where we wanted a year-long supply of something in particular – we'd need a good few apple trees to keep us in juice and cider. Apples, pecans, almonds, quince, medlars and sweet chestnuts were the prime candidates to be planted.

Having been bowled over by a visit to Martin Crawford's forest garden in south Devon, I wanted to create something here that used some of the same principles. Forest gardens are modelled on natural woodlands, designed in tiers of differing height, from trees, through shrubs and herbaceous layers, to groundcovers, with underground harvests and climbers completing the layers. Plants that naturally feed their neighbours are integrated with the edibles. Nitrogen fixers take nitrogen from the air and make this key nutrient available via their roots or through the leaves when they fall; mineral accumulators draw nutrients and minerals into their deep roots from low in the soil profile and, when they are chopped back or parts die, make it available to plants at the surface.

Forest gardens can take time and effort to get underway but they are also home to a range of plants and flavours that are ready across the growing season. Both of these were factors that influenced the decision to put the forest garden fairly near the house, where we can pay them the attention they need. Once established, forest gardens are low-maintenance, low-energy, highly productive spaces that maintain a natural balance with only occasional interference – largely to ensure one plant's expansion isn't at the expense of another.

The perennial garden takes the forest garden model, but does away with the tall tree layer, tailoring the idea to a space smaller than an allotment and emphasising the herbaceous and shrub layers. Diversity is maximised, with a weed-suppressing groundcover of creeping strawberries, chocolate vine and mints lightening the workload while providing delicious harvests.

The veg patch is home to all of the annual veg and many of the perennial vegetables – everything from potatoes and courgettes to 'Good King Henry' spinach and oca. Annuals, with their yearly cycle of sowing, growing and harvesting, need regular attention – hence their position near to the house.

Edible hedges subdivide and punctuate the farm. Szechuan pepper, autumn olive, hedgerow rose and hazel hedges not only form linear orchards of sorts, but also act as a windbreak for the plants on the leeward side.

Main features

- Forgotten fruit, such as quince and medlars
- Climate-change plants including almonds, peaches and pecans
- Planted to provide many of the nutrients required within the system
- Driven by flavour more than yield
- Areas requiring most attention are nearest the house
- Four acres of vineyard
- Edible hedges, including Szechuan pepper and autumn olives
- Orchards of fruits and nuts
- A perennial garden, based on forest garden principles but smaller in scale
- Veg patch

Particular plants and why

- Szechuan pepper – a beautiful plant with aromatic, delicious leaves and peppercorns. One mature plant will give you all the pepper you'll ever need. Also an edible hedge
- Autumn olive – with leaves similar to the familiar olive, this plant forms a nitrogen-fixing hedge that moves beautifully in the breeze, fertilises neighbouring plants and provides delicious fruit late into autumn
- Japanese wineberry – the reddish-pink bristled canes light up the perennial garden in winter, while the gorgeous fruit (like raspberries but more wine-like in flavour) fill the lull between summer- and autumn-fruiting raspberries perfectly
- Pecans – one for a large space, and slow to mature, but what incredible nuts
- Moroccan mint – productive, aromatic, and needing no attention at all, this variety is clean, fresh and lively, the perfect one for mojitos, tea and mint sauce. My desert-island mint
- Quince – not widely available in the shops and expensive when they are, quince

322

have a depth of flavour and aroma that is completely unique, and as much a spice as a fruit. Now available as a true dwarf, which makes it a possibility for container growing in even the smallest of gardens
- Society garlic – a gorgeous perennial plant with white-pink flowers that taste strongly, yet not harshly, of garlic, while leaving no trace on the breath – hence its name. Flowers abundantly from April into autumn
- Broad beans – as much for the scent of the flowers (which are as fine as any ornamental) as the beans. Prolific, delicious and easy to grow
- Mulberries – the finest fruit there is, and only available to those who grow it or their friends. A tree with a beautiful, lazy habit and glorious heart-shaped leaves
- Asparagus – the sign that spring has arrived and the best advert there is for the superior taste of homegrown vegetables. Sweet, succulent and perennial

PLANTING KEY

1. QUINCE
2. MEDLARS
3. ALMONDS
4. PERRY PEARS
5. SWEET CHESTNUTS
6. PERSIMMONS
7. PECANS
8. PEACHES
9. MULBERRIES
10. APRICOTS
11. VINES
12. JAPANESE PLUMS
13. APPLES (DEVON ORCHARD)
14. ROSA RUGOSA
15. SZECHUAN PEPPER
16. AUTUMN OLIVE
17. VEGETABLE GARDEN
18. FOREST GARDEN
19. PERENNIAL GARDEN
20. PHACELIA AND CLOVER
21. FRUIT CAGE

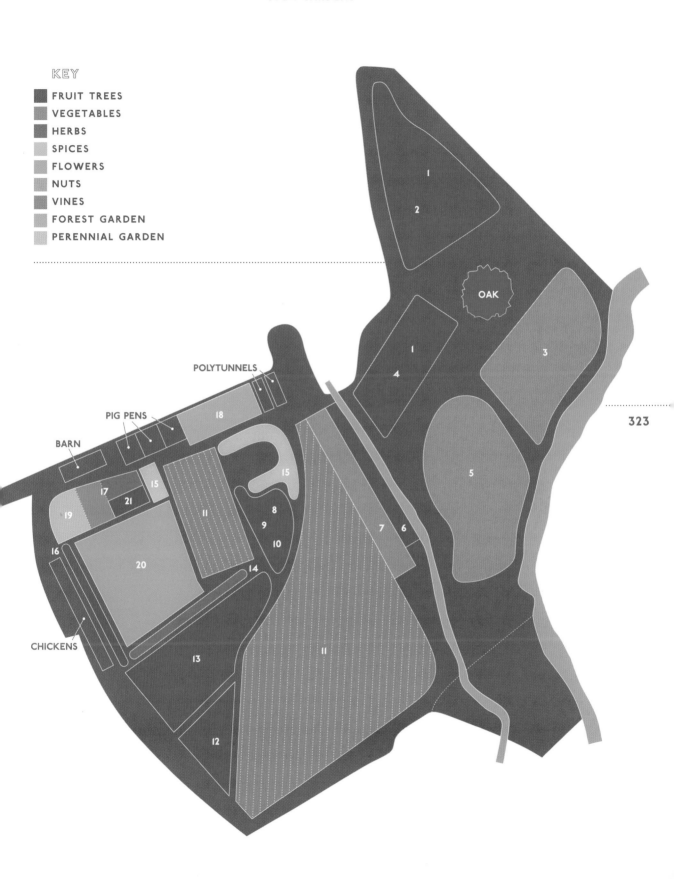

KEY

■ FRUIT TREES
■ VEGETABLES
■ HERBS
■ SPICES
■ FLOWERS
■ NUTS
■ VINES
■ FOREST GARDEN
■ PERENNIAL GARDEN

OAK

1
2

1
4

3

POLYTUNNELS

PIG PENS

BARN

18

5

323

15

17   15
21

19   11

8
9
10

7   6

16

20

14

CHICKENS

13

11

12

CHAPTER 5

CREATING YOUR KITCHEN GARDEN

WHATEVER FORM YOUR garden takes, whether it's measured in acres or inches, be it a classic allotment, forest garden or a clutch of pots, a good start is vital. As with most things, building momentum encourages success and reduces the likelihood of failure.

Get to know your soil, minimise the presence of weeds or any other unwanted groundcover such as grass, and start thinking about getting started with the business of growing.

There are choices still to be made: which rootstock for trees, whether to start with seeds or plants and, if seeds, whether to start off under cover or direct, and to plan for successive harvests or gluts, among them. It's all straightforward; it just needs a little consideration before you leap in.

GETTING TO KNOW YOUR SOIL

There are two types of gardener: those who dedicate the majority of their time caring for the plants, and those who spend most of it looking after the soil. Be in the latter camp. I must've said that in every book I've written and on every course I've given, and why not: it is at the heart of what makes an abundant, healthy garden.

Whether your kitchen garden is a newly colonised field, a reclaimed urban space, an allotment or a collection of containers, the health and vitality of the growing medium is something you should concern yourself with from the off. With a healthy soil and a reasonable position in which to grow, your plants will need little else to help them on their way.

Largely hidden, soil is easily neglected – get to know it from the off and you'll have started a fruitful relationship that will keep you in abundant harvests.

Before you plant a thing, plunge your hands into the earth and thoroughly acquaint yourself with it – it helps you to understand any potential growing issues you might face. Once you know its basic condition, it's all about improvement, if needed, and then good habits to keep it fertile and in good heart.

SOIL STRUCTURE

Structure is all about the physical make-up of your soil, it indicates something of the way the soil particles cling together, and does much to determine how easily your plants will thrive and the relative availability of nutrients and water.

This is easiest to picture if you imagine yourself as a root, pushing into the soil. Within a clay soil the soil particles are small, smooth and shiny, and packed close together. It is a struggle for a root to penetrate, but once there it is strongly anchored. Clay soils are cold and unwelcoming in spring, but good at holding on to moisture, which comes in handy in summer. They can become claggy and hard to work. Sandy soils are the opposite. The particles are large and gritty, and they don't readily stick to each other. These soils are easy to work and warm up quickly, and a root can push its way through with ease, but they also dry out fast and often lack nutrients, which drain away with the water. A loamy soil is somewhere between the two: more nutrient rich and water retentive than a sandy soil, easier to work than a clay soil. Very much a happy medium.

You can find out which of these soils you have by performing the far-less-fun-than-it-sounds 'sausage test'. Take a handful of soil and try to roll it into a sausage shape (add some water if needed). If your soil is high in clay it will form the perfect sausage; you may even be able to smooth it with your thumb and create an almost shiny surface. If your sausage falls apart easily you have a sandy soil, and should you rub a little between thumb and fingers you will be able to feel those big particles: the soil will feel gritty to the touch. A loamy soil will be something between the two.

You might think that each soil issue would have an entirely different solution, but no. The horticultural magic wand is organic matter.

Organic matter can take several forms – garden compost and well-rotted farmyard manure are the most common. This universal panacea will lighten a clay soil and add body and heart to a sandy one, gradually turning each into a well-balanced, healthy soil, ideal for growing in.

Dug into soil or laid on top to be slowly worked in by weather and worms, organic matter rots down further into humus, a fairly stable form of organic matter that benefits any soil. In the case of clay soil, it forces the particles apart, creating a more easily worked structure, and allowing water and roots to move through it more freely. In the case of a sandy soil it provides something to cling to, for both water and the soil particles themselves. It sticks those abrasive, gritty particles together. This makes a soil more water retentive and less prone to drying out, and gives it more substance. In short, it brings soils to a happy middle ground and helps to keep them there.

THE pH OF YOUR SOIL

The pH scale is a measure of relative alkalinity or acidity, which in the case of your soil will do much to determine which plants will thrive (or not) in your garden. In a garden situation, mildly acidic soils

are more common than alkaline ones, and while some plants will do well in extremes of acidity and alkalinity, most are happiest in reasonably neutral conditions, somewhere in the centre of the pH scale. Unless you intend to largely grow plants that favour the extremes, I'd suggest you aim for this middle ground.

First up, you need to check on the pH of your soil. An inexpensive kit is all you need: they're widely available online or in garden centres. Home testing kits are easy to use – dissolve a little soil in the liquid, dip the litmus paper into the solution and check the resulting colour against a chart – giving a quick and dirty indicator of your soil's pH.

If your soil is heavily acidic it's possible to add lime to draw it back towards neutrality, but in most instances you'll find the pH in need of only a little adjustment. Whether yours is acidic or alkaline,

327

needs 'diluting' away from strong alkalinity or acidity, or just needs maintaining at a reasonable neutrality, compost is the key.

If you are intent on growing plants that flourish in pH extremes (such as blueberries, with their need for acidity), I'd suggest doing so in containers where you can more easily set up and maintain the conditions they need.

COMPOST IN CONTAINERS

A container is its own little world. None of the concerns about your underlying soil structure matter here, because you can make of a pot whatever you wish. You may live in an area with stony or clay soil, but in a container you can make the growing medium friable and loose, and grow perfect long, straight carrots. You may have boggy soil in your garden that kills all silver-leaved herbs, but in a container you

can mix grit and compost until your oregano thinks it is nestling on a rocky Mediterranean hillside. Whether your container is a huge raised bed or a tiny pot, this is the joy of growing in containers: you are in complete control of the growing medium.

The basis for all pots should be good-quality, peat-free compost. From this starting point you can add other things to create the perfect mix for your chosen plant. Add horticultural grit if you want to grow plants that like more drainage, such as the Mediterranean herbs. If growing acid-lovers such as blueberries, opt for peat-free ericaceous compost, or add plenty of leaf mould. Biochar is a good addition to every container as it is so good at creating and maintaining a healthy structure, and at hanging on to water and nutrients and then releasing them as the plant needs. I would add a good dose of it to every container planting.

A CLEAN START FOR YOUR GARDEN

The nearer you start to a perfect, weed-free space the easier you are likely to find growing and the more time you will spend on the pleasure of gardening rather than what most people find is the tedium of weeding.

There are a number of ways of getting to a great starting place, some of them covered in Chapter 4 (*Open Gardens*) where experienced, knowledgeable growers share their thoughts.

First, be sure that your plant is really a weed. It's all about context: a weed is an unwanted plant rather than just an unexpected one. Perhaps 30% of my salad comes from self-sown lettuces, leaves and flowers – plants that crop up wherever chance has taken them – and for the most part they are welcome. I guess what I'm trying to say is, be sure the 'weed' is something you can't take advantage of: if you (and your crops) can live with it, and especially if it will be productive, perhaps let it stay. If it only has a negative impact, get it out sharpish.

A weeded bed may look tidier, but weeding is really about reducing the competition your plants are facing and creating an environment in which they will thrive. It's a tricky balance to strike as other little seedlings growing up beside your intended plants may look harmless enough, but if they compete for water and light, your plants may struggle as a result.

Some weeds (as with edible plants) are present for only one growing season, and their main threat is through multiplication by sowing their seeds through your garden. Perennials are an altogether more tedious prospect, reappearing year on year, as well as multiplying either by seed, lateral spread or if their roots are inadvertently chopped.

ANNUAL WEEDS

Some weeds have a light presence. Many common annual weeds – chickweed, hairy bittercress, fat hen among them – are edible and were once commonly eaten in the UK, and still are in many parts of the world. Annual weeds can be a little annoying and will certainly compete for light and nutrients, but they are very easy to deal with. Their attempt on world domination is limited to the casting about of seeds, so if you can get to them before they set seed – or even better before they flower – you will have nipped them in the bud. A quick hoe just under the surface will sever leaves from roots and they are gone.

A hoe is a hugely useful piece of equipment, particularly if kept clean and sharp. The idea is that it should slice through the ground just under the surface, chopping the weeds in two. It is particularly useful for keeping the ground clear between rows, but within the rows themselves you may have to hand weed with a trowel.

PERENNIAL WEEDS

Perennial weeds are those that regrow year after year: docks and nettles are among the most common. As a rule you can identify them by their roots: thick and white and looking like they are packed full of energy. They are. These are far trickier customers than the annual weeds, persistent and swamping, if they get the chance. A perennial weed doesn't die when you chop its head off. It has vast reserves in those roots and will shoot again from the tiniest piece. Once present, they are almost impossible to eradicate completely from your soil, but they can be mastered.

Whether you favour a dig or no-dig approach (see page 330), have an allotment largely of annuals or a forest garden, your first line of defence should be digging out the worst of the weeds, as it weakens the weed bank and stacks the odds in your favour. Next add plenty of organic matter. This will make the weeds grow more lushly, for sure, but it will also make them easier to remove: it is very tough trying to prise a couch grass root out of solid clay. Beyond this point your weapon is vigilance. Keep looking for new shoots that arise and dig them out with a hand fork every time. Never pull at them or chop the tops off, but carefully delve down into the soil and gently pull up as much root as you can get hold off.

If you are looking for an easy way out, the best method is to cover the soil with something that excludes light, such as plastic sheeting, and leave it there for at least six months over the growing season, even better a year or two. Given enough time this will completely kill the weeds beneath. Given a little less time it will certainly weaken them.

Effective options depend on the extent and nature of the weeds present: perennials need more determined removal than annuals. Run a rotovator over your ground and likely as not it'll look good; two weeks later, any perennial weeds you inadvertently chopped into small pieces will have happily re-sprouted, multiplied. If the weeds are largely annuals, a good hoeing or a thorough rotovating may be all that is required to prepare a weed-free garden. Perennials require either a thorough digging over and removal of all parts of the plant (to be safe), or an equally thorough suffocation. Both can work well, and have their pluses and shortcomings.

I've taken three approaches here at Otter Farm: I dug over the annual veg patch removing what perennials there were when we started growing here, but it usually requires a bit of weeding once or twice a year for those that spring up; I created raised beds using cardboard over the grass and infilling with compost, à la Charles Dowding (see page 284); and in creating the perennial garden I used mulch mat to plant through. Whichever you do, do it well, because perennial weeds can drain the enthusiasm out of even the most lively gardener.

TO DIG OR NOT TO DIG

It used to be thought that in order to keep your soil in good working order you should partake in 'winter digging'. This involved digging over your entire plot to a spade's depth (a 'spit') in an orderly and organised fashion, no spit left unturned, often adding in organic matter to the depths as you went. Done at the beginning of winter the digging itself was fairly rough, leaving the soil in jagged peaks to be worked on by the frosts. By spring the frosts would have caused all of this to crumble down into a relatively fine and workable tilth.

This is a perfectly fine way to go about your business if you have the strength and plenty of time on your hands, and it generally does leave the soil in a lovely, friable condition come spring, plus it provides an easy opportunity to pull out any lingering perennial roots. But it is serious work and may not

actually be the best thing you can do for the soil.

No-dig is both a gardening philosophy and a practical instruction. The idea behind no-dig is that the soil should not be disturbed, and certainly not annually and thoroughly, in the winter digging style. Soil left to its own devices naturally forms into various subtle strata, with its own micro- and macro-organisms inhabiting the layers that suit them best. When we turn this subterranean ecology upside down we upset this balance. Far better, goes the theory, to lay organic matter on top of the soil and leave it there, letting the worms do the hard work.

The one drawback of the no-dig system is that it requires a reasonable amount of organic matter each year, and this can be hard to track down if you do not have a ready supply of manure or compost. But if you can overcome this obstacle it works wonderfully: soils are slowly and brilliantly improved by this. The most stubborn and unworkable clay becomes irresistibly civilised.

Even the most weedy and neglected of soils can be conquered without the need for digging. For overgrown patches, first cut down the growth, next lay thick cardboard over the soil, then a layer of manure, then several layers of newspaper, watered, and finally a thick layer of compost. This can be planted into immediately. The layers will smother out most of the weeds, and any that eventually find their way through will be easy to pull out because they are growing through soft, friable soil. Read more about Charles Dowding and his no-dig approach on page 283.

STARTING WITH SEEDS

When seeds make contact with earth, water and a hint of warmth they germinate and start to grow; for most, it really is as straightforward as that. However, there are several methods for placing your soil and your seeds in contact with each other, and each will serve you slightly differently.

PREPARING FOR OUTDOOR SOWING

Sowing seeds directly into the ground where they are to grow is easy and straightforward, and is usually

most successful if you wait for the soil to warm a little: most seeds flourish when sown from mid-spring onwards.

Whenever, wherever you sow, fine-textured soil is best. Picture your emerging seedlings' delicate roots setting off down into the earth hunting for stability and water — if they don't find it quickly they'll wither. A fine tilth allows the roots to sink below the surface easily, with the air spaces allowing water and dissolved nutrients to access the roots.

You may find, especially if creating a garden from scratch, that your soil isn't in this ideal condition. Depending on whether you favour a no-dig approach or not (see opposite) this means either a little digging and working over with a rake until the surface is crumbly with few big lumps, or adding compost. Lavish a little time on getting the soil into welcoming shape — it'll pay you back in spades.

BROADCAST SOWING

This style of sowing best suits cut-and-come-again salad leaves that are happy to grow cheek by jowl. They are harvested when small so never need much space to stretch out, and harvesting is simplest where they grow like this, close together in a swathe of leaves.

- Draw the back of a rake across the prepared soil to create a level surface with no large lumps.

- Take a small handful of seeds and scatter them across its width from side to side, starting furthest away from you and working backwards until you have covered the entire area evenly.

- Use the rake to lightly tickle the very surface soil so that most of the seeds are slightly covered.

- Use a watering can with a fine rose attachment to lightly water the seed drill — keeping the stream of water light is vital; too heavy and the seeds will wash off. If in doubt, water the soil a little before rather than after sowing.

331

DRILL SOWING

Drill sowing suits little, tough, easy-to-grow plants where each seedling produces a single crop, such as carrots, turnips and celeriac.

- Use a string line to mark out the line for your drill. Draw the edge of a hoe or the corner of a rake through the soil next to it to create a v-shaped furrow or 'drill'.

- Pour a small amount of seed into one palm, then use the thumb and forefinger of your other hand to pinch out some seeds and sprinkle them finely along the base of the drill, all the time picturing the eventual size of the carrot or beetroot and attempting to sow at a spacing that roughly equates to the spacing you'd like the plant to have.

- Chances are you won't sow thinly enough, and will have to come along and thin out those seedlings a few weeks later when they appear clumped together or just too close – just be careful not to dislodge those left behind, which you should then carefully water to settle back in when you have finished thinning out.

CREATING A STRING LINE

If you are sowing in rows, make them straight: you'll fit more in and sacrifice less space to bare soil, you'll find it easier to tell what is weed and what is not, and it just looks better. A string line is a useful tool in a vegetable garden, and you can create one with the use of string and two short pieces of wood: bamboo cane is ideal. Cut a length of string several inches longer than the row you want to create. Tie one end of the string to one of the sticks and the other end to the second stick. Push one stick into the soil at one end of your row and the other stick at the opposite end, creating a line of string inbetween the sticks, which marks out your row. Wind any excess string around one of the sticks so that the line is taut. This then acts as a useful yet unobtrusive guide.

LABEL

As you sow your beetroot seeds, you will believe that there is no need to label the row. You have a photographic memory. You have pored over catalogues carefully choosing this heritage seed and then chosen the perfect spot for it. You are sure you'll remember the name and location perfectly. You won't. You will stare baffled at this very same spot a couple of weeks down the line, scratching your head at the mysteriously emerging seedlings, or worse, as you run out of space you will rake over the whole area and sow again. Label everything. Label when you first sow. If you pot on from a seed tray into pots, label again, a fresh label for every single pot.

STATION SOWING

Some seeds are big and tough enough that you can just push them into the ground and be reasonably confident that they will come to something, broad beans and peas among them. However, as a backup it often pays to 'station sow', that is: you sow at the eventual spacing you want the plant to grow at – with no expectation of thinning out later – but you plant two seeds at each station. This acts as a little insurance should one fail, and if both germinate you pull out the smaller one as early as you spot it.

SOWING UNDER COVER

All but the most marginal vegetables and herbs will grow well sown outside at the right time of year, but some – chillies and aubergines for example – need to be started indoors to allow them the long growing season they require to ripen before the season ends. Sowing under cover is also a way of getting ahead on other crops; the warm, protected conditions allow plants to germinate and grow weeks or even months ahead of when they should be sown outside.

Starting plants off under cover also gives them the relative comfort of the indoors – slugs and other would-be nibblers are fewer in number, the

winds absent, the temperatures milder: it's hardly surprising that plants get away so well.

Light and heat are both key to germination and good early growth. If you are sowing early – e.g. for chillies in February – the outdoor temperature will be too low, but under cover you can make it seem like April or even May.

The very best spot for light and heat is on a greenhouse or polytunnel bench over a heating mat or in a propagator (essentially, a mini-greenhouse that may be heated) indoors by a sunny window. The heat encourages germination and good root growth, while good light levels ensure the plants develop steadily.

Sowing under cover allows you to care for your plants through their most vulnerable stage, and plant them out when they are well able to fend for themselves.

Anything grown under cover will need to be 'hardened off' before planting outdoors – this is the process of preparing young, cosseted plants for life outside. Do this in stages: put the plants out first for a few hours during the middle of the day, then bring

them back in; next leave them out for a whole day, then back inside for night-time; then leave them out for a day and covered overnight with garden fleece; finally leave them out for a few days and nights uncovered before planting them out. This is the ideal – follow it as well as you can, but the main thing to bear in mind is that hardening off should be done gradually over a week or two, so repeat each stage for a few days before moving on to the next stage.

STARTING OFF IN MODULES

Many of the plants that can be sown direct can also be sown in modules indoors first and planted out later. Modules are plastic trays divided into sections that when filled with compost act as small pots, perfect for a seedling to develop in.

- Place a mound of compost on to the module tray then push it across the surface so that it fills all of the holes.
- Brush off the excess then give the tray a little tap on a flat surface to settle the compost.
- Sow one or two seeds only per module and just cover with a little compost.

- Water gently using a fine rose attachment. These are tiny amounts of soil and will dry out quickly, so keep an eye on them.

An alternative is to use seed trays – essentially just a shallow tray filled with compost – and sprinkle the seeds across. This has a couple of drawbacks: firstly, it creates an extra stage of work as seedlings need to be gently prised out of the compost (this is known as 'pricking out') and grown on in a slightly larger container before they can be planted out; the second drawback is that roots can become entangled in each other and get damaged in the process. A module tray costs a little more and takes slightly longer to sow, but you save yourself all of this palaver.

STARTING OFF IN POTS

There are some plants – tomatoes, aubergines and chillies among them – that are inconveniently both frost tender and take a long time to grow mature enough to flower and fruit. If sown outside after the frosts have passed they would only ever find enough time to fruit in the hottest and sunniest of summers. These plants need to be sown early indoors, and

336

planted out when the weather has warmed.

These are generally large seedlings, and they can be sown one or two seeds to a small pot to save on potting up later. They are also lovers of heat, and if sown in cold conditions or even at room temperature will sit about for weeks doing nothing. A small heated propagator will kick-start them into growth, as will a spell in the airing cupboard: a low but constant heat is what you are after. Move them out the moment they have germinated and place somewhere sunny and bright. All of these plants grow quickly and need to be potted on several times into larger pots before they will be ready to plant out in their final position.

If you don't have a greenhouse you can keep these plants in the house until frosts have passed and the weather has warmed, but choose your brightest spot and regularly turn the plants so that they don't grow leaning towards the light. Gently brushing their tops a few times a day simulates the effects of the wind in strengthening stems and can help to keep plants small and stocky. Do also time sowing so that

plants aren't overcrowding the space you have for seedlings. Chillies grow slowly so can be sown as early as January. Tomatoes grow fast so should be sown no more than six weeks before you plan to plant them out. Courgettes are even quicker.

STARTING WITH SEEDLINGS

You can sidestep the seed sowing by buying young plants. Expert growers can send you perfect, stocky little plants, allowing you to avoid the tricky first steps — someone else gets to nurse the plants through their most vulnerable stages, while you save on compost and equipment — and it allows you to play catch-up if you forgot to or couldn't sow when they needed to be started. Planting bought-in seedlings is also a great way to overcome losses to pests or weather.

The one drawback is that you'll have access to fewer varieties than if you sow your own seeds, but there

are enough to choose from that you are unlikely to be left wanting.

Although you can source a wide range of veg and herbs as seedlings, I'd suggest prioritising those that involve greenhouses, heated propagators and fuss to get started, thereby saving you the hassle. You can start the easier plants that can be sown directly, straight from a packet, from seed, if you want to do a mixture of the two.

Vegetable seedlings usually arrive as plug plants: just a few leaves tall, having been grown in a module tray and popped out into a plastic bag for posting. On arrival give them a good splash of water and plant them as soon as possible. Those that can go straight into the ground should do so within a few days. Others may need to be grown on first: pot them up into a small pot of fresh compost as soon as you can and water them in. A good supplier will give you all the information you need.

STARTING WITH PLANTS

Plants are usually supplied as containerised or bare root. Containerised plants are those that have been grown in pots, and you'll probably have seen them in garden centres and nurseries. They can be despatched and planted at any time of year, and they can sit in your garden (keep them watered) until you are ready to plant them.

Bare root plants have been lifted from the soil in the dormant season (November to March) and despatched immediately. They are only available when the plants are dormant in winter and the leaves have dropped, and you need to get them planted within a few days of receiving them. You rarely see them in garden centres as they can't be stored out of the ground. They tend to be cheaper than containerised plants and are often available in a wider, more interesting range of cultivars.

A little care when planting can have a huge effect on how well your plant grows, setting it up well (or otherwise) for perhaps years to come. First, whether bare root or containerised, seedlings, small pots, shrubs or trees, give the plant's roots a soak — a light spray for plug plants and an hour's dunk for trees.

MYCORRHIZAL FUNGI

Mycorrhizae are helpful fungi that form a symbiotic relationship with plant roots. They occur naturally in soils and are particularly prevalent in woodland soils — but you can also boost your plants' root health by using mycorrhizae in powdered form to be sprinkled around the roots on planting. As plants start to grow the mycorrhizae grow with them, and are able to stretch farther out and deeper down into the soil than the plant's roots, often over large distances. This sets the plant up with a back-up system, with water and nutrients being relayed back to the roots, particularly useful in times of stress such as droughts. Plants with mycorrhizal support systems typically grow stronger and are more resistant to disease.

Mycorrhiza is most often used as a planting treatment on woody plants such as trees, shrubs and fruit bushes, but all plants benefit and formulations have been developed for use with annual plants such as vegetables.

PLANTING VEGETABLE PLANTS

If you have regularly improved your soil with organic matter and it is easy to work you may not need to add anything to it at planting time: just create a hole, plant and water the plant in. Some plants are particularly greedy though, and will benefit from having a big hole dug for them and backfilled with manure or garden compost. Courgettes, pumpkins and winter squash love this treatment. The same plants tend to be thirsty. Create a little depression in the ground as you plant, so that rainwater and watering-can water runs towards their roots, rather than just off elsewhere.

PLANTING TREES

As I never tire of saying, don't plant a £20 plant in a 20p hole. A moment's extra care when planting can make all the difference to the plant's ability to flourish.

Don't make the roots fit the hole: dig to suit the shape of the roots, be that shallow and wide or narrow and deep. And dig a little deeper and wider than you need, loosening the base and edges to allow the roots to make easy progress after planting.

If the soil is quite clayey, you can fork in a little organic matter to help loosen the soil and improve drainage.

Set the plant into the hole at the correct height (see box overleaf) and loosen the compost from around the roots if it's a containerised plant. Backfill the hole by a third and take time to settle the compost around the roots. Add another third, allow to settle again, and then add the final third. Tread

around the plant to consolidate the soil a little. Water in thoroughly, even if rain is forecast.

Many people add fertiliser or composted horse manure when planting – I tend not to as I feel the roots have more incentive to go in a wider search of nutrients rather than remain in a pool of goodness.

PLANTING AT THE RIGHT LEVEL

Trees need to be planted at the same level they were previously growing at in the field or pot. Too much compost piled around the stem is suffocating and can cause grafted plants (such as most fruit trees) to grow from the rootstock, and if you plant too high the roots will become exposed and dried out over time. A neat trick is to lay a bamboo cane across the planting hole when positioning your tree. First find your tree's previous planting level by looking for the point at which the stem turns a darker shade of brown; if it's a plant supplied in a container, plant it to the same depth as it is in the compost. Lay the cane across the hole and fill in with or take away soil until this point meets the cane.

STAKING TREES

A stake pushed into the ground next to, and attached to, your newly planted tree can help stabilise it during its first years of growth. There are many ways to do this; I'll tell you what works best in my experience.

I use a stake of around 1m in length and hammer it 60cm into the ground, vertically. A rubber tie holds the tree to the stake, allowing the plant to expand without strangling it. Using a longer stake and tying the tree at a higher point is counter-productive: the aim is to secure the roots, allowing the upper part of the tree to move in the wind and develop its own strength. In the most sheltered sites staking might be unnecessary, but if you're in any doubt, stake them for their first couple of years (see photo above right).

PLANTING IN POTS

You don't need swathes of land to grow fruit, vegetables, herbs and spices. In many cases a pot of compost will do just as well, sometimes better. You can grow pretty much any of the plants you can grow in the open ground in a pot, but you may find it more rewarding to grow those that produce over a long spell: a chilli plant, which can produce hundreds of fruits from each plant, might come higher on your desire list than a cabbage, for instance, which will produce one meal's worth of food.

Similarly, consider underplanting – a peach tree will happily have strawberries fruiting at its feet – and using a cut-and-come-again approach to leafy crops including lettuces.

While the final container for your plant should accommodate its needs when fully established, make its journey from infancy to adulthood a gradual one, through incrementally larger pots. While too small a pot will hinder a plant's development, over-potting can lead to problems including too much water in the compost.

Whatever size the pot, it should have good drainage holes in the base as you don't want roots to be drowned in water. Place a single piece of broken crock over each hole before filling, to prevent them from blocking up.

PROPAGATION

Propagation is the art of increasing your stock by taking one plant and turning it into many. When growing food, seed sowing is the most important propagation technique to master, as the bulk of the vegetables we grow are annuals that must be sown fresh each year. But there are a few other techniques that will serve you well if you want to make your plants go further or pass on plants to friends. Each entry in Chapter 3 (What To Grow) tells you which, if any, method of propagation works well for that food.

GRAFTING

This is the art of joining a young piece of wood, known as a scion, from a fruit tree on to a set of roots with a short stem, the rootstock, that has been grown separately. Grafting brings a number of potential benefits:

- Grafting a scion of your chosen variety to a rootstock ensures that the fruitful part of the tree will be true to your chosen variety, whereas trees grown from seed can give unpredictable results as a consequence of cross-pollination.

- Rootstocks can control the rate of growth and size of the fully grown tree.

- A grafted tree usually produces fruit much earlier than a seed-grown tree.

- Some rootstocks will allow you to grow particular fruits or nuts in soil conditions where they might not otherwise thrive.

- Grafted trees can offer resistance to some diseases.

The vast majority of fruit and nut trees available from nurseries and garden centres have been created using this process. It's perfectly possible to do this yourself, if you want to save some money or for the simple pleasure of it.

It's not a definite, reliable process – some will inexplicably fail to take, so do a few spares. If they all work, you might discover a roadside sideline business in fruiting trees. It works well for apples and pears, but most of the stone fruit need extra heat and are a little less reliable.

There are a few approaches to grafting, but I have always used the somewhat specialist-sounding whip-and-tongue technique. First, you'll need to find a tree of the variety you want to create. In December or January, when the tree is at its most dormant, snip off a length of last year's growth, ideally 5–15mm in diameter. Cut the end that was nearest to the trunk with a straight cut (so you create a round-faced cut), and snip the end furthest from it with a diagonal cut (to give an oval-faced cut) – this ensures that you will never confuse which is the right way up. Store in a plastic bag in the fridge to keep it dormant until needed.

341

The time to graft the scion on to the rootstock (see pages 376–377 for suppliers) is in February, March or April. This needs to be carried out under cover: a polytunnel, greenhouse or even in the house is fine.

With a very sharp knife, cut through the base of the scion (the end that currently has the round-faced cut) at a diagonal angle to create an exposed oval-shaped face about 4cm long. Make sure it still has 2–4 buds remaining above the diagonal cut. The prepared scion is now known as the 'whip'.

Make a second cut about a third of the way along the face of the sloping cut – this cut is almost parallel to, but back against, the direction of the first cut, creating a 'tongue'. Repeat these cuts on the stem of the rootstock, matching them as closely as possible; the two pieces will then slide together, held in place by the two tongues. The closer the fit, the better chance of success. Tape the graft immediately – ideally with specialist grafting tape, but I have used masking and electrician's tape when I've run out. Grow in a pot for a few months under cover to give the union opportunity to take and the tree chance to establish. Remember to remove the tape by midsummer – the union will have taken place if it is going to, and leaving the tape longer can constrict growth.

DIVISION

Plants that grow in clumps can be lifted and split. Rhubarb is a prime candidate for this, but it can also work well with other perennial vegetables. As a clump gets larger it declines in vigour. Dig out the whole clump and use two forks back to back to split it into two, and then again into four if it is large enough. If the forks aren't cutting it then use a sharp spade and some force, and if all else fails revert to a saw. The pieces, replanted, will be like young things again. Autumn is the best time to divide plants.

OFFSETS

Some plants will naturally produce infant plants. Strawberries do this with abandon, sending out runners – long stems with mini plants on the ends – that can be left to grow where they fall, or gently lifted and potted up. This is particularly handy in

the case of strawberries as they are short-lived plants that need replacing after a few years, so try to plant up a new patch of offsets each year. Similarly, globe artichokes produce mini-plants at their base, which can be separated from the parent and grown on to maturity.

CUTTINGS

One of the best ways of increasing your herbs is to take cuttings.

Softwood cuttings are taken around midsummer, when there is plenty of new growth to play with. Select a non-flowering shoot a few inches long. Cut it from the plant with a sharp knife or secateurs and remove most of the leaves, just leaving a few at the top. Push the cutting almost to the bottom of a small pot of well-drained compost. Seed compost is perfect, otherwise mix peat-free compost with plenty of grit. Water well and then cover the pot with a clear plastic bag and seal with an elastic band. Place the

cutting somewhere warm but shaded and keep an
eye on it, making sure it doesn't dry out. As soon as
you see new leaves growing you will know that it has
rooted and can be removed from its polythene bag
greenhouse and even potted on into a larger pot. Use
this method to increase plants of oregano, thyme,
mint, rosemary, sage and lemon verbena.

Some fruit bushes and trees such as gooseberries,
black-, red- and white currants, figs and mulberries
can be propagated by hardwood cuttings, taken in
winter when the leaves have dropped and the season's

new growth has hardened. Look for straight, new
growth, cut a whole shoot from the plant, and then
cut this into sections at least 15cm long, using a knife
or secateurs. Create a trench to push the cuttings
into by digging the soil over well and incorporating
compost and grit – do this beforehand if you can.
Push the cuttings about 10cm or so into the trench at
15cm intervals and then water in well. These cuttings
are slow to take but need little attention, just water
them during dry periods and firm the soil around
them occasionally. They should be well rooted and
ready to be transplanted the following autumn.

Whether you are taking softwood or hardwood
cuttings, make sure you observe the following:

- Your pruning knife or secateurs should be very
  sharp and very clean – a fine cut makes success
  much more likely.

- Make horizontal cuts at the lowest end of the cutting (the end that was nearest the trunk) and angled cuts at the top. This ensures you are never confused about which way is 'up'.

- Cuttings should have at least two leaf nodes: the bottom one forms the roots; new growth appears from the top one.

- Use specialist cutting compost to ensure the correct drainage and nutrient levels. Ericaceous compost is best for blueberries.

- Keep your cuttings somewhere bright and under cover, but not in direct sunlight.

- Ensure the compost is moist when you add the cuttings, then water again only when the compost has dried out. When the cutting has rooted, water as usual.

- Dabbing the rooting end of a cutting into organic hormone rooting compounds before placing it in the compost increases success rates.

LAYERING

Make new plants of cane fruits such as hybrid berries by tip layering. This involves gently bending the tip of a young cane, still attached to the plant, towards the ground and pinning the tip just below the surface of the soil with a stone or a tent peg. Bury the tip and leave it like this until autumn. By then shoot will have turned into root, and the new plant can be severed from the mother plant, dug up and potted on. This will also work for raspberries but they are so vigorous you are unlikely to want more of them.

ROOTSTOCKS AND TREE FORMS

I have an apple in the garden that grows as an upturned umbrella in shape, reaching no more than 1.5m in height and spread now it is fully grown. Every year, it gives me dozens of delicious fruit. Out in the orchard, 7-year-old apple trees easily spread for 6m and I have to climb into them to prune in winter. In summer and autumn, each produces potato sack after potato sack of fruit. The differences in the two are largely defined by the rootstock on which they are grown and the shape into which they are allowed to grow.

ROOTSTOCKS

Most fruit and nut trees are grafted on to separately grown roots known as rootstocks (see page 341). There is a bewildering choice of rootstocks, each attributed with a selection of numbers and letters or a seemingly meaningless name: fear not, you don't need to memorise them. A good supplier will recommend a rootstock for whatever your requirements, which should give you the option (say) of an apple tree that grows to 6m or more in spread or will stay happily productive in a pot on your patio.

FREESTANDING TREES

As well as choosing a rootstock that suits, there are also options as far as the shape of your tree is concerned. None are 'better'; whichever you fancy is best.

STANDARDS: forming the largest trees, with at least 1.8m of clear trunk, before branching to form a sizeable canopy.

HALF STANDARDS: similar to standards, though with an unbranching trunk of around 1.5m. Tend to make trees of 4–5m.

BUSHES: short trees, with a clear trunk of 90cm or so at most.

PYRAMIDS: while the three forms above are usually grown in an open goblet shape, pyramids resemble the classic Christmas tree shape, with branches incrementally longer from apex to base. They require regular pruning to maintain the shape and are best grown on relatively dwarfing rootstocks.

TRUE DWARFS: relatively recent developments in grafting and rootstocks allow us to grow a great selection of fruit and some nuts as trees that reach only 1.5m in height and spread, and require very little pruning – perfect for container growing and small gardens.

345

TRAINED FRUIT

The fine art of training fruit trees into beautiful and productive shapes has been perfected over the centuries, and many of the classic forms make excellent options for the garden. Most are particularly suited to those with limited space, as they are pretty much two-dimensional, but also provide structure and height in a large garden.

You can undertake the training yourself, but it is skilled, time-consuming and means a number of years until the plant has reached a position to bear fruit. I would highly recommend buying a plant that has had at least some of the initial training done for you – your job will be largely about maintaining the form in such a way as to produce well.

The most common forms of trained fruit:

ESPALIERS: a vertical trunk with two or more pairs of horizontal branches growing from it. Often grown against a fence, wall or series of posts and wires. Usually apples and pears. Can be kept to two tiers and to 2m or so in breadth, or allowed to extend further.

FANS: as the name suggests, a series of radiating branches, fanning out from a short trunk. Often grown against a fence, wall or series of posts and wires. Usually stone fruits and currants, and grown to around 2–3m in breadth and height.

CORDONS: a single trunk, with fruit growing on short spurs along its length. Can be grown vertically or at an angle. There are numerous variations, from U-shaped cordons to very convoluted shapes. Most commonly apples and pears, and grown to 1–2m in height.

STEPOVERS: essentially, low single-tier espaliers forming a T-shape.

CHOOSING COMPOST

You'll find any number of arguments between those in favour of using peat and those not. Peat certainly stabilises composts, holding on to water and nutrients and making for a stable growing medium; this is countered by the fact that peatlands are an ancient carbon sink, a valuable and threatened habitat, and (effectively) a finite, irreplaceable resource.

My view is that contributing to climate change, destroying habitats and threatening the species that depend on it, as well as destroying beautiful landscapes, is simply way too high a price to pay for slightly easier gardening.

Many growers, from part-time allotmenters to professional nurseries, have plants and businesses that thrive perfectly well without it. I've never used it; and I'm not about to encourage anyone else to.

Choose a good-quality, peat-free compost that suits the task at hand: seed compost for starting with seeds; container compost for plants; ericaceous compost for acid-loving plants. You'll find some outstanding suppliers on pages 376–377.

For container growing, you may want to add grit to the compost to improve drainage, and place a piece or two of broken crock (or similar) over the holes in the base to ensure the compost neither runs out nor blocks the drainage.

SUCCESSION

It's all good to choose a list of flavours and textures you want to enjoy from your garden, but one of the crucial considerations that can make the difference between a garden that feels successful and one that doesn't is succession.

A unexpected sea of apples can be tricky to deal with, whereas the same haul delivered in small instalments from a few trees that produce one after the other can give you delicious fruit for months. Of course, gluts can be good: if you're hoping to make cider, that sea of apples is just what you are after. The 'unexpected' element is what you have to remove from the equation.

Similarly, you don't want to tear up the squash and courgettes at the back end of summer and think, 'What next?' You need to plan for what fills the space, even if that is nothing.

SUCCESSION ACROSS THE YEAR

Consider when your harvests come. If they are concentrated within a short period of time in the prime high harvest of late summer and early autumn, ask yourself whether this suits you. There are no rights and wrongs: some people like a busy time of preparation, growing, picking, eating and preserving in the warmest months followed by a quiet time through winter, but if you want a steadier, more consistent supply of food, plan for it. Refer to the table on pages 212–231 for ideas.

SUCCESSION THROUGH VARIETIES

Often this is as simple as growing a spread of varieties – three apple trees of the right varieties will give you fruit from late July into the new year; choose a good spread and Brussels sprouts can be yours for six months of the year. The detail of variety can make all the difference.

The table (on pages 212–231) is invaluable. Check your wish list against it and if there are lulls where you want something from your garden, check out your options and add in.

SUCCESSION OF ANNUAL VEG AND HERBS

An allotment plan can look full and like a source of abundance, but consider what comes after the first harvests. An early sowing of radishes will be grown and eaten in a few short weeks: what's to follow? Pairing up these quick-to-harvest crops with ones that are ready to plant out in early summer is one of the secrets of a productive plot. Again, use the table to consider your options: choose plants that are ready to go out as seedlings when quick croppers are done. Or don't – it is perfectly fine to have a more haphazard approach, fitting in plants as space allows. Whichever way, get used to asking yourself, 'What comes after X?' Even if the answer is 'a long drink by the fire and a winter indoors', it's important to ask the question.

347

CHAPTER 6

ONGOING CARE

VEGETABLES, HERBS, SPICES, fruits and nuts have a lust for life just like any other living thing; they want to grow. Familiarise yourself with what they need and equip yourself with a few skills, and you can help them on their way.

Problems in the garden often arise when your plants run into other living things that see them as helpful in their own journey to stay alive or reproduce. A garden or allotment is an ecosystem, filled with creatures and plants fighting for survival: pop your little seed out and leave it to fend for itself, and chances are fairly high that it will soon be swamped by weeds competing for the same sunlight and water, eaten by a hungry predator, or hijacked as a breeding ground by an opportunistic pest.

We need to be a little overprotective if we want to get anything to eat for ourselves. We need to place our baby plants into the best possible, least competitive environment we can create, and mollycoddle them until they are big and tough enough to go it alone.

Even when a plant is growing well, the aims of a gardener and a plant are not always in perfect harmony. There are things that we can do to encourage them to produce more fruit, to produce leaves for us to eat rather than seeds, and to stay upright and keep their harvests clean and appealing, rather than scrabbling around in the mud with the slugs. You can get along perfectly adequately without mastering some of the techniques in this section – most unpruned fruit trees will still give a crop, for example – but the rewards will be greater if you do.

Even if your plants are growing well and producing abundantly, the source of much of that success – the soil – needs maintaining in good heart.

And so this section is really about getting the most out of the plants you have chosen: caring for them in such a way as to keep them happy, but above all else, to encourage them to produce well for you. Much of it is about creating a healthy environment rather than employing heavy-handed interventions, and about bending things slightly in the plants' favour. None of this is tricky, and armed with a few techniques and a healthy smattering of paranoia, you can't go too far wrong.

WATERING

All life requires water, and ensuring your plants have a reasonable amount for their needs is one of your primary concerns.

This does not mean more water is better: I suspect that more plants – herbs especially – are killed from too much love (in the guise of water) than not enough.

WATERING ANNUALS

Annuals, by their 'sow, grow, harvest within a year' nature, need welcoming conditions consistently available so they can spring from seed to crop within a short time – regular water is critical on the journey to harvest. 'Little and often' is almost always preferable to the occasional huge deluge; where something different is required, I have included it in the plant profiles in chapter 3, and it will usually say so in the care guide that comes with your plant or seed.

WATERING SEEDS

Bear in mind that most seeds require just the barest damp to germinate – any more than that risks the seed rotting – and the amount of water needed only increases slowly as the seedling develops. The key is to not allow plants to fully dry out in the first place, rather than soaking them to compensate when they do. For most, the ideal is for the compost or soil to be damp beneath the surface.

WATERING PERENNIALS

When planted in the ground, most perennial plants – especially trees – need watering throughout their first year until they become established. If you plant in autumn, then watering once in a while through any dry periods in the winter will be enough. Planting at any other time of year means roots and top growth are both using up resources through the establishment phase, so water regularly, never letting the soil or compost dry out. Once established, trees grown in the ground rarely need watering as they have a root system that draws nutrients and water from deeper in the ground than annuals, and they are less susceptible to fluctuations in weather.

WATERING CONTAINERS AND UNDER COVER

If you are growing in containers or under cover, you will need to water your plants frequently throughout their lives: they are almost entirely dependent on you for their water supply. Water thoroughly, soaking them through, and then leave them unwatered until they start to dry out at the surface.

If you have lots of plants, consider a drip irrigation system – essentially just a length of hosepipe with either drip-holes along its length or a number of mini-pipe offshoots, which you can position so that water drips slowly into your pots whenever the tap is switched on low. Easy and relatively inexpensive to put together, they are great for simplifying container watering or, when linked up to a timer, for keeping your plants happy when you are on holiday.

Overhead watering is another option for watering plants grown under cover. As with a drip system, an overhead system is easy and inexpensive to construct (see pages 376–377 for suppliers), and most effective when there is a sea of plants to water rather than just a few specimens and/or tall plants – I find a drip hose is better in these cases.

MAKING A BOTTLE RESERVOIR

A neat trick when planting tomatoes (which are very thirsty plants) is to cut the base off a small plastic drink bottle and half-bury it vertically, upside down, lid off, alongside the plant. Water poured into the upturned bottle will reach the roots far quicker than water poured on to the soil's surface. You need to water tomatoes every day at the height of summer, and this will make your efforts more effective.

TACKLING WEEDS

Assuming you've prepared the ground well (see pages 329–330) and have a reasonably clean start, weeding will be very much about maintaining the status quo. Hopefully, you'll have a strategy for weeds based on the type of gardening – be it forest gardening, dig or no-dig etc – that you're adopting (see pages 320 and 330). Whether you are thinking of a largely annual veg patch or a perennial food forest, weeds will arise.

Consider mulches (see pages 351–353) as a way of minimising their presence, but when they appear be prepared.

Ensure you deal with weeds early enough in their lifespan, before they become a drain on water and nutrients to the detriment of your crops, or set seed. Your focus needn't be to keep a garden completely weed free – though some people, such as Charles Dowding, aim for just that (see page 283).

For annual weeds, a hoe is invaluable. Young plants can be stopped in their tracks with a swift slice of the sharp blade, and left to desiccate on the surface. If left to grow, you may need a trowel to ease bigger weeds from the soil, with the upside being that, provided they haven't set seed, they'll add to the wealth of composting material.

Perennial weeds need a more determined approach. Getting them early and small saves work, and resolves the problem long before they can set seed. It's easy to ignore them when they are small, but imagine them at their full size and the prospect of pulling them out while still small will become more appealing. A trowel is usually the best tool for taproot plants such as docks, and a fork for anything larger and/or with a web of roots.

MULCHES

A mulch is a layer of material that suppresses unwanted growth, retaining moisture beneath it. There are a number of options; the 'best' depends on the nature of your garden, personal preferences, and what you have to hand and is easily available to use.

The right mulch, planned well ahead of planting and used well, can make life much easier in the garden; it can keep weeding and watering to a minimum, and – depending on which mulch you use – enrich the soil and improve your garden aesthetically.

With traditional, annual vegetable gardening, the plentiful bare soil between rows of vegetables leads to regular watering and weeding – it is part of that culture of gardening. At the other end of the spectrum, forest gardening involves leaving little or no bare soil, with mulches a crucial part of the establishment cycle, and creating an ongoing natural balance between plants an overall aim. Whichever spot along the line between the two that you inhabit, if you adopt a friendly relationship with mulches your garden is likely to benefit, and you'll spend less time bending your back with a trowel and hoe getting the weeds out.

Each type of mulch – living, loose and membrane – can be highly effective and often work well combined. A membrane covered in wood chips, for example, makes a fine semi-permanent path, with more of a natural feel and weed-suppressing capabilities than bare membrane; planting apple mint and other lateral colonisers through mulch mat keeps the space between plants weed free, and the mat can be cut back as the plants establish.

LIVING MULCHES

Growing plants that exclude weeds is by far my favourite way of dealing with otherwise bare soil. In a garden largely of annuals, where crops are typically grown in a new location from year to year, annual living mulches are ideal. Green manures are made for the job (see pages 356–360). Typically, they grow rapidly and give little room for other plants to germinate and establish. This is crucial.

Annual green manures can do the same job in a perennial system (such as a forest garden), but perennial living mulches serve the same purpose but over a longer period. Apple mint and Nepalese raspberry are two of my favourites here: they both spread laterally, covering the ground and denying weeds the resources they need to establish.

LOOSE MULCHES

That layer of compost you add to maintain good soil structure and fertility (see page 326) can also act as a mulch, if applied in a thick enough layer (at least 10cm) and not incorporated into the soil. It kills many birds with one stone. There are other options though, and some of them can turn what would otherwise be a waste product into something that makes your garden an easier, more beautiful place to be (see below).

MULCHING MEMBRANES

As well as acting to clear weeds so that you can create your garden, mulch membranes – be they plastic, cardboard or coir – can be really effective in keeping weeds at bay and clearing areas of grass for planting into, with the mulch being moved on to another patch for clearing.

LIVING MULCHES

ADVANTAGES

- Often the most beautiful option

- Can bring many other positives – including attracting beneficial insects and improving the soil

- Can be edible

EXAMPLES

- SHORT LIVED: (from a couple of months to a year) green manures, such as phacelia and buckwheat: quick growing, can be cheaply grown from seed, can improve soil/attract beneficial insects, but need re-sowing

- LONGER LIVED: (from 1–4 years, depending on conditions) green manures, such as trefoil and clovers: same benefits as with short lived, above, but some take time to establish

■ PERENNIAL GROUND COVERS, SUCH AS APPLE MINT: a long-term, effective solution, but typically slower to colonise than green manures

LOOSE MULCHES

ADVANTAGES

■ Can turn a waste product into something very useful

■ Often available in large quantities free/cheaply priced

EXAMPLES

■ WOOD OR BARK CHIPPINGS: effective and often available cheaply/for free in bulk from tree surgeons or local authority recycling centres. Fresh wood bark/chippings can rob the soil of nitrogen, so best over mulch mat if this is an issue for the plant

■ STRAW: widely available and looks good, but can be expensive

■ COMPOST: easy to produce at home though perhaps not in large quantities

■ GREEN WASTE: many local authorities can supply composted house and green waste in bulk. Often full of nutrients, feeding the soil

MEMBRANE MULCHES

ADVANTAGES

■ Some options are free/cheap and easy to source, but may need replacing once in a while

■ Plastic and woven membranes can be costly but provide a long-term solution

EXAMPLES

■ CARDBOARD OR LAYERED NEWSPAPER: usually easy and cheap to source. Works well for a year, often longer when supplemented with a layer of loose mulch on top

■ COIR MATTING: a medium-term (2–4 year) solution, made of waste product from the coconut industry, and should be anchored with wire staples

■ PLASTIC MEMBRANE: effective in the short to medium term (depending on thickness) and a relatively cheap option compared to woven membrane, but can tear; tends not to withstand foot traffic and doesn't allow water through

■ WOVEN MULCH FABRIC: the most expensive option and the most effective, a use-once solution with a long lifespan and durability. Most allow water through

353

MAINTAINING A HEALTHY GROWING MEDIUM

The structure of even the heartiest growing medium — be it soil or compost — declines over time, and as plants grow the nutrients within the soil or compost are either exhausted or leached out by water. If you want your plants to thrive, you need to take care both of the structure and fertility of your soil or compost. Fortunately, it's a very straightforward business.

MAINTAINING GOOD SOIL STRUCTURE

Air spaces are crucial for easy plant establishment and to allow movement of the water, along with dissolved nutrients. A heavy soil and/or plenty of foot or wheel traffic can easily compact the soil, inhibiting root development and nutrient and water take-up. Assuming you have started from a good position (see pages 326–330), either from thoroughly digging over, establishing no-dig beds or using the correct compost in containers, your primary task is to avoid compaction.

Be realistic about your movements and allow enough space for adequate core pathways. Reducing the width of access becomes damaging if the result is you end up walking on the beds.

Acquire some planks. When laid over bare soil they are surprisingly effective at spreading the weight of a person, minimising any compaction. Having a few wide boards to walk on – giving you moveable access to your beds for weeding, planting and harvesting – gives you flexibility and keeps the ratio of garden to pathways in your favour.

Even the action of the rain, especially in winter, can compact the soil. The less you leave uncovered, the better. There are a number of ways of achieving this, depending on the type of garden you have.

If you have a classic vegetable garden that's dominated by annuals, growing plants closely together where possible ensures little soil is exposed to the elements. Green manures (see pages 356–360) can be a great part of the strategy whatever type of garden you have, both sown between annual plants that need wide spacing (e.g. climbing beans), or across wider areas if there are times of the year when your patch is less productive. They work as well in perennial systems as they do in annual gardens, but in perennial gardens permanent ground cover is often desirable. Nepalese raspberry, apple mint and some of the long-lasting clovers are particularly effective groundcovers, protecting the soil, offering a harvest and (in the case of clovers) fertilising the soil naturally.

Whatever your garden, a regular supply of organic matter is vital – it provides the soil with an ongoing supply of material that serves to lighten and improve clay soils, or give substance and increase water retention in light soils, and is the single most important factor in maintaining good soil structure.

There are many sources of organic matter; all have their advantages, and your chosen source(s) are likely to be driven by convenience and the type of garden and gardening you favour.

COMPOST

For many, the most convenient form of organic matter is compost – it's easy to make and virtually free. There is a little everyday magic about making compost: position a compost heap at the end of your garden, chuck everything once living (but without a heartbeat) into it – vegetables past their best, prunings from the garden, grass clippings – and six months or so later, beautiful, rich, crumbly brown compost results, ready to spread on your garden. You almost can't go wrong. I have a neighbour who once (not knowing he shouldn't) composted a dead fox; not recommended but it works.

There are some food-related ingredients you should avoid adding to your heap. Top of the list come meat, eggs and anything cooked. As well as potential health issues, they will attract rats, which are not something you want to be dealing with – hence, I recommend finding another resting place for your dead foxes.

The key to making compost is the balance of dry, brown matter and soft, sappy green material. This is the carbon to nitrogen ratio.

CARBON-RICH INGREDIENTS, THE BROWNS, INCLUDE:

- Dry twiggy growth
- Newspaper and cardboard
- Straw
- Fallen leaves
- Sawdust and shavings
- Animal bedding, from herbivores

NITROGEN-RICH MATERIALS, THE GREENS, INCLUDE:

- Vegetable scraps
- Grass cuttings
- Weeds (annuals only, as perennial seeds and roots can survive the composting process)
- Coffee grounds

Try to mix the two, with slightly more browns than greens, ideally blending them together: add too much green growth and the heap will collapse into an anaerobic, slimy mess; too much brown material

and it won't do anything at all. Unloading a barrel of grass clippings to form a slippery slow-to-decompose layer is as close to cling-filming your compost heap as it gets. Not recommended.

There are some non-essentials that will accelerate the process of composting. Nettles, comfrey leaves and urine are all nitrogen-rich and readily available. Treat them as additional greens, diluting the urine before adding if rain is not due.

Turning the contents of your heap over is the key to quick compost making. If you have the space, have three compost boxes. Add your compostable material only to Heap 1. Once Heap 1 is full, use a garden fork to transfer its contents into Heap 2. Refill Heap 1 with new material and when it is full again, fork Heap 2 into Heap 3, and Heap 1 into Heap 2. Again, refill Heap 1 and hopefully, by the time Heap 1 has been filled for the third time, the material in Heap 3 will have turned into compost, which you can now use and make room to repeat the transfer of Heap 2 into Heap 3, and Heap 1 into Heap 2. If Heap 3 hasn't fully composted at this point, you may need to create more space for your compost, and/or turn the compost in each heap once every few weeks to accelerate the process.

If you have room or inclination for only one bin, either make it a bin that can be spun around its central axis (called a compost tumbler), or be prepared to turn the contents of a static bin by emptying out the material and forking it back in again.

TO WORK WELL, A COMPOST HEAP NEEDS:

- A balance of greens and browns – add more browns if it becomes slippery and dense; add more greens if it is too twiggy or dry
- To be wet but not too wet – leave it uncovered and open to rain
- To have material added that is fairly small – chop up twiggy growth, rip up cardboard
- To contain plenty of air – so don't chop up those pieces too finely
- To have its contents turned to speed up decomposition

There are plenty of styles of compost bin and which you choose to buy or make is down to personal taste as much as anything else. Wooden slatted compost heaps are the classic, as they look good and allow air to penetrate in through the sides of the heap, but plastic bins keep the ingredients warm and can help the contents to heat up faster. Even an open heap with no bin will decompose eventually.

It's worth remembering that for most purposes you don't need to produce perfect compost. If your bins fill up and you need the space before it is perfectly crumbly and even, just spread it – as long as there is no unrotted, identifiable matter – on to your beds anyway. It will continue to rot down in situ and will do just as much good as more mature compost; it'll just take a little longer to work into the soil.

ANIMAL MANURE

Animal manure, most commonly available from horses, pigs and cattle, makes a wonderful bulky soil additive. Horse manure can often be picked up from stables at little cost (or even for free: they have to get rid of it somehow), and cow manure is sometimes available from farms. Unless you are sure it has already been well rotted, pile it up and leave it to mature for six months before using. As with compost, you can either dig it lightly into the top layer of soil in autumn, or spread it across the surface for the worms to work in. Well matured, it makes a wonderful addition to the planting hole of a big feeder such as a winter squash or a courgette, and a highly nutritious feed around the base of fruit bushes and trees.

GREEN MANURES

Green manures form a group of plants that act as a sort of soil rejuvenating treatment, improving soil structure and enriching it with organic matter and nutrients. They are widely available and almost always grown from seed. With the right choice of varieties, it's possible to grow green manures at any time of year, covering otherwise bare ground, and interplanting with your edible crops.

Depending on which varieties you choose, they provide one or more of the following benefits (see the table on pages 358–359 for more details):

- Minimise soil erosion
- Prevent nutrients washing or leaching away
- Build fertility (e.g. through nitrogen fixing)
- Improve soil structure
- Suppress weeds
- Retain moisture
- Attract beneficial insects

Sow seeds thickly across prepared soil and allow them to grow and cover the ground. How long this takes and how long you leave them there depends on the green manure, the time of year and your plans for the garden (see table below).

A particularly useful technique is to sow seeds in early autumn so the green manure covers the ground over winter. During this time it will act as a blanket for the soil, protecting it from the slings and arrows winter throws at it. Essentially, you sow and do nothing over winter, and return to a garden with its soil in better heart than when you left it. Green

manures prevent soil erosion and, when chopped down and dug in during late winter, they leave the soil in perfect planting condition for spring. Suitable types for winter sowing include winter grazing rye and winter tares, both very much tough enough to withstand the weather.

I use green manures a lot during the main growing season too, sneaking a row between other crops or to cover an area after crops have been lifted. As well as enriching the soil, the coverage can also help smother out weeds and retain water at the height of the season, when both can be an issue; buckwheat and fenugreek, which both have thick, weed-suppressing growth, are ideal for this. One of my favourites is sowing yellow trefoil beneath climbing and runner beans — it's a nuisance weeding around the beans and beneath the structure they're growing up. The trefoil keeps most of the weeds out, while adding nitrogen to the soil and attracting beneficial insects. A pretty big bonus, for the cost of a few penceworth of seed.

White clover

GREEN MANURE	SOW	LASTS	PRIMARY BENEFITS
ALFALFA	May–July	1 year	Nitrogen fixer. A mineral accumulator that's rich in elements which promote good plant growth.
BLUE LUPIN	March–July	6 months	Nitrogen fixer. Deep rooting, which breaks up heavy ground and draws nutrients up to enrich the topsoil. Thrives in most soils but especially useful for light sandy soils. Attracts beneficial insects if allowed to flower.
BUCKWHEAT	April–Aug	3 months	Fast growing and deep rooting, which breaks up heavy ground and draws nutrients up to enrich the topsoil. Thrives in heavy soil. Attracts beneficial insects if allowed to flower. Can release chemicals that inhibit germination in some plants so leave at least a month between digging in and direct sowing.
CRIMSON CLOVER	March–Sept	3 months or over winter	Nitrogen fixer. Attracts beneficial insects if allowed to flower. Best in loam to sandy soils.
FENUGREEK	May–Aug	3 months	Nitrogen fixer. Fast growing and if left to flower will attract beneficial insects. Excellent even in a heavy soil.
FIELD BEAN	Sept–Nov	Over winter	Nitrogen fixer. Fast establishing and particularly effective for covering ground through winter.
FODDER RADISH	May–Aug	6 months or over winter	Deep rooting, which breaks up heavy ground and draws nutrients up to enrich the topsoil. Thought to release chemicals that inhibit nematodes, which might attack root veg in particular.
HUNGARIAN GRAZING RYE	Aug–Oct	6 months, through winter	Fast growing, even into winter. Good in most soils, especially clay. Can release chemicals that inhibit germination in some plants so leave at least a month between digging in and direct sowing.

GREEN MANURE	SOW	LASTS	PRIMARY BENEFITS
PHACELIA	March–Sept	3 months or over winter	A striking blue-purple flowering plant that attracts beneficial insects, especially bees.
RED CLOVER	April–Sept	Up to 2 years	The best nitrogen fixer of all the clovers. Attracts beneficial insects if allowed to flower.
WHITE CLOVER	March–Aug	Up to five years	Nitrogen fixer. Lower growing than most other clovers. Attracts beneficial insects if allowed to flower.
VETCH (AKA WINTER TARES)	March–Oct	3 months or over winter	Nitrogen fixer. Thrives in a heavy soil, but not in acidic or dry soils. Can release chemicals that inhibit germination in some plants so leave at least a month between digging in and direct sowing.
YELLOW TREFOIL	March–Aug	6 months	Nitrogen fixer. A low-growing, yellow-flowering plant which attracts beneficial insects.

Phacelia

Whether it's a change of season, the conclusion of their lifespan or just that you're ready to plant that brings a green manure's tenure in your garden to an end, they can be worked into the soil with the end of a spade or cut down and left to decompose. They will work just like any other bulky organic matter in improving your soil structure. Roots that have pushed down into the soil will add organic matter as they break down and leave pathways for water to trickle down as they rot. This is a particularly useful soil improvement technique if you live in a city with limited access to manure, or if you don't have the physical strength or inclination to move and spread manure. It is grow-it-yourself organic matter, with no heavy lifting involved.

Legumes such as clovers and alfalfa are particularly nutritious for the soil, drawing nitrogen from the air and fixing it into nodules in their roots. Plants are always desperate for nitrogen, so this is the green manure to bump up fertility in well-used soils.

LEAF MOULD

If your garden isn't as strewn with autumnal leaves as mine, go to the nearest park with a rubbish sack or two and fill them with fallen leaves. Bring them home, sprinkle enough water into the bags to lightly wet the leaves, tie the tops and punch a few air holes in the sides. Throw these bags somewhere you will forget about them for a year. When you finally remember to dig them out, you will have two bags of rich, moist compost: a wonderful soil additive. Left for two years it becomes fine enough to be used as a seed compost. It also makes a great addition to container mixes. Though you will find deciduous leaves in the most abundance, you can also compost the leaves of conifers, though they take much longer to rot down. The resulting compost will be acidic and useful for keeping acid-loving plants (such as blueberries) happy.

BIOCHAR

In the poor yellow soils of the Amazon are patches of rich dark soil, the 'terra preta', or 'black earth'. These are areas once worked by Amazonian communities, and the soil is black from a build-up of a particular type of charcoal that has been used on the soil: biochar. It is formed by burning waste at particularly low temperatures and with little access to air, and it turned these soils from unfertile to rich and sustaining.

After having been ignored for over a thousand years, biochar is back on the radar as a soil enhancer, and gardeners can now buy biochar to sprinkle on to the soil or to dig in to planting holes. Putting biochar into soil brings many of the same benefits as adding other sources of organic matter, but the difference is that biochar does not break down and need replacing every year. Biochar is a sort of permanent organic matter, and once in the soil it will stay there, improving structure, drainage and the soil's ability to hold on to nutrients. It also provides the perfect environment for mycorrhizal growth (see below), therefore boosting the plant's support system. One of its many benefits is that it helps soil to hold on to moisture. This makes it particularly useful in propagating mixes where it helps to regulate the fluctuations in moisture that can lead to poor germination rates. It is also wonderful in container mixes for the same reason; it helps keep composts stable and moist, rather than quickly drying out.

BOKASHI

Bokashi is a compost pickling system, originating in Japan. You place kitchen waste into a lidded bin or container and then sprinkle with a bran that has been inoculated with particular micro-organisms. Once it is full, seal the whole thing and wait. The micro-organisms get to work on the kitchen scraps and two weeks later the result is a block of semi-broken down matter that has taken on a glassy, pickled look.

You may not think you need to pickle your compost, but this system does a couple of very useful things. It renders everything edible compostable, including meat and fish scraps. It also makes the scraps entirely repellent to rats, and rats usually love compost. But above all else it speeds up the composting process to breakneck speed. You can tip the contents of your pickled bokashi bin into your normal heap if you wish, but it is unnecessary. Spread straight on to the soil it will break down rapidly.

WORMERIES

Wormeries engage a posse of worms in the process of munching through your kitchen waste, and the result is a fine, high-quality and very nutritious compost. The benefit of this system is that it can be fitted into a small area: it is the perfect answer for roof or balcony gardeners. There is some stress involved in keeping the worms alive; this is by no means a straightforward task. Put too much of one thing or another in, and the contents can become too acidic or too wet and the posse perish. If you can cope with a little jeopardy and guilt in the early days it is worth persevering, as once the worms are properly settled and have a good bit of compost under their belts, they become more gardener-proof, and will keep you well supplied with beautiful compost. This is rich stuff, and may be too strong for use when propagating. It is absolutely perfect for using in containers, or for top dressing older containers that need a compost top-up and an injection of nutrients.

ORGANIC MATTER AND CONTAINERS

Long-lived plants such as dwarf fruit trees, or short-lived annuals, can be grown in containers equally happily with a little bit of regular attending to. Perennials can be potted on into increasingly larger containers, and new compost will be added as you do. For this you will need a pot slightly bigger than the one the plant is already growing in, but not much larger. A couple of inches' extra space on each side is perfect. Place fresh compost into the base of the new pot and then gently ease the plant out of the old pot. Tease out a few of the roots to encourage them to move out into the new compost, and then position the root ball in the new pot, adding or removing compost until the top of the plant's root ball is a couple of inches below the rim of the pot. Take more compost and feed it down the sides of the pot, compacting with fingers as you go. Cover the surface with a little fresh compost and water in.

There comes a time in every container plant's life when it reaches its optimum size and doesn't need potting on. Once your plants have reached the heftiest proportions, you need a new way of freshening them up each year. Over time, the bulk of the compost will start to reduce as the organic matter in it breaks down. In long-term plantings, say of dwarf fruit trees, the compost level will slowly lower and need topping up. You can do this by top dressing, just covering the surface with a layer of compost a couple of inches thick, once or twice a year. Spring is the best time, as this is when the plant will be able to make most use of the fresh burst of nutrients. Worm compost is perfect for this, being fine and nutrient rich, but you could also use a well-matured garden compost or leaf mould.

When growing annuals in containers, I tend to replace the compost every year, adding the old compost to the compost bin to be incorporated with the kitchen and garden waste.

MAINTAINING FERTILITY

꜍ Plants need a range of nutrients in order to grow well. Their three main requirements are for nitrogen, which particularly stimulates leafy growth, phosphorus for root growth, and potassium, which helps promote flowering and fruiting. There are several other secondary macronutrients (needed in relatively large quantities) and a whole host of micronutrients (needed in tiny quantities, but still necessary for good growth).

If you keep your soil well topped up with organic matter, or grow green manures, a good proportion of the nutrient requirements for most of your plants will be taken care of. Each type of bulky organic matter contains its own nutrients, on top of which the addition of organic matter over the soil makes the soil far better able to hang on to nutrients.

However, some plants are particularly hungry — especially fruit, and Mediterranean vegetables such as tomatoes, chillies and aubergines — and will respond to supplementary feeds.

Plants in pots, on the other hand, have no access to nutrients other than those you give them. Try as they might, there is nowhere for their roots to go off in search, and so you must anticipate their needs and keep them fulfilled or they will decline in vigour and productivity. Compost manufacturers include slow-release plant food in their mixes, so your plants are well kept for about the first six weeks. After that you need to step in and top up.

LIQUID FEEDS

It is possible to buy chemical fertilisers that will provide everything a growing plant could need, but while they do the job perfectly well, their production is usually far from sustainable. There are a few more appealing alternatives, a couple of which can be home made.

You can feed plants with plants. Some perennials are particularly effective at drawing nutrients up from the soil and holding them in their leaves. Known as mineral accumulators, if you have a patch or two in a corner of any kitchen garden they will

provide a precious resource. When left to rot, their leaves release their nutrients to produce a potent fertiliser. Two of the best plants for this treatment are comfrey and nettle. Comfrey is particularly rich in potash, which is the nutrient that pushes plants to produce more flowers and fruits, and tea made from their leaves should be used to water tomatoes and other fruiting plants liberally once they have started to flower. Nettles are rich in nitrogen, perfect for feeding plants where green growth is desirable.

To make a feed using either nettles or comfrey, first avail yourself of a bucket with a sealing lid, as things are going to get smelly. Really smelly. Chop the leaves up and weigh them down inside the bucket with a couple of bricks, put on the lid, then put the whole thing aside for a few weeks — preferably as far from humanity as possible. After a few weeks, a little brown liquid will have gathered at the bottom. Pour it off into a bottle with a lid, place some fresh chopped leaves into the bucket along with the old ones, weigh down, seal and leave again. This drained-off liquid is now a potent fertiliser, and can be diluted and watered on to plants: use one part fertiliser to 10 parts water. An effective, if less exact alternative, is to add water to the bucket with the leaves and allow the leaves to break down into it until it smells appallingly (how long this takes varies with the weather), strain and use direct.

PELLET FERTILISERS

Pelleted manures pack nutrients into an easily used form. Chicken manure pellets typically contain roughly equal amounts of the three main nutrients, making them a very balanced feed. Comfrey is also often made into pellets, if you don't wish to make your own feed from the leaves. Like the liquid, this is high in potash and so good for flowering and fruiting crops.

MAINTAINING A HEALTHY ENVIRONMENT

꜍ A thriving garden owes much to creating an environment where the balance between your plants and potentially hostile organisms is in your favour.

If you can give up any urge to eliminate all pests and diseases, and instead focus on fostering a set of circumstances where potential problems are kept in natural check, your workload and blood pressure will be much reduced.

That said, it's not paranoia if they really are out to get you. Plonk your plants out into the garden to fend for themselves, and chances are something with a mouth will have a go at them. It is no good reciting incantations to the sun god of a solstice evening, in the hope that the rabbits will bypass your lettuces.

The best strategy involves a mixture of excluding undesirables, inviting beneficial creatures, taking advantage of natural positive pairings, not growing annual crops in the same spot in successive years, and, when needed, introducing populations of predators to do the dirty work for you.

EXCLUSION

Sometimes the surest way to keep a pest at bay is to put up a big old barrier that stops them getting anywhere near your plants. I use a strong chicken wire fence to keep out the four-footed nibblers – 60cm is about the minimum effective height. Make your fence sturdy and hole free: it is utterly dispiriting to have the cheeky beggars levelling beautiful seedlings you've nurtured – a single evening's feasting by a lone rabbit can take care of weeks of plants. You'll need something altogether higher (or a friend with a gun and a carnivorous disposition) to dissuade deer.

A tree guard of the appropriate height will protect the trunk from nibbling deer or rabbits.

Beyond that, I'd recommend designing into your garden solutions that deter pests and attract beneficial insects. Here are some suggestions for how to deal with common nuisances.

CARROT FLY BARRIERS

Carrot fly lay their eggs in the tops of the roots of young carrot plants. As the roots develop, so do the larvae, and they eat ugly holes in your carrots. Happily, carrot fly are not the cleverest or most adaptable of creatures, and we can use this against them. They fly fairly low to the ground sniffing out carrots, but when they hit a barrier they make no

attempt to negotiate it and ricochet off in another direction. Use this to your advantage by erecting a 60cm barrier of fleece on both sides of your row. You can also cover rows of carrots with fleece or cloches to the same effect, and they will have the added advantage of warming the ground in spring and bringing about earlier crops.

BRASSICA NETTING AND ROOT COLLARS

Brassicas are the sheep of the vegetable world, attracting disease and predators at the drop of a hat. They might be stripped to the veins by cabbage white butterfly caterpillars, shredded by pigeons, or have their roots attacked by root fly. Or a combination of the three. To guard against the root fly, place a 7–10cm high collar of cardboard or thick fabric around the base of the stem on planting. This will physically stop the flies from laying their eggs, and is particularly useful for cabbages and cauliflowers, which suffer from root fly most. To guard against the others, build a framework big enough to completely cover the full-grown plants – canes tied together, loops of hosepipe – and then cover it completely with fine netting.

FRUIT CAGES

Given any opportunity, birds will eat much of the fruit from your bushes. Berries, currants and cherries are their favourites, and if you are growing them expect your plot to appear as a big, succulent fruit platter to them come high summer. They will swoop at the very moment of perfect ripeness, be that at 6 am or 8 pm. In other words, you can't beat the birds to it, unless you want to pick your fruits while really quite unripe, and there seems very little point in growing your own fruit if you're going to do that.

Nets can be employed to keep birds off the most vulnerable plants. It needs to be thoroughly done as if there are any gaps in the netting they can get caught inside, so make sure there are no gaps and that the sides are as taut as possible, pinned down with tent pegs or stones. If you intend to grow a lot of fruit, consider a fruit cage.

TRAPS

Trapping pests very rarely deals with the problem entirely, but it can be a useful way of reducing numbers or of monitoring just how many of the blighters are eyeing your precious developing harvests.

- Codling moth traps: Codling moths are the winged part of the maggots-in-apples cycle. After mating, the females lay their eggs on to the tops of the developing fruits, which then hatch and the caterpillars burrow down into them. The opening is small and the problem often only discovered on biting into the apple. An open, sticky trap is laced with pheromones that lure in the males, whereon they get stuck firmly. These were originally used in commercial orchards to monitor the numbers of male codling moths pre-spraying, but they are also useful in their own right in reducing their numbers and the females' chances of mating.

- Slug pubs: Slugs are attracted to the fermented yeast in beer. They clamber in and drown in a drunken stupor, and somehow this makes me feel a little better about the whole ugly business. Given a chance, other creatures will also clamber in and we don't want a drunken wildlife massacre on our hands, so care is needed. Chop the bottom 10cm or so off a large plastic drinks bottle and sink it, base downwards, into the soil, leaving 2–3cm above ground. This creates a cup to be filled with beer, which the slugs are drawn to. Slugs will be keen enough that they will climb up and into the trap, whereas beetles and other creatures will deflect and continue past on their journey. If you create a pitched roof over the slug pub using a couple of slates or similar, it will provide the shady cover slugs favour and prevent evaporation. Replace the beer every few days, as a mass slug grave is a fairly clear advertisement to other slugs not to follow suit.

COMPANION PLANTING

No plant is an island. Every one of the plants that we grow interacts with the other plants around it, dominating their space or perhaps being kept in check by their footprint, offering shade or perhaps taking advantage of support. A whole range of interactions takes place, often beyond our gaze, and with an understanding of these interactions we can plant to harness the benefits (see photo right).

Companion plants can offer one of more of the following to their neighbours:

- Support
- Shade
- Weed suppression
- Attracting potential pests away from crops
- Drawing beneficial insects into the garden
- Distracting potential pests through smell
- Making nitrogen and/or other nutrients available

There are almost endless pairings that are useful to keep in mind – see below for some of my favourites – but the easiest way to deter pests is to mix up your plantings. Avoid large blocks of the same plant (once their pest finds them, it will gleefully rip through the lot unimpeded), grow plenty of flowers to draw in pollinators, and plenty of scented herbs to confuse those pests guided by scent. Not only will this make your crops less predated upon, but it will make for a more beautiful garden too.

COMPANION	BENEFICIAL FOR	BENEFITS
BASIL	Tomatoes, aubergines, most fruit	Attracts aphids from primary crops, also said to improve the flavour of tomatoes. The scent is thought to help prevent fungal diseases in fruit.
BORAGE	Tomatoes, squash, strawberries	Attracts beneficial insects and repels tomato worm, reputed to increase strawberry yields.
CHERVIL	Lettuce	Repels aphids when interplanted with lettuces.
COMFREY	Any fruiting plant	High in potassium, which boosts fruit production, and flowers early attracting bees.
CORIANDER	Most edible plants	Attracts beneficial insects when in flower, and repels carrot fly and aphids.
DILL	Most edible plants	Attracts a range of pollinators and natural predators to the garden when in flower.
FENNEL	Most edible plants	Attracts a range of pollinators and natural predators to the garden when in flower.
GARLIC	Most vegetables, raspberries	Disguises other scents, e.g. keeping carrot root fly from carrots, repels aphids from raspberries.
HYSSOP	Brassicas	Attracts beneficial insects when in flower and repels cabbage white butterflies.
LEMON BALM	Most fruit	The scent is thought to help prevent fungal diseases in fruit.
MARIGOLDS (Tagetes)	Most edible plants, especially root vegetables	Deters nematodes, wireworms and slugs.
MINT	Cabbage, tomatoes, radish, most fruit	Deters cabbage white butterflies, aphids, flea beetles and the scent is thought to help prevent fungal diseases in fruit.

COMPANION	BENEFICIAL FOR	BENEFITS
NASTURTIUMS	Brassicas, apples	Attracts beneficial insects when in flower and repels cabbage white butterflies. Repels codling moth if grown through an apple tree.
NETTLES	Legumes, brassicas	Attracts cabbage whites and aphids away from more precious crops.
ONIONS, CHIVES, LEEKS	Most vegetables, apples	Disguises other scents, e.g. keeping carrot root fly from carrots. Prevents apple scab.
OREGANO	Brassicas	Attracts beneficial insects when in flower and repels cabbage white butterflies.
PARSLEY	Most edible plants	Attracts a range of pollinators and natural predators to the garden when in flower.
POT MARIGOLD (*Calendula officinalis*)	Any plant that needs insect pollinating; tomatoes, asparagus, courgettes	Attracts pollinating insects, repels tomato worm, asparagus beetle and white fly.
ROSEMARY	Legumes, brassicas, carrots	Attracts beneficial insects when in flower and repels cabbage white butterflies, bean beetle and carrot fly.
SAGE	Brassicas, carrots, radish	Repels cabbage moth, carrot fly and flea beetle.
SUMMER SAVORY	Broad beans	Repels aphids that like to take up residence in the beans.
THYME	Brassicas	Attracts beneficial insects when in flower and repels cabbage white butterflies.

Bees and other pollinators are hugely useful to anyone growing anything edible, because in pollinating flowers they nudge the plant into the next stage of development, creating food for us. Many pollinators are struggling and in decline, and it is in the gardener's long-term interest to help to reverse that. Unfortunately, bees cannot live on apple blossom alone. They need an array of nectar-rich flowers to keep them supplied all year round. Plant as many pollinator-friendly plants and flowers as you can fit into your garden, and you will help to ensure their survival, as well as concentrating them handily around your crops.

Along with those highlighted in the companion plant table above, here are a few suggestions for pollinator-friendly plants that work their magic at different times of the year:

- Spring flowers: rosemary, daffodil, hawthorn, primrose, Pulmonaria
- Summer flowers: comfrey, sweet pea, lavender, cardoon, fennel, foxglove, thyme
- Autumn flowers: Angelica, Buddleia, Sedum, Echinops
- Winter flowers: Hellebores, Mahonia, ivy, winter aconite

ENCOURAGING BENEFICIAL WILDLIFE

It may be slightly counter-intuitive, but encouraging wildlife into your edible garden helps reduce damage to your crops. The idea is to restore a balance that is missing from so much of our environment through the use of chemicals and the loss of habitats. Essentially it comes down to this: it doesn't really matter if we have a few aphids on our plants, they only become a problem when there are no natural predators around to keep their numbers low and damage minimal. To create a good balance we have to relax about a few pests, but encourage a population of predators that will keep them (and their impact) in check. Frogs, toads, beetles, hedgehogs, hoverflies, bees and even wasps are our friends.

Make a log pile, to encourage in beetles and spiders. The more the logs rot and collapse, the more useful they become to a whole host of

beneficial creatures, so resist any tidying urges. A pond is a little more ambitious to build, but hugely welcoming to frogs and toads, both of which devour slugs. You might also create homes for mason and solitary bees by drilling differently sized holes into a block of wood and placing it somewhere sheltered. These bees are marvellous pollinators. Also try creating a 'wildlife hotel'. Stack a pile of bricks leaving good gaps between them, and then stuff each with a different material: straw, twigs, cut bamboo canes, the stems of perennial plants – each will suit a different creature. Hoverflies like to overwinter in straw, and will emerge in spring starving for aphids and ready to pollinate every flower in sight.

CROP ROTATION

Crop rotation has traditionally been used to help fight pests. The theory is a good one, and it goes like this: repeatedly grow the same crops in the same patch of soil and you will get a build-up of pests of that particular crop. You create the perfect environment for pests, where they can just lazily slink from soil to favourite bit of food, and use all the excess energy they would have spent searching for it on having more cabbage- or tomato-loving offspring. By moving the crops around, you at least make them hunt for their supper.

It is possible (and, again, traditional) to worry a little more than you strictly need to about this. The traditional vegetable garden is divided into quadrants: one for brassicas, one for roots, one for legumes and one for alliums. These crops are strictly moved around the quadrants each year, so that you are guaranteed that no piece of soil sees the same group of plants twice in four years. I have never done it like this and I haven't seen any ill effects. To my mind, it doesn't particularly suit the way most of us grow. What do I do after I pull out my broad beans in July? Planting with more legumes would be nonsense, but if I use anything from the other quadrants I mess up the system. It is much more helpful to just bear the principle in mind. Make a rough sketch of where your crops end up and try not to grow them in exactly the same place the following year.

BIOLOGICAL CONTROLS

As well as sending invitations to beneficial insects and other creatures to come to the party, once in a while you may have to call on the bouncers. Biological controls are the bouncers – helpful creatures that can be introduced to your plants to maim, kill or do battle with your pests so you don't have to. They are your pests' natural enemies, and are often creatures that are present in the environment anyway, but in low numbers. Bumping up their population will help you to keep the upper hand. These microscopic creatures are generally supplied semi-dormant in a powder that is mixed into water and then watered on to plants.

One of the most useful of the biological controls is *Phasmarhabditis hermaphrodita*, a parasite of slugs sold as Nemaslug. Watered on to soil, they give around six weeks' protection, and it is a particularly useful treatment early in the season when you are planting out lots of young, vulnerable plants. You won't entirely beat slugs this way, so have other measures in place, but nematodes can reduce the population and stack the odds in your favour.

A second pest worth treating with biological control is vine weevil. Vine weevil attacks the roots of plants in pots and is particularly keen on those of strawberries (which it will even attack in the open ground). An autumnal pre-emptive watering every few years with nematode *Steinernema kraussei*, sold as Vine Weevil Killer, will keep them at bay.

PRUNING

Do not fear pruning. You really have to try quite hard to kill a tree or fruit bush with secateurs, so don't be afraid to snip. A little of the right sort of attention can make for a healthier tree and more fruit, so become familiar with the essential hows and whys.

Left unpruned, fruit trees and bushes will usually go on producing fruit, but over the years production will decline and the plant becomes more susceptible to disease.

Pruning does a few helpful things: it removes dead material that can encourage disease; it shapes the tree, aesthetically; it allows greater air circulation and light penetration; and it helps guide how the plant produces fruit. In many instances, it actually encourages the plant to produce more fruit.

There are a couple of other points to grasp that will help you to wield your secateurs with confidence. First: have good secateurs to wield – buy once and well. Secondly: a sharp blade is essential for a clean cut – sharpen it either before or after each time you use it.

When cutting anything thicker than your thickest finger, upgrade to long-handled loppers, and when those start to struggle, move up to a pruning saw – a small curved saw designed to fit in between other branches without damaging them.

Unless you have good reason for wanting otherwise, aim for a goblet shape – an open centre with a gently curving cup of branches surrounding it. Completely cut out any crossing stems and those pointing towards the middle. When pruning back, look along stems and cut just above a bud that is pointing outwards. When sap rises, this is the bud that will be spurred into action, and you will encourage growth away from the centre.

Beyond this, there are a few finer points that will help you to deal confidently with particular crops.

APPLES AND PEARS

Apples and pears should be pruned in winter, while they are leafless and dormant. Remove dead and diseased wood, prune out any branches pointing in to the centre, and cut out crossing stems to increase air circulation. Cut back new growth by a third, pruning to just above an outward-pointing bud.

Most apples and pears produce fruit in clusters, known as spurs, along each branch's length; a few, such as 'Irish Peach' and 'Cornish Gilliflower', are tip-bearers, fruiting on new growth borne at the tips. For these, do not cut new growth back by a third each winter, like you would with spur-bearers, as you will cut off all potential fruiting buds; just prune lightly for shape and air movement.

STONE FRUIT

The stone fruits – plums, peaches, nectarines, apricots and cherries – generally produce the most fruit on fairly young growth. This means it is a good idea to occasionally take out some of the oldest branches (back to the trunk or other convenient point), to give more room for younger branches to come through.

Prune all stone fruit in summer, as winter pruning leaves them open to the devastating fungal disease silver leaf. I tend to prune late in summer, after the fruit has been picked.

VINES

There are several methods to pruning grapevines. To grow them as lines, as you might in a vineyard or against a fence, it's easiest to grow them in a similar way to an espaliered apple, with arms trained horizontally either side of the main stem. You'll need two or three horizontal wires (depending on how many horizontal arms you want to train) – the lowest is usually 1m above the ground, the others spaced 40–50cm apart, above – held firmly in place by posts. Plant your grape(s) under the wire, with a cane pushed vertically into the soil behind it. Tie the trunk of the grape and the wires to the cane.

Allow the strongest shoot that emerges from your grape to grow up the cane, tying it in as it goes, pruning off all other shoots – you won't get any grapes on the plant in this first year. Cut this shoot back in winter to just below the lowest wire.

The following late spring/early summer, when new shoots emerge, allow the strongest that grows from the top of the main stem to remain, and rub off all other ones from the top. Depending on the number of wires, allow two or three well-placed shoots to grow from either side of the stem along the horizontal wires. These side shoots are known as laterals. Tie them loosely to the wires and remove all other side shoots.

When the laterals and growing tip have grown 30–40cm, prune off the growing tip to prevent it growing further. Allow 2–3 bunches of grapes to develop on the plant, but don't be greedy – any more will deplete the plant's energies at this stage in its life. Remove all other bunches while still tiny.

Come winter, cut the main stem back to just below the top wire again, and prune the laterals back to only three buds to create what is known as a spur.

In late spring, when the buds start growing, select the strongest shoot from each spur and prune off the rest. Tie each shoot to its wire as it grows. This year, you can allow two bunches on each side shoot to develop. Remove any others. Prune the end of each side shoot three leaves beyond its second bunch of grapes to direct the plant's energies to the grapes rather than more leafy growth. Remove any shoots growing from the top of the main stem. In following years, follow the same process, allowing three bunches per side shoot.

If you have a structure such as a pergola to cover with a grape vine, train the vine up one of the uprights and along the horizontal. When it reaches the edge of the pergola nip out the growing tip to stop growth. This will encourage side shoots to form and these can be tied into your pergola at right angles to the main stem. This is your permanent framework, you should cut back to this in early winter, and the shoots that emerge from this each year will bear your fruit.

MEDLARS AND QUINCES

Quinces make beautifully shaped trees and require very little pruning. Medlars can be twisted and oddly leaning trees, but there's not much that pruning can do to save them from this. It's generally better to plant them where there is plenty of space to let them do their strange thing, than to try to manipulate them into line. Light winter pruning as you would apples will suit both trees, when necessary.

FIGS

Figs make beautiful stand-alone bushes, or they can be fan-trained against a wall. Take out damaged and crossing growth in winter, along with any shoots appearing at the base of the plant, and nip out a few centimetres of each growing tip in summer to concentrate the plant's energy towards the ripening fruit.

SOFT FRUITS

Soft fruit pruning falls into two camps: there are bushes that need to be pruned for air circulation and renewal, and canes that just need to be pruned right down to the ground.

BUSH FRUIT: *gooseberries, redcurrants, white currants, blackcurrants and blueberries*

All of these plants grow roughly bush-like in shape, with woody, twiggy growth. Gooseberries, redcurrants and white currants make proper little bushes. Blackcurrants and blueberries grow more like little thickets of woody stems.

Redcurrants and white currants flower and fruit on spurs. Allow a main framework of several stems to form and then prune back to this every winter by cutting back side shoots to one bud and removing the tip of the main branches.

Gooseberries should have their oldest stems removed each winter or they will become congested and unproductive. They have a tendency to trail their

stems across the ground which makes for poor-quality fruit, so completely cut out any low branches and – unlike with all other pruning – always prune to an upwards or inwards pointing bud, to encourage upright, compact growth.

Blackcurrants and blueberries both send up woody, twiggy growth direct from the ground. Winter pruning should be to cut out the oldest of these completely, which will leave room for new stems to come through.

CANE FRUIT: *raspberries, blackberries, and hybrid berries such as tayberries and lingonberries*

Most of these plants fruit and flower best on one-year-old wood, i.e. canes grown in one year, and fruit the next. This makes their pruning very simple: after fruiting, cut the stems that have borne fruit right to the ground and tie in any new, unfruited stems in their place. You can tell the fruited canes in winter, as they have side branches and look generally brittle and lifeless, while still-to-fruit canes are smoother and newer looking.

Raspberries come in two varieties: summer- and autumn-fruiting. Summer raspberries fruit in their second year, so fruited canes should be cut down; autumn raspberries fruit on this year's canes, so all can be cut back to the ground every year after harvest, with new canes growing (and fruiting) each year.

WINTER PROTECTION

꩜ The growing season can be short, and the cold months in which light and temperatures are too low for speedy growth are always too long. So, in dreaming of summer, we have to make allowances for winter too, and make plans to protect plants from its harshness.

Plants in containers are your main concern when it comes to frosts. During a very cold spell the whole root ball can freeze, and while this in itself doesn't necessarily kill the plant (though it might), it locks up all of the moisture around the roots so that the plant dehydrates. Water also expands on freezing and an expanding frozen block of soil can crack a terracotta pot. Start each winter by putting terracotta pots up on 'pot feet', little pieces of terracotta that lift pots an inch away from the ground and allow them to drain well after rains. Grouping pots together will make them less exposed and can help to prevent freezing, but particularly precious pots should be wrapped in an insulating layer of bubble wrap in late autumn.

Use straw to protect vulnerable crops still in the ground from the harshest frosts, as well as any plants (such as Chilean guava) that are susceptible to dieback in the cold. Tuck a 5–7cm layer of straw around plants and pin down lightly with hoops of wire if they're in an exposed position.

Fleece is a delicate material that lets in air, light and water, but draped over plants will help keep them that tiny bit snugger than they would be without it. Although they don't strictly need it, broad beans sown in autumn benefit from being covered by a layer of fleece, stretched over the row and pinned down taut on either side. The plants will be less battered by frosts, winds and hail come spring. The same goes for autumn-sown winter salads, which are perfectly hardy, but just get a little too pockmarked and tough for the salad bowl when left to face the elements all winter. Fleece is also hugely useful in giving a helping hand to fruit trees, such as peaches and apricots, which flower early and so are often hit by frosts. A little fleece draped over them during blossom time (though only when frosts are forecast as the bees do need to reach the flowers) will save them from themselves, and convince them that they are in the Mediterranean after all.

GROWING UNDER COVER

It's not all defensive action where winter is concerned. There are also many ways of extending the season into autumn and winter, and kicking it off earlier in spring. Go beyond frost protection and you start to delve into the world of growing under cover. Here you can create a far longer season than your plants would have outside. There are plenty of options for this, whatever the size of your garden, your budget or style of gardening.

CLOCHES

Cloches are just a step up from stretching fleece across your plants. They are small structures, usually around 25cm high, often composed of hoops with fabric or clear plastic stretched over them. The more

money you spend on them, the more solid they will be and the better protection they will afford. Some cloches are made of glass and others of solid plastic, but consider where you might store them before you buy. The more flexible hoop-and-plastic-sheeting types do a pretty good job and are easy to store. Stretch them over rows of winter salads and use them to warm the soil pre-sowing in spring, or to bring on crops sown at the same time as those not under the cloche for a staggered harvest.

GREENHOUSES

Even unheated greenhouses can be hugely useful at extending the season, pushing the temperature up a few degrees. A greenhouse is the place to start off your seedlings in spring, and to grow the plants like tomatoes and chilli peppers, which respond well to a long hot season.

Give your greenhouse a tiny bit of heat and it becomes the perfect place for overwintering a few of the more delicate plants, including citrus, which fare much better if kept above freezing. Grown in pots, they can be moved back outdoors come summer if preferred. A large greenhouse will make a great home for those more unusual plants that are hardy but unreliable outdoors, and will guarantee some fabulous crops: vines, apricots, peaches will all fruit beautifully under cover.

As well as providing a favourable home for sun-loving plants, greenhouses are good for early crops of those plants that are perfectly fine in the garden later in the year – such as carrots, lettuces, baby beetroots, French beans and strawberries. At the end of the season, you can replace them with oriental leaves and hardy salads to see you in peppery greens all through winter.

Being basically a box of glass, greenhouses will heat up fiercely in the summer sun and get very cold in winter. These extremes don't suit many plants but there are a few things you can do to even out the temperature a little.

- Shade paint: as the weather starts to warm, paint shade paint on to the outside of the glass, to block out a little of the sun and keep the temperature down. It is chalky stuff that can be easily wiped off at the end of the season.

- Water the floor: if you have a concrete or paved floor to your greenhouse, water the floor on hot days. This water evaporates, pushing up the humidity and lowering the temperature.

- Have a full water butt inside the greenhouse: water has great thermal properties. It holds on to the heat it receives during the day and releases it at night, and likewise it acts as a coolant during hot days. Several large, full water butts can help to keep a greenhouse just above freezing in winter.

- Insulate: as autumn approaches, insulate your greenhouse with bubble wrap. You can buy attachments from garden centres that will hold the wrap away from the glass, so creating an extra insulating layer of air between the two.

- Heating: only consider heating once you have insulated. An electric heater with a thermostat is simple to use but expensive to run, and gas and oil heaters are a little cheaper but fussier. Remember that for most purposes you only need to keep the temperature at just above freezing, so heating should be minimal. Try creating a cheap convection heater by burning a candle with two upturned terracotta pots (the inside one small, the outer one large) covering it. (Obviously consider safety at all times.)

- Heating mats: at propagation time, a heating mat can be a very useful thing in an otherwise unheated greenhouse. Place your trays of seedlings or cuttings on to it and it warms the soil they are in, so encouraging good rooting. At the same time the air around them is cool, which helps prevent the drawn-up, leggy growth you would get in warm surroundings.

POLYTUNNELS

A polytunnel is constructed of arches with a thick but transparent plastic sheet stretched over, keeping out the wind and rain while letting in every drop of sun. They have most of the advantages of a greenhouse, while being less harsh environments in the height of summer. What some see as perhaps not so aesthetically pleasing is counterbalanced by a less extreme atmosphere and being cheaper in price.

RESURCES AND SUPPLIERS

SEEDS, SEEDLINGS AND PLANTS

Agroforestry Research Trust
www.agroforestry.co.uk / 01803 840776 (Fax)

Blackmoor Fruit Nursery
www.blackmoor.co.uk / 01420 477978

Delfland Nurseries
www.organicplants.co.uk / 01354 740553

Edulis
www.edulis.co.uk / 01635 578113

The Heritage Seed Library
www.gardenorganic.org.uk/hsl / 024 7630 3517

Kings Seeds
www.kingsseeds.com / 01376 570000

Nickys Nursery
www.nickys-nursery.co.uk / 01843 600972

Otter Farm
shop.otterfarm.co.uk

Pennard Plants
www.pennardplants.com / 01749 860039

Reads Nursery
www.readsnursery.co.uk / 01986 895555

The Real Seed Catalogue
www.realseeds.co.uk / 01239 821107

Sarah Raven's Kitchen and Garden
www.sarahraven.com / 0845 092 0283

Sea Spring Seeds
www.seaspringseeds.co.uk / 01308 897898

Thomas Etty
www.thomasetty.co.uk / 01460 298249

Victoriana Nursery
www.victoriananursery.co.uk / 01233 740529

OTHER SUPPLIES

Carbon Gold
www.carbongold.com / 0117 2440032
Biochar products

Chicken supplies
www.omlet.co.uk / 0845 450 2056

Defenders
www.defenders.co.uk / 01233 813121
Biological pest control for the garden.

Fertile fibre
www.fertilefibre.com / 01432 853111
Organically certified peat-free compost,
and more.

The Green Gardener
www.greengardener.co.uk / 01493 750061
Range of biological pest control, plus general
veg patch supplies.

Greenhouse Sensation
www.greenhousesensation.co.uk
0845 602 3774
For superb propagators, and more.

Harrod Horticultural
www.harrodhorticultural.com / 0845 402 5300
Wide range of fruit (and general garden)
supplies, including excellent fruit cages.

Implementations
www.implementations.co.uk / 0845 330 3148
Bronze/copper tools - hardwearing and
beautiful.

Link-a-bord
www.linkabord.co.uk / 01773 590566
Instant raised beds made from recycled plastic.

Rooster Pelleted Manure
www.rooster.uk.com / 01325 339971
Pelleted chicken manure from non-battery
chickens.

UK Juicers
www.ukjuicers.com/dehydrators / 01904 757070
Excellent dehydrators for drying/preserving
harvests.

West Riding Organics
www.wrorganics.co.uk / 01706 379944
Organically certified compost.

Wiggly wigglers
www.wigglywigglers.co.uk / 01981 500391
Worms, wormeries and general veg patch
supplies.

Wood Ovens
www.woodovens.net / 01636 678653

World of Felco
www.worldoffelco.co.uk / 020 8829 8850
The best secateurs.

Garden Organic
www.gardenorganic.org.uk / 024 7630 3517
A charity (formerly the HDRA) dedicated to
organic growing. Well worth joining to give you
access to a wealth of advice. Also an excellent
source for seeds and everything to do with
growing.

GIY
www.giyinternational.org / 00 353 51 302 191
The international community of food growers.

The National Fruit Collection
www.brogdalecollections.co.uk / 01795 536250
Tours, events, courses and identification of
varieties.

The National Garden Scheme
www.ngs.org.uk / 01483 211535

Royal Horticultural Society
www.rhs.org.uk / 0845 260 5000
A great source of advice, with numerous
excellent gardens to visit, and also offers a soil
analysis service.

Slow Food
www.slowfood.org.uk / 020 7099 1132
Promoting the locality, diversity and
enjoyment of food.

ACKNOWLEDGEMENTS

For most of my life I have been relatively unemployable, but somewhat late in the day I seem to have found a facility for growing and writing about food. I owe that to my wife, who got me into the garden in the first place; to my daughter who keeps me planting things in the hope that she'll enjoy harvesting and eating them; to Hugh Fearnley-Whittingstall, Martin Crawford, James Alexander-Sinclair, Cleve West, Alys Fowler, Sarah Raven, Nigel Slater, Monty Don, Debora Robertson, Trish Deseine, Diana Henry, Steven Lamb, Pam Corbin, John Wright, Tim Maddams, the GIY gang, Xanthe Clay, Lia Leendertz, Jason Ingram, Keith Floyd, Nigella Lawson, Jane Grigson, Lucy Inglis, Fi KP, Emma T, AMP, Dawn I, Nads, Futch and Nikki, Stu, Laura, Nick, the Hateleys, my mum and Derek, Anthony and Sarah; to my ever-enthusiastic agent Caroline Michel; and the many followers of and commenters on the Otter Farm blog, who have kept and keep me gastronomically, horticulturally, emotionally and comedically nourished via one medium or another at regular intervals. Thank you.

This book has been a pleasure to create, largely due to the creativity, skill, good humour and carrot juice supplied in varying amounts by publisher Elizabeth Hallett, senior editor Kate Miles, editor Laura Herring and designer Tony Lyons: thank you, thank you. I have fought to keep your names and the prominence that your fine work deserves from the cover and keep the glory for myself. Thanks too, to Rosie, Vickie and Laura and the other fine folk from Saltyard who help to promote the finished thing.

Lastly, a huge thank you to the people who have allowed me to use their gardens to convey just how special a kitchen garden can be. I hope everyone who reads this book will feel moved to visit them all and learn even a little from the bright minds and busy hands that have created each of these gems.

INDEX

First published in Great Britain in 2015 by Saltyard Books
An imprint of Hodder & Stoughton
An Hachette UK company

1

Copyright © Mark Diacono 2015

Photography © Mark Diacono 2015

Photography © Jason Ingram on pages 15 (right), 17, 18, 21 (left), 34 (bottom left), 51, 158, 248, 320, 321, 334 (left), 335, 336, 355

A CIP catalogue record for this title is available from the British Library.

ISBN 978 1 444 73478 2
eBook ISBN 978 1 444 73480 5

Book design by Estuary English
Typeset in Mrs. Eaves and P22 Underground

Copy editor Laura Herring
Proof reader Margaret Gilbey
Indexer Caroline Wilding

Printed and bound in Germany by Mohn Media.

Saltyard Books
338 Euston Road
London NW1 3BH

www.saltyardbooks.co.uk